AMONG REMARKABLE BEINGS

Dare to discover yourself as Soul

GASTON J. OUELLET

PublishAmerica
Baltimore

© 2013 by Gaston J. Ouellet.
All rights reserved. No part of this book may be reproduced, stored in a retrieval system or transmitted in any form or by any means without the prior written permission of the publishers, except by a reviewer who may quote brief passages in a review to be printed in a newspaper, magazine or journal.

First printing

This publication contains the opinions and ideas of its author. Author intends to offer information of a general nature. Any reliance on the information herein is at the reader's own discretion.

The author and publisher specifically disclaim all responsibility for any liability, loss, or right, personal or otherwise, which is incurred as a consequence, directly or indirectly, of the use and application of any contents of this book. They further make no representations or warranties with respect to the accuracy or completeness of the contents of this work and specifically disclaim all warranties including without limitation any implied warranty of fitness for a particular purpose. Any recommendations are made without any guarantee on the part of the author or the publisher.

PublishAmerica has allowed this work to remain exactly as the author intended, verbatim, without editorial input.

Softcover 9781627723336
PUBLISHED BY PUBLISHAMERICA, LLLP
www.publishamerica.com
Baltimore

Printed in the United States of America

Dedication

This book is dedicated with deepest love and affection to my life partner Annie-Claude Ranger. Her love, wisdom and strength inspire me each day to be the best I can be and encourage me to share with the world what lies within my heart.

To Karl,

To Love is to Listen &
To Listen is to Love...

Gaston J. Ouellet

Acknowledgements

I would like to humbly express my love and gratitude to the following people:

First and foremost to my friend, guide and mentor Steve DeWitt, author of "The Golden Kingdom" and "Warriors of the Sound Current."

I would like to pay special tribute to three people who have given freely of their time, heart and resources to support this work: Michael Mann, Sandrine Dugas, and Raymonde Rivard.

As well to friends who have supported me through the years in accomplishing this work: Bruce Thompson, Serge Amyot, Alamaia Will, Carol Humlie, Dr. Anne Cowden, Michele Soule, Patricia White, Rollande St-Jean, Richard Martin, Claire Bergeron and Jacque Perrault.

Finally, my deepest gratitude to my four children who have taught me about unconditional love, mutual respect, and accepting the presence of Divine Love in daily life.

FOREWORD

This book was made possible by the contributions and assistance of several spiritual guides who have accompanied me throughout my life. Many readers may find some of the experiences I mention to be far-fetched; however, they were not written to convince anyone of their validity. Rather, they are meant to inspire, to dare the readers to have some of their own out-of-body experiences.

It may be important to note here that the knowledge of Divine Truth is not something one can absorb from books or learn by discussing it with others. It shall always be something we experience by ourselves, for ourselves, and for no one else.

These inner journeys are the means great spiritual guides have always used to access the Secret Kingdom, which awaits everyone's discovery while still living in the physical body.

Soul's destiny is to learn to rediscover Its true self while expressing Its spiritual heritage, one experience at a time. Once we realize that, we know we are Souls. The inner door opens to begin our passageway through the heart of creation, the eye of Soul.

Our world is rapidly reaching a crossroads, where the inner worlds are becoming more and more accessible. Why? Truth is available to everyone now. There's a very good foundation for this. Collectively we've entered into a spiritual golden age. So be bold, be ready and dare yourself as Soul to journey within and become the spiritual pioneer you've always dreamed of being.

Welcome to *Among Remarkable Beings* and the inner net, the most traveled pathway in the universe. Read this book and discover for yourself how you can awaken the spiritual virtues in you. The sacred worlds have always been beyond the sight of man. Yet they are as real today as the air which supports us all!

CONTENTS

FOREWORD.. 7
I THE GREAT VISIT 11
II THE ARRIVAL.. 32
III ON THE MOVE... 50
IV MATERNAL LOVE 73
V THE VISIONS OF SAINTS 96
VI WE ARE NEVER ALONE..121
VII LEARNING TO SHARE..147
VIII GRATITUDE LEADS US TO LOVE.......................169
IX SURRENDER IS THE KEY..199
X SOUL TRAVELS...227
XI EXPERIENCE, THE MOTHER OF CONSCIOUSNESS 251
XII TOGETHER OUR MISSION IS TO LOVE................269

THE GREAT VISIT

I

Have you ever stood in line at an airport wondering where everyone is going or where they're all coming from? That is the very question I was asking myself while I waited at the Honolulu International Airport with thousands of other travelers, all going in different directions.

On this day in July of 2004, an elderly Hawaiian lady in front of me began to display signs of anxiety as we neared the ticket counter. She was a large woman in a brightly-flowered Hawaiian dress. Her toes were nearly bursting out of her too-tight sandals. I wondered how painful it must be for her to walk around in those shoes with so much weight on her feet.

The people in line took one step forward, and then she turned and exclaimed in a fearful voice, "I'm very sorry, sir, but I don't think I should be in front of you!" Desperation radiated from her.

"Why?" I said.

"I'm not sure if I should depart on this trip!"

During my travels I've experienced many unusual coincidences, and this one seemed to be no exception.

"Where are you going?"

She told me in great detail about her son, Kimo, and her granddaughter, Lulu, who was stricken with terminal cancer. Several other passengers close to us listened intently to our conversation. When we finally reached the ticket counter, her voice grew shrill, and her shoulders hunched forward with the tension of her fear. She pleaded with me to go ahead of her. I insisted she go first because she was in line ahead of me. Behind us people began grumbling at the delay. Then the Hawaiian lady began sobbing like a lost child. Without stopping to think, I wrapped my arms around her large form.

The passengers listening to us looked at me with approval. Their collective anxiety eased as quickly as it had risen.

The ticket agent offered the Hawaiian lady a quiet place to sit down. I gently released her from my embrace. Within moments, two airline agents arrived to escort her to the VIP lounge where she could find comfort and peace. She wiped her tears and wobbled away through the crowd.

When I stepped up to the counter, the ticket agent spoke to me with a pronounced Asian accent.

"Hi! My name is Mrs. Pearl. Welcome to China Air Line. May I have your passport, please?"

"Of course"

"Where are you going today?" she asked. Her intense curiosity made her seem like an FBI agent performing an interrogation.

"I am leaving for Koh Samui, Thailand."

"Oh. You're going to Bangkok via Taipei flight 38."

"Yes, indeed."

"Since you live on Maui," she said quizzically, "may I ask why you'd want to vacation on a tiny island in Thailand?"

It seemed she took great pleasure in probing passengers to discover the reasons for their trip. However, before I could answer, she continued in a tone of disapproval, "Oh, let me guess. You're going for the women. Most men I book on these flights have this grin on their face, about their, you know, *excursion.*"

She was acting even more like an FBI agent now. But then she suddenly pulled back. Maybe she realized her curiosity had gotten the better of her, or maybe she was remembering what had just transpired between me and the Hawaiian woman in line. She bowed her head.

"Please forgive me," she said contritely.

"I understand why some people would think this about men traveling to Thailand," I said. "But rest assured to me Thailand is far more than that. It's the Land of the Smiling People, some of the happiest people on earth. They're at peace with each other and with themselves."

"Tell me then," she said, this time with genuine interest. "Why are you going to Koh Samui?"

"If you really want to know, I'm going to take care of myself for the first time in my life."

"What do you mean?"

"Well, I'm a 44 year-old single father of four, and this is the first time in six years I'll have the opportunity to care only for myself. You know, like resting or reading in bed all day long if I want to. Doing things I love. You understand, right?"

In her position she had probably heard many stories from passengers, but Mrs. Pearl looked at me as if this was the best story she had heard in a very long time. Nevertheless, her probing continued.

"But why would you travel to Koh Samui when you already live on the best island on earth? Don't you know that Maui was voted the best island in the world for nine years in a row?"

I did know this; they say Maui is *No Ka Oi*, which means 'the best' in Hawaiian. "Actually, I'm going there for three weeks of fasting at the Dharma Healing Center. Then it's onward to Katmandu for a spiritual pilgrimage, or quest, or call it what you will."

"Wow!" she blurted. "I've been working for China Airlines in Honolulu for over ten years now, and I've never met a man who's traveling to Thailand to fast for three weeks—never mind holding elderly crying Hawaiian ladies along the way!" She paused for a moment, then nodded. "I believe you." Her smile grew wider. "And because you were so truthful with me, and so kindhearted with our passenger, I will make your journey more enjoyable."

By then all I wanted was the boarding pass and my passport back so I could be on my way. I had spent the past four nights preparing my children for their own journey to Alaska to visit their mother. I was exhausted and emotionally drained; experiencing the mixture of emotions only a parent can feel when the safety and well-being of his children are at stake. I had never left my children for more than a week at a time; now I was leaving them for two months. Still, I knew I was doing the right thing, both for them and for myself.

During the weeks before our separate adventures began, we spent night after night discussing what we expected to experience during our summer travels. They would tell me about the wildlife they hoped to encounter in Alaska, and I'd tell them I'd never be the same after this trip.

"Wait and see," I kept telling them, "I'll be a different father when you get back from your summer vacation."

And of course, they laughed disbelievingly. But deep in my heart I knew something profound was going to occur on my journey. I just didn't know where or how or when. I had prepared for this fast for the past three months and I was ready, I thought.

I felt so strong in my pursuit of this new me, and so vulnerable at the same time. Raising four children as a single father requires strength and perseverance usually wielded only by the heroes of ancient tales. Somewhere along the journey before me, I sensed a new kind of strength waiting.

While Mrs. Pearl looked over my documents, I wondered whether my children would be okay in Alaska. Hawaii and Alaska are universes apart: one is a tranquil, tropical paradise, the other is the land of survival of the fittest.

My excitement mounted; I was only an hour or so away from leaving! Then Mrs. Pearl drew me back to the present.

"Here's your boarding pass, your tickets, and your passport, Mr. Hulet. I have also upgraded you to First Class."

"What? I don't have that kind of money," I protested.

"Oh no, don't worry Mr. Hulet. China Airline has oversold this flight again, so I've taken the liberty of giving you this gift. I believe you've earned it. And by the way, Mrs. HonoOpono—the elderly Hawaiian lady you helped earlier—she's also traveling First Class this evening. She's seated just three rows behind you. Could you please keep an eye on her? She's quite perturbed with her family situation, as you are well aware."

"I will," I said.

First Class! Upgrading to an upper class? Is that what life had in store for me? Had I really earned this? Sometimes in life you work with such single-minded determination you can't always see all the upgrades life has in store for you. I had no intention of dishonoring this gift.

My appreciation for Mrs. Pearl's generosity made my eyes brim with tears.

"Thank you so very much, Mrs. Pearl. Your gift means a lot to me. I've had to work so hard just to make this journey possible. Your gracious gesture makes my journey even more worthwhile."

Before handing me my ticket and passport, she walked around the counter to shake my hand properly in the Asian tradition of bowing first, then giving a heartfelt handshake.

As I walked away, the passenger in line behind me asked, "Will you shake my hand too, after booking my flight?"

Mrs. Pearl laughed. "Yes, of course! But only if you promise to take care of our passengers and others wherever you're going!"

Have you ever spent just a few moments with someone who gets you immediately? Someone who sees who you really are? Sometimes it seems only complete strangers have this ability. Or maybe we are so constantly on guard with those who know us that we rarely reveal our true selves. We remain guarded to avoid being judged, even when we've spent years developing a friendship. The feeling of unconditional acceptance from Mrs. Pearl was like a ray of sunshine.

As I walked away towards the security checkpoint, I looked back and called, "Aloha!"

This Hawaiian expression can mean many things, depending on what you wish it to mean. You can use it to say, *goodbye*, or *welcome*, and much more. Mrs. Pearl waved as I walked away.

The security line seemed a mile long. Standing there, I wished this process would just go away so passengers could feel comfortable traveling again. Once I passed through security, I headed for Gate 9 and waited for the boarding call. Finally the announcement came over the intercom.

"All passengers traveling on China Airline Flight 38, we are now boarding at Gate 9. First class passengers and passengers traveling with young children please come forward."

My great journey had finally begun. With a sense of profound contentment, I took my seat in first class and settled in to rest. The crew went through the usual motions of getting the flight in order, and we taxied to our runway. Exhilaration swirled in my heart. Here I was in first class, with no one sitting beside me! It was like a double blessing.

Have you ever traveled on an airplane next to a passenger who loves to talk, even through the night? This would be a nine-and-a-half hour flight, so the last thing I wanted was someone who needed my attention. I had already given it all to my children, the kind of focused attention that drains you so completely that not even three weekends in bed could rejuvenate you. I was ready for rest and quiet.

I brought out my leather journal and began to write as the plane climbed ten, twenty, thirty thousand feet. I had barely begun a to-do list for my journey when suddenly, without warning, a colossal wave of turbulence began to toss the plane about like a toy. It fell abruptly into powerful downdrafts and then experienced even greater bumps when we stabilized again. The turbulence continued for quite some time.

Passengers were shouting and crying out loud. Minutes went by, the storm showing no signs of loosening its grip. The flight attendants were strapped into their jump seats, and when they delivered their emergency messages, fear shook their voices. The captain tried to comfort the passengers over the intercom, but without success.

Over the roar of the engines battling the elements, I could hear passengers praying out loud. Not the typical, reverent prayers reserved for church, but fervent, determined attempts to make true contact with God. Time seemed to be of the essence.

Though I too was in the grip of fear, I looked around to see how people were reacting to one another. I've always been curious about human nature. My curiosity has often shown me how generous and kindhearted people can truly be. But sometimes you have to wait for a potential disaster in the making to witness humanity's true glory.

Chaos reigned; children, women, and men screamed louder and louder with each descent. Amid the mayhem I saw passengers comforting their loved ones and neighbors. I even saw young children comforting their parents. But with each jolt, the atmosphere of fear grew thicker.

During all this, the strangest thing was also happening. A tall, distinguished gentleman in a blue suit walked down the aisle as if nothing out of the ordinary were occurring. He stared directly at me with the most piercing blue eyes I had ever encountered. When he reached my row, he greeted me with a traditional Asian bow, though he was far from Asian looking.

"May I sit here with you, please?" His voice resonated through me like a summer wind through a screen door. The plane was still being tossed up and down at an alarming rate. Everyone was in a state of panic except for this man. How he managed to stay upright was a mystery to me.

As intriguing as his presence was, I had mixed feelings about him. Sort of like when our favorite uncle comes over for an unannounced visit—part of us is happy to see him; another part hopes the visit will be brief.

"Of course," I said.

Since I was sitting on the aisle, I moved my knees aside to allow him access to the window seat.

The moment the strange man sat down, the captain announced we were clearing the storm. The plane leveled; the seat belt sign was turned off. Within seconds, everything changed. My fatigue vanished; suddenly I was wide-awake. Even my worries regarding my children evaporated. I felt rejuvenated.

Meanwhile, the man's gaze did not leave my eyes. Time stood still for what seemed like an eternity, and a deep sense of joy overcame me. It was as if I was fully alive for the first time in a very long while.

With a start I noticed the flight attendant leaning over me.

"My name is Brielle," she introduced herself. "I'll be your host for this part of your journey. Would you like anything to drink?"

I glanced over at the man next to me, but he had turned to look out the window. Suddenly very thirsty, I said, "Yes, thank you. May I have some green tea, please?"

My tea arrived within moments. As I took a careful sip, the man turned to introduce himself.

"My name is Justin Toldeck. What's your name?"

Listening to his voice, my attention was drawn to his eyes like a bee to a flower. For some reason my emotions seemed to spin in all directions at once. I stammered out a quick response, like a game show contestant on the spot.

"My name is Gaston J. Ouellet. But please call me Gaston."

I felt an odd sense of relief at even being able to reply. His gaze went right through me, like when a parent looks at his child and sees everything. My discomfort must have been obvious, but soon his easy manner and relaxed conversation put me at ease.

After some small talk, he asked the question that would begin an hours-long conversation.

"How far back can you remember, Gaston?"

When I opened my mouth to reply, at first no words came out. Finally I recovered my voice.

"What do you mean?"

"How far back can you remember?" he asked again, this time punctuating his words with a slight nod of encouragement.

No one had ever asked me this before. All my life I had longed to tell the story of my earliest memories to someone but had feared to do so. I was afraid people would think I was crazy.

As a young child I had learned that if you don't want to answer a question, you simply deflect it with another question.

"Do you mean can I remember my first day of school?"

He shook his head slowly. "Your very first memory, Gaston," he insisted, his voice soft but unyielding.

I considered repeating the question again, shaping it so that I could answer however I wanted. But this occasion was different, this man was different, everything was different. I took a deep breath to gather some courage.

"Alright, Mr. Toldeck. If you really want to know, then I'll tell you."

My stomach tied itself in knots. Part of me wanted to tell him, and another part wanted to run away and hide. But of course I was stuck on a plane, so hiding was impossible. I chose, for the moment, to give the shortest answer I could think of.

"I remember many moments prior to being born."

There it was: I had said it out loud for the first time in my life. Adrenaline surged through my veins and my heart raced. I was finally going to tell someone about my journey here, a journey that began very long ago, long before any memories were recorded in my physical body, long before I even had a physical body.

Mr. Toldeck seemed unsurprised. "So tell me, what, precisely, do you remember?"

I took another deep breath. Something about this man inspired me to share my truth. I felt oddly safe in his presence.

"What I'm about to tell you may challenge your beliefs or your understanding of how life works, but I hope it will also inspire you to choose love over anything else in life." I suppressed a tickle of fear. "Or maybe you won't believe a thing I say. I'll leave it to you to determine the truth behind my experiences. I won't try to convince you or even influence your perception of reality. Before I begin, however, I want you to know that I respect your religious beliefs, whatever they might be."

Mr. Toldeck waved his hand in a rolling gesture. "Go ahead, Gaston, and give me as much detail as you can. You know what they say about the truth being in the details."

What remained of my anxiety disappeared. I felt accepted; I felt as if I were in the presence of a true confidant.

"I've always thought of it as the Great Visit. It began in one of the most venerated wisdom temples in all creation. Believe it or not, Mr. Toldeck, ever since the Great Visit my heart yearns to serve the community of Soul once again." My tone of voice shifted; I was seeking reassurance.

Mr. Toldeck nodded. "Don't worry, if I don't understand something or don't believe you, I'll ask questions. Please continue."

With a sigh of relief, my shoulders relaxed.

"At the beginning of the Great Visit I stood, solid as you're sitting here with me right now, in the most beautiful temple

I'd ever seen. I still ache every day with all my heart to return there, the place where my long journey began."

I looked into the timeless distance, remembering the beauty of that place.

"The temple is called Jart Chiong, and it's located in the eighth dimension of the spiritual worlds."

I paused to gauge Mr. Toldeck's reaction. Mention of Jart Chiong and the eighth dimension was where my story took a turn into the truly strange. The man's piercing blue eyes calmly regarded me, showing no sign of disbelief.

Taking this as encouragement, I continued. "The Master of Jart Chiong is Asana Kaya. He comes from an ancient line of Masters in charge of the spiritual evolution of Souls throughout the entire universe. However, Master Asana Kaya would rather be referred to as a spiritual guide than a Master, because in the higher spiritual regions mastership is a relative state."

I stopped talking to take a sip of my tea and glance out the window past Mr. Toldeck. Far below, the vast Pacific Ocean was as blue as the sky.

"I shall describe what took place with as much detail as I can. One day my dear friend, Ule, and I were standing on a huge walkway admiring the vast waterfalls pouring pure light from the distant mountains into the valley below the temple.

"'This place,' I said to Ule, 'is so immense and beautiful… no words or thoughts could ever describe it.'

"Ule nodded agreement, his eyes fixed on the falling light in the distance. 'Did you know, Gaston, that this walkway surrounds the whole temple? It's a hundred and fifty feet wide in some places, and the columns are hundreds of feet tall.' Ule's eyes shone with awe. 'Even more amazing, the walls vibrate at a specific frequency rate that allows young spiritual travelers to navigate here.'

"Young spiritual travelers are called Newcomers," I explained to Mr. Toldeck, before I continued with my story. "I turned to Ule. 'Actually, I don't know all that much myself. I haven't visited all the rooms of this temple. And I haven't walked the entire walkway, either. You know, I'm almost a Newcomer myself.'

"Ule listened to the sounds of the temple for a moment.

"'You know, this temple was created long before the lower worlds. The lower worlds are the dimension where Souls receive their education in the knowledge of the spiritual laws, the laws which govern the realm of creation. The higher worlds contain the other dimensions where the purity of Soul resides. The Souls dwelling there are beings who have reached spiritual maturity due to the development of their innate knowingness and their creative application of the spiritual laws. Spiritual maturity leads Souls to consciously choose their spiritual mission, which is to serve our Creator, just as you have. Most Souls come to the temple to expand their knowledge of creation. They stay long enough to gather spiritual strength before returning to their spiritual mission.'

"Ule remained silent for a moment, his deep eyes searching mine. When he continued, he spoke with a reverence that told me I would do well to imprint this information onto my heart.

"'When Souls travel into these inner worlds, some enter realms that most Souls only dream of. Like this world, for example. Souls travel here to learn from the great teachers. Most spiritual guides have specialized spiritual knowledge, just like you and I have developed our skills as scouts.'

"Ule paused for a moment. I looked down at the stepping-stones of golden marble arranged in a harmonic pattern.

"Ule went on, 'You probably remember that, before entering this temple, Souls must take on the form that ancient myths refer to as a Light Body because here only pure, white light exists. There is nothing else here except the holy, humming melody that travels throughout creation to sustain all life. Only Light and Sound exist here.'

"I considered what Ule had just told me. We were both scouts in this region. That was our duty."

Mr. Toldeck held up his hand. "Tell me about the scouts."

"scouts travel to unknown regions of creation, what some of us call the Ancient Sacred Worlds. We bring back explicit details and report our findings so that other Souls can eventually find their way there. We are similar to the old pioneers who crossed the Rockies for the first time and reported their experiences back to their communities."

Mr. Toldeck nodded his thanks and gestured again for me to continue.

"Well, I suddenly noticed that at the Wisdom Temple in the far distance, many Souls were gathering for a debriefing ceremony. A scout had just returned from the Far Country. I realized it had been a long time since Ule had gone on a mission, whereas I had recently returned from one myself.

"The tradition of the scouts has always been that when one of us returns we share the tale of our adventures and report our findings to each other. For most scouts the debriefing ceremony is the greatest reward for journeying into the Far Country, or, as we also call it, the Unknown Worlds. Most everyone at the temple comes to witness these events. The returning scout stands at the center of the Oracle Assembly Chamber and recreates his experience by delivering the details of his journey into a pulsating sphere of golden light.

"Once the scout has completed this re-creation, the other Souls gather around this sphere and, in a sense, experience the journey themselves.

"During the debriefing, scribes enter the new discoveries into the Sacred Scriptures of the Book of Life. Once the ceremony is completed, the returning Soul is allowed to rest until its balance is restored. Then the scout is able to travel once again into the Unknown Worlds.

"'Kalani is the scout reporting this time,' Ule stated.

"'How did you know that?' I asked him.

"'I heard it from one of the guardians earlier, just prior to our love song ritual. Everyone was talking about it. Some say he just returned from the lowest region of all.'

"I was excited about being in Kalani's presence again. He was one of the most experienced Spiritual Travelers at our temple.

"Ule and I followed the crowd of three or four hundred Souls to the Oracle Assembly Chamber.

"'We seem to be a lot fewer than usual,' I observed.

"Ule said, 'Remember, when fewer are gathered, it's because fewer are able to understand what is about to unfold.'

"We were all preparing to chant the word HUK during our sacred love song to God, but before we began, Kalani advised us we'd better be prepared to touch the essence of realities that were once part of most of us.

"After the main debriefing, some of us followed Kalani to another hall to receive additional information about his journey. Kalani waited for everyone to quiet down. The air itself seemed to tremble with excitement.

"Kalani had visited a Soul named Melee who had just translated from the physical form and journeyed to the capital of the astral plane. Her cry for truth was so great that Kalani journeyed there to help her remember her spiritual origins. Before continuing, the scout looked at each of us in turn. For some reason, he looked last at me, and as he spoke his attention kept returning to me.

"'When traveling into the regions below it can at times require great courage and love to be able to return back here again. The tremendous pull on the attention of Soul to remain there is greater than I can describe. Throughout eternity, countless masters, gurus, saints, and others have tried to lead the way to these higher regions, but none may enter until they've first mastered the lower worlds.

"Ule interrupted him. 'Please, Kalani, tell us why.'

"Kalani let his deep gaze play over everyone present, and again, his eyes lingered on me. 'The force at play in the lower regions is the dark force. It has many names, such as Satan, Kal, the devil, or the great evil spirit. This being is endowed with the negative power. His spiritual duty is to keep Souls in the lower worlds for their spiritual education.

"'If a traveler forgets for the slightest moment where he originally comes from, he runs the risk of succumbing to the desire to remain where he is. And let me impress this upon you: this desire is very seductive, and it works very fast. Forgetting where we originate from is the first spiritual violation a Soul commits upon entering the lower worlds. The veil over the eyes of Soul creates the illusion of being separated from the Sound Current, or the Holy Spirit. To dissolve this veil requires the greatest, most difficult spiritual journey of all: the quest of recalling and knowing who we are as Soul. Remember this: our love song is the creative key to rediscovering our connection with the Great One. Never forget that the reason we exist is because of the Great Spirit's Love for us.'"

"Kalani stood and made the sign of blessing with his right hand. 'May the Blessings of Spirit Be!' He began to float away.

"Several hundred Souls had attended the original debriefing ceremony, but only a few of us had followed Kalani to this other hall. These Souls now drifted away in various directions as well.

"I pondered Kalani's last statement. 'Never forget that the reason we exist is because of the Great Spirit's Love for us.' Kalani's words reminded me how important it is to remember where I came from and that I am loved for eternity, no matter what happens to me or how far I journey into the Far Country.

"As a scout, I had already received all the necessary training through my spiritual exercises. Hence, I knew that no matter where I might be sent I would always be able to tune into the Divine Sound Current and ride It to wherever I desired to be. As long as I could remember to listen, that is.

"Ule pulled me back from my thoughts and we strolled along the walkway. The pathway was laid out in a perfect circle, offering a panoramic view from every vantage point. The sound of a celestial symphony of a thousand violins followed us like waves of laughter, happiness, and joy. I couldn't help but merge with its presence.

"Suddenly, Rena, one of the guardians of the Wisdom Temple, floated into our path. The guardians are the chosen few who stand at the doorways of the temples to screen each Soul before allowing It in. No one ever enters the temple without permission.

"Ule and I both knew that whenever one of the guardians moved about, someone was about to be invited on a journey. I was sure it would be Ule because I had just returned from a journey myself. Ule was ready and well prepared. He had more experience than most scouts.

"Rena fixed me with his eyes.

"'Gaston, your presence has been requested by three of the *Mahavakyis*. You are to follow me into the Grand Hallway.'

"The *Mahavakyis* are also known as the Silent Ones. Only nine of them exist in the entire universe, and they're in overall charge of the affairs of each Soul, Its training, and even the Sound Current Itself.

"I turned to Ule. 'Have you ever met any of the Silent Ones before?'

"'No. Most Souls who meet them aren't seen again for a very long time.' His voice vibrated with reverence.

"To be summoned before the Silent Ones was an enormous blessing for a scout, even for a great Master. This was what we lived for. This was our duty, our way of life, to live on the edge of creation and discover It.

"I bowed farewell to Ule and followed Rena. I had never been in the Grand Hallway before. Rena stopped and pointed to a double door at least three hundred feet high.

"'Your presence is welcome,' he said. Then he vanished.

"I stood all alone in front of the biggest door I'd ever seen. I hoped it would open if I pushed hard enough. But before I could step forward to try, I sensed a presence to my right. Master Asana Kaya himself had appeared next to me. The Light of his presence was so overwhelming I stood transfixed, honored, and awed.

"Master Asana Kaya took my hand and he placed a tiny, brilliant pearl of pure light in my palm. The moment the pearl dropped into my hand, a great Truth took shape in my consciousness. I tried to transform this Truth into visible images, but the more I tried, the more it slipped away. The light in my palm began to fade until my hand was empty, the great Truth dissolving like mist. I felt panic raising at the loss of this gift, but Master Asana Kaya shook his head slightly and smiled. When he spoke, his voice was like thunder and violins from the heart of God.

"When you need this Truth, when you are ready, my words will come to you."

The moment he finished speaking the huge double door swung inward. I turned to peer into the Grand Hallway, and when I looked back, Master Asana was gone. I proceeded towards the doorway and stepped inside.

Inside the Grand Hallway the light was almost unbearable. The door closed audibly behind me, but when I looked back, they were no longer there.

"The sweetest white light imaginable washed over me, and then three vibrant faceless beings appeared dressed in radiant purple robes. Accepting their presence took all my spiritual strength. If the Divine Love radiating from them had been the tiniest bit more intense, I might have dissolved on the spot.

"The being in the middle moved forward and placed a white tablet in front of me. It radiated Golden Light. When he spoke—though *spoke* is an inadequate description of his communication—the words came at me from all directions.

"'We have a mission for you. If you choose to accept it, you will learn about Divine Love in ways you have never before imagined.'

"I tried to look directly at these spiritual giants, but I couldn't. The strength, the spiritual fortitude required was beyond my capacity.

"I gathered all my inner resources and replied. 'May I know what this mission consists of?'

"I couldn't believe that I hadn't simply said *yes*. Spiritual Travelers yearn for such a blessing, but here I was requesting more information before making my decision.

"The Silent One to my right moved forward and instructed me to scrutinize the tablet. Light poured from its center, transmitting clear instructions for the spiritual mission I would pledge to undertake.

"After a moment I stopped looking at the tablet to regain my balance. My focus was immediately drawn towards the third Silent One. I summoned as much grace as I was able.

"'I am honored to serve your cause.'

"The third Silent One moved forward and raised his hand. The words 'Baraka Bashad,' echoed through my consciousness like a distant flute. *Baraka Bashad*. The ancient benediction which means 'May the Blessings Be.'

"As soon as I heard the last syllable, the scene in front of me vanished. In an instant I was traveling a billion light years per second, flying what appeared to be downward through a long, multi-hued tunnel, then upward. One moment I was speeding in one direction, then unexpectedly into the opposite direction. Traveling in all directions at once, it seemed. Or maybe I wasn't moving at all. Every atom of my being was screaming as if I were being pulled apart, unable to do anything to stop it. The longer my movement continued, the deeper and denser the colors became. I longed for it to stop; I had to stop; I could no longer bear it. In the vast distance, the symphony of a thousand violins was fading away.

"Then the great illusion took place; the sensation of being separated from the Great Spirit overwhelmed me and a new longing arose. These new sensations collided with the excitement of fulfilling my mission, which was strongly present in my consciousness. Suddenly, I found myself suspended in a resting point, looking down at a new scene. A woman in a hospital bed was screaming in agony. Several concerned people bustled around her. A baby was emerging from her body.

"My vision blinked out and I drew my first breath of life. And with that first breath I settled right into my new, tiny physical body.

"A series of the most surprising and uncomfortable sensations overwhelmed me. The physical state captured me, contained me, and immobilized me. For the first time throughout this entire experience, I felt abandoned, sentenced to mortality.

"Wide awake in this tiny body, I realized I was upside down, looking at a man wearing a white mask. He held me by the ankles with cold, rubber-clad hands. From the depths of my Soul I cried out—I had lost all my freedom and all my mobility.

"Memory of the holy love song drifted farther away, and this new, foreign reality bombarded me with a sensation that I somehow understood was called *fear*. My awareness was compelled to perceive all the physical sensations my little body was experiencing. They demanded my absolute attention.

"The Divine Sound Current continued to fade. I could barely hear the Holy Spirit singing to me anymore. Not that It had stopped loving me; rather, I could no longer hear It because my focus was now driven to answer physical needs that, as of yet, I could not comprehend. I felt like a prisoner in my body.

"It was April 9th, 1960, in Montréal, Québec. I was born. I had entered a new world."

I returned Mr. Toldeck's gentle gaze. "Believe it or not, that's how far back I can remember."

Taking a deep breath, I waited for his reaction.

THE ARRIVAL

II

Mr. Toldeck turned partially away and looked out at the cloud formations far below. The silence was palpable. I looked at him, anticipating a response that one would normally receive after telling such an eccentric story. But this was my childhood experience, my true memory. This was where I had come from.

His silence persisted, but his face radiated a fatherly smile. Silence, at times, can be a good barometer of how people feel towards one another. You can really witness who you are in the presence of silence. I bathed for a moment in the profound stillness. Then, just as I was about to break this peaceful moment, Brielle arrived.

"Are you finished with your tea?" she asked.

"I am," I replied. "Thank you"

She didn't even look at Mr. Toldeck, just took my cup and continued down the aisle. I thought that perhaps she disapproved of him sitting here with me, but since we were having such an intense conversation, she probably allowed him to remain. In a moment, Brielle was back.

"I'll return soon with the menu," she said.

"Thank you," I said, my desperate tone suggesting I might be in danger of starvation. I had not stopped talking since I began telling Mr. Toldeck my story. In my previous travels I had learned to counter hunger by rolling my tongue along my gums to generate saliva in order to balance and nurture my appetite. I had practiced this technique earlier and my hunger had vanished. But hunger only goes away for so long.

I wondered what Mr. Toldeck thought of my story, and of me. He still had not responded.

This profound experience had been stored in my heart for the longest time. I longed to be understood and to feel that I wasn't crazy. Yet I didn't anticipate being understood right away. All I really wanted was to be heard so that my heart could find relief from my inner struggle. Sometimes we live through experiences that fundamentally transform us, experiences that no words could ever describe. I was on the verge of returning to the familiar terrain of self-doubt.

Mr. Toldeck turned away from the window and looked directly into my eyes.

"You felt overwhelmed when you were born," he said. "A state of being captured, you said. Could you describe that?"

Instantly my confidence returned. He believed me—or at least he was willing to suspend his disbelief.

"Imagine an elderly person stuck in bed and unable to move," I said. "His entire life he's had his full mobility, and now that freedom has been taken away. It was very much like that.

"Sometimes you can witness the same love, humility, and sadness in the eyes of the elderly as you can in the eyes of an infant. It's a very similar state of surrendering, and of yielding to whatever life asks of you. On the Spiritual Planes, the place from which I had just arrived, Soul has complete freedom.

But at birth, paradoxical feelings rush through you, from a devastating loneliness to an infinite state of blessing. This paradox overtakes all of your senses. Sometimes the feelings are so unbearable that you're driven by nothing more than to fulfill the crashing desires that demand all your attention. You are being literally pulled away from listening to the Holy Spirit, the Love Sound of God. Anyone can hear It, if they take the time to listen. But in the body, your attention is constantly drawn towards answering needs that scream from every cell to be fulfilled. Freedom is replaced by the determination to achieve one purpose only: to respond to your physical needs.

"I was left alone in an incubator. For the first three hours, I cried nonstop. All I wanted was for someone to remove me from this prison so I could regain my freedom and return to my true home.

"Then a young nurse picked me up and carried me to my mother's side. Within moments my little heart was immersed in her maternal love, which was Divine Love to me. Is there any other Love? I melted into her arms. I could hear her heartbeat, and soon my own heart beat had the same rhythm. For the first time since my arrival, I felt the presence of the Great Spirit. It lived in my mother's heart.

"Have you ever watched an infant cry? The mother holds the baby in her arms and, once her Love penetrates the little one's heart, peace is restored. Love is the universal language. Love removes all darkness and fear. Babies' cries touch us so deeply because newborns still remember the Divine Home from which they have just arrived. Hidden within a baby's cry, we hear the Holy Spirit and Soul's yearning to return home to God."

I paused; Brielle was approaching. She dropped a menu in my hands and moved on. I was about to call her back to bring another, but Mr. Toldeck shook his head. I shrugged. A few minutes later she was back.

"Have you made your choice for dinner this evening, Mr. Ouellet?" she said.

"Of course, Brielle," I said. "I'll have the filet mignon. Thank you."

"Good choice," she said.

The enthusiasm with which she answered made me think that she was hoping there would be some left over for her. She walked up and down the aisle, taking other passengers' orders, and when she had finished she returned and bent close to me. I thought for sure that she was about to comment on my conversation with Mr. Toldeck, possibly even expressing her point of view on the matter. I was accustomed to such reactions whenever I shared about my out-of-body experiences with others. But to my surprise, Mr. Toldeck nodded toward her to indicate that she needed my help.

I chuckled. I doubted that she needed any help at all. Brielle was clearly a woman who had mastered every aspect of her work environment. Nevertheless, she leaned close to my left ear and spoke softly.

"You know," she said, "Ms. HonoOpono needs help with her menu. Would you be able and go over there and assist her, please? Since you know her?"

I smiled, both at the opportunity to help Mrs. HonoOpono again, and at the realization that Mr. Toldeck's insight had been correct. Brielle did need my help after all.

"Yes," I said. "I'd be delighted to do so."

I considered the possibility that this would be a good way for me to give Mr. Toldeck a break. But before I could even get up, Brielle continued.

"She doesn't seem to have her glasses," Brielle said. "Or she just can't find them. I can't tell which it is. Before we left Honolulu, Ms. HonoOpono and I talked. She told me all about you. I thought of asking for your help, since you already know of her family predicament. So I'll let you go before everyone in here gets the wrong idea."

She rose and straightened her uniform. It was apparent that she was drawn to me, possibly because of what Ms. HonoOpono may have told her. I glanced over at Mr. Toldeck with a smile, then stood up and waited for Brielle to move out of the way so I could make the short journey back to Ms. HonoOpono's seat. I sat beside her, and she looked at me with a mischievous smile on her face. She had planned this all along. She took hold of my right hand; her own hand was shaking, but she spoke with a steady voice.

"On the left side of your seat you have a window with a great ocean view," she said. "And yet I have noticed you looking to your right. So..." She fixed me with that mischievous gaze. "Why don't you go and talk to that pretty girl?" She nodded her head toward the beautiful, Polynesian woman reclining a few seats forward, across the aisle from my seat. It was obvious that Ms. HonoOpono still believed very much in Love. "Her name is Lea," she said. "Why don't you go over there and sit with her?" She paused and smiled that smile again. "I know she would love to know you!"

"How is that so, Ms. HonoOpono?" I said.

"Oh," she said. "Call me by my first name please. It's Akina. Especially after everything we've been through together. Do you know the last time someone gave me as big a hug as you did at the airport?"

"No," I said, shaking my head.

"Almost a year and half ago," she said. "When my granddaughter Lulu could still visit me. Those hugs, when you get older, they become priceless. Especially when they come from a loved one." She looked again at Lea, then back to me. "That's why I told Lea all about you while we were waiting together in the executive lounge."

"Oh, really," I said. "And what did you tell her about me?"

This time she looked at me with amazement in her eyes, as if to say "Come on. Grow up."

"When you get to be my age," said Ms. HonoOpono, "everything you once held dear is taken away. You're left only with the truth about yourself and the ones you love. I told Lea all about you. That's all." Her mischievous smile was back on.

"And what might this be?" I said.

"That you are a man filled with the Aloha Spirit," she said. "Do you know that when I was a little girl my grandfather was a Kahuna? He would always say that the mark of a great warrior is one who leads his life selflessly, and that's how the Aloha Spirit takes hold of you and never lets you go." She stopped and looked me up and down. A tone of hope crept into her voice. "You know about the Aloha Spirit, right?"

"After living on Maui for the past fourteen years, I'd better," I said. "It's all over the place."

She burst out laughing. At the same time, Brielle passed by and smiled.

"Ha!" Ms. HonoOpono laughed. "You're a little bit of a smart ass aren't you?" But she said it with affection. "So," she continued, "be honest with me. Tell me—are you shy? Why don't you go and talk with beautiful Lea?"

I couldn't bring myself to tell her that my attention hadn't even once drifted over towards Lea, since Mr. Toldeck and I had been involved in our conversation. Instead, I dodged the question by excusing myself to go to the bathroom. But when I was walking back from the lavatory, there she was, this slim, stunningly beautiful, Polynesian woman. She turned in her seat and took a good look at me as if to say, "I know who you are."

Her long, dark hair covered most of her seat back. That's a Hawaiian tradition. How could I have not noticed this noble princess? Her feminine gentleness radiated a delicate scent. The other passengers certainly had noticed her; why hadn't I? Had my fear of intimacy blinded me once more? Everyone has met a person whose beauty is so astonishing it is almost intimidating. That happened to me, right then and there. Awkwardly, I hazarded a smile at Lea. At the same moment, my leg bumped into my metal arm rest. Mr. Toldeck looked at me with a grin on his face as if to say, "What the hell are you trying to do?"

Ms. HonoOpono began to laugh out loud. The more I heard her laughing the more my face reddened. I continued down the aisle, finding my place at her side once more. She stopped laughing and recaptured her breath.

"Tell me," she said. "Why didn't you just sit down there with Lea? She was looking right at you after all the commotion you made. And what the hell was that noise?"

"Oh, I bumped my knee on the arm rest," I said. "And since you really want to know, well I guess I was afraid and embarrassed."

My cheeks were still burning. I leaned closer to pick up her menu so I could read it to her. At the same time I whispered in her ear. "You're right. She is a beautiful lady."

"Ha!" Ms. HonoOpono said. "A beautiful lady! That's what I am!"

She continued to laugh, this time even louder. From where we were sitting, we could see Lea laughing as well from Ms. HonoOpono's last comment.

"What's with you, Gaston?" she continued. "Lea is one of the most beautiful women I've ever seen in my life. Wow! You aren't one those men who's threatened by beautiful women, are you? I have never understood that about men. In my life I've meet a lot of handsome men. I wasn't always obese, you know. I turned a lot of men's' heads. But those days are long gone now. I mean, it really has been decades since those days. Now they're just funny memories." She shook her head. "So what would it take for me to convince you to go over there and sit with Lea?"

Everyone in our section could hear her loud voice; my embarrassment grew with each passing moment.

"Please speak softly," I pleaded. "I am here to help you read your menu so you can make a choice for your meal."

"Oh," Ms. HonoOpono said. She waived her hand dismissively and her voice took on a gentle, apologetic tone. "I already know what I want. I heard the other passengers making their choices earlier, so I made mine. I only asked Brielle to send you over here so I could pay you back for your kindness in Honolulu. I spent time in the VIP lounge with Lea, and she's gracious, just like you. All I really wanted is for both of you to meet. That's all. You'd make such a great couple." She leaned near so I would pay close attention. Her eyes had that mischievous twinkle again. "She's single, you know," she whispered. "Old ladies like me? We can see through veils. People like Lea and you are filled with the Aloha Spirit. That's becoming rarer each passing day." She looked directly into my eyes. "Understand me now, Gaston. I am speaking from experience here."

"I believe you, Ms. HonoOpono," I said.

Brielle stopped by. "So, Ms. HonoOpono what will it be for dinner this evening?"

"I am having the filet mignon," she said. "Just like all the other passengers. And if you could, ask them please to add extra potatoes to my serving. I would really appreciate that."

"Yes, I'll ask. And thank you, Mr. Ouellet, for your assistance here. It's very much appreciated. You may want to return to your seat now. I'll be serving your dinner soon."

I held Ms. HonoOpono's shaky hand and expressed my gratitude to her. Just as I was leaving the seat, I leaned close to her so no one could hear us. Softly I whispered, "If we are meant to meet, Lea and I, nothing in the universe can stop that from occurring, not even you or me."

She smiled; her face was beaming with hope. As she released my hand she winked. When I stood up, Lea looked at me again, this time with a gaze of approval. I returned to my seat, my shy feelings even stronger than before.

Mr. Toldeck was patiently awaiting my return.

"That was quite the journey you had back there," he said. "A lesson on women, on their beauty, and on courage all at the same time. And all the while you were traveling over 570 miles an hour 35,000 feet in the air. That's worth paying attention to. So! Are you ready to continue with your story?"

He was implying that I might want to reconsider. My whole attention was still very much captivated by the possibility of introducing myself to Lea. Lea and I were the only young people in First Class. It seemed just natural that we would be together. But the more I listened to Mr. Toldeck's voice, the more everything else vanished, even my desire to be in Lea's company.

As if reading my mind, Mr. Toldeck said, "Don't worry. You'll get to meet Lea and spend time with her tomorrow." His voice resonated with profound certainty.

"What the heck do you mean?" I replied. "How can that be when I don't even know where I'm staying in Bangkok yet? Never mind where I'll be after that. I can't even guess."

He ignored my protests completely. "So here's my question," he said. "Have you ever met one of these spiritual guides or gurus? I mean, when was the first time you encountered a Master?"

I smiled at the memory and nodded. "Within the first few hours of my arrival," I said. "At my birth to be precise.

"At first, all I did was cry. Then, once my mother began to comfort me, I found sanctuary in her Loving presence. As this experience continued, I found that I was also outside of my little body, observing my mother and me intertwined in a sacred bond of Love.

"And suddenly, there he was. Master Asana Kaya, right by my side in his Light Body. I was overwhelmed with joy. Just as I was about to express my gratitude for his visit, I noticed a tall, dark haired, striking Tibetan man with a well-trimmed beard standing beside him. He was clad in one of those maroon robes like you'd find in an ancient monastery.

"'This is Rebatarz,' Master Asana said. 'He'll be accompanying you during this journey.' I looked at him and greeted him with respect. Shortly afterwards, Master Asana faded away, and I was left alone with Rebatarz.

"'I am in charge of your spiritual education,' he said. 'That's part of the spiritual contract you made.'

"He explained that he would visit me in the astral world whenever I needed him, mostly in my dream state. His piercing, dark brown eyes were filled with irresistible Divine

Love. They drew me inward to a very familiar place. But at the same time, his countenance said, 'Prepare yourself, Dear One.' When I could no longer look into his eyes, his very essence filled my being. Then, within seconds, I awoke once more in my little body.

"My beautiful mother caressed my cheek with her gentle fingers. There was such a contrast between these two kinds of Love, my mother's and that of Master Rebatarz, and yet each was from the same source, and just as transformative. My mouth was now by her warm breast. She looked at me with the Love that only mothers know. This felt so good. She nursed me until I fell asleep. I tried to fight it, tried to remain awake, but I was so very tired. This was my third human contact. Moments like these are life-transforming experiences. I can assure you of that, Mr. Toldeck."

He nodded, indicating not only that he understood, but that he fully agreed. I continued.

"Within several weeks we established a routine. Her Love for me grew. Our mutual communion expanded every time I awoke in her protective arms. I slept most of the time, and each time I'd fall asleep, I'd awaken in the astral worlds with Master Rebatarz. He escorted me on inner journeys, reassuring me all along that all was well. Night after night these experiences continued, until one evening when he reminded me in detail of the spiritual contract I had agreed to regarding my current incarnation. After that, I made peace with these new captivating sensations of living in the physical.

"Even though I had reached an inner state of acceptance, physically I still felt like an old man trapped in my bed. Still, reaching that state of surrender had become my salvation. I had learned this lesson. Or so I thought.

"Did you know, Mr. Toldeck, that most children, if not all, leave their bodies constantly during the early months after their birth? That's why, when we look into an infant's eyes, we can witness Divinity staring right back at us. Infants have not yet been encumbered by mental faculties, which constantly try to trap Soul in the illusion that we're separated from our Creator, God Itself."

Brielle suddenly stopped by and tapped me on the shoulder.

"Ms. HonoOpono is asking to see you again," she said. "Hurry if you can, please, because dinner is almost ready to be served."

"Of course," I said.

I turned to Mr. Toldeck. He lifted his right hand in a supporting gesture. "Go ahead," he said. "When you're popular, you're in demand."

We both laughed, knowing full well that I might be getting publicly drilled about Lea once again, especially with Ms. HonoOpono's stentorian voice carrying across the entire compartment.

As soon as I stood up, Lea bathed me in the warmth of her beaming smile. My knees might have felt a little weak for a moment. I noticed the colorful, attractive dress she had on. It was the kind of dress worn at diplomatic functions. I walked three rows back and sat by Ms. HonoOpono.

"Did you notice?" Ms. HonoOpono asked. "Did you?"

"What are you talking about?" I said.

"Ms. Lea's dress, of course," she said. "Don't pretend that you didn't notice her beautiful outfit."

"Yes," I said, wondering if maybe Ms. HonoOpono was psychic. "Indeed I did."

I was already regretting moving these three rows back. Her voice filled our whole section.

"Did you know that Lea made that dress herself?" she boomed. "And that fabric comes from one of the artists in our area who hand-prints silk."

"No," I said with a smile. "That I did not know."

"The artist is my Aunty Makena," said Ms. HonoOpono. "She creates a lot of our traditional Hawaiian dresses, like the one I'm wearing."

"You mean she creates the colors and the patterns that are printed on the fabric?" I asked.

"She does," Ms. HonoOpono said. "And she made that hand printed silk pattern just for Lea. Because Lea is famous, you know."

"Oh, is that so?"

"Lea is Ms. Hawaii 1980," she said. "And she's one of the most sought after hula dancers in the whole state of Hawaii."

"Wow," I replied. "I really enjoy going to luau and watching the hula dancers. They dance in perfect harmony. Each move is filled with so much grace. I love hula dancers."

"I knew you would love Lea!" Ms. HonoOpono almost shouted. This time her voice rang out so loud the captain and his co-pilots must have heard her. Everyone in our section turned to look towards us. She didn't mind at all. She's a confident Hawaiian woman. Lea looked back in our direction, too, and smiled. I was overwhelmed with embarrassment and shyness once again. Near the front of the aisle, we could see Brielle getting ready to serve dinner. I tried to pull Ms. HonoOpono's attention away from Lea by asking her a question.

"Ms. HonoOpono," I said. "Do you know where the hula dance originates from?"

"Of course I do," she said. "I'm a Hawaiian lady and a hula teacher." It was clear that she was very proud of her heritage.

"Years ago, when I was young girl, I was a good hula dancer myself, you know. Everyone in my family are hula dancers. I first started dancing at the age of three; my great grandfather, Kahuna Haiku, told us all about it. When great grandfather spoke, we all listened. He told us the hula's the oldest Polynesian dance of all, and that each movement is a prayer of gratitude to the Aloha Spirit for providing everything for us."

"As for myself," I said, "I believe hula dancing is much older than that."

"Oh really," she said. "Go on, then. Tell me."

"Okay," I replied. "Well, Hawaiians are descended from the land of Lemuria. I believe the hula, and all other spiritual traditions of the Hawaiians originated there."

Now Ms. HonoOpono addressed me in a softer tone, obviously not wanting to be overheard.

"It's funny you mention that," she said. "Great grandfather Kahuna Haiku told us often about the legends of Mu, and reminded us how special we are as Hawaiians."

Just then Brielle stopped by again.

"Better wrap it up, guys," she said. "We're starting dinner service in next to no time."

I turned to Ms. HonoOpono. "I know you didn't ask me over here to talk about the land of Mu. So what was it for?"

"You're right, Gaston," she said. "But I really enjoyed what you shared with me. It reminded me of my childhood with my great grandfather. But yes, I asked you over here for a very good reason. Earlier I couldn't read the menu because I couldn't find my glasses." She pointed with her index finger under the seat in front of me. "They're down there," she said with a smile. I slipped to the floor and scrunched forward, looking underneath the seat. I saw them stuck far away, beneath one of her carry-on bags that had shifted during the flight.

"Come on, Gaston. Go ahead," she said. "You can do it. You know I can't reach down there."

Just as I got down on my knees to reach with my right hand under the seat, Ms. HonoOpono said, "Can you see Lea's beautiful shoes from down there? Can you?"

I made no reply. By now I had made several attempts to reach her glasses, but so far I'd had no success. I was practically down on my belly. Now she shouted out, even louder than before.

"I asked you, can you see Lea's gorgeous shoes down there?"

Brielle walked briskly towards us. "That's got to stop, guys," she admonished. "Right now!"

Her stern expression clearly indicated her disapproval of what she imagined was taking place. I finally managed to reach under the bag to retrieve the glasses. I stood up and shook my head. Everyone in first class was staring at me. Some were laughing, while others were only smiling. Lea, however, wore an expression that indicated this was the first time anyone had ever tried with such determination to get a glimpse of her shoes. Even so, her look was approving. All I had wanted was to recover Ms. HonoOpono's eyeglasses. I gave the glasses to her, and just before hurrying back to my seat, I leaned in close. "Yes, by the way," I said. "I did see Lea's beautiful shoes."

By the time I sat back down, it was evident from my red face that I had just participated in possibly the most humiliating experience of my life. Mr. Toldeck gave me my space; he must have sensed what I was going through. Not long after I was seated, Brielle served my filet mignon. Mr. Toldeck looked out the window while I devoured my dinner, choking with conflicting emotions. God knows I had done a lot of that. Once I completed my dinner, Brielle removed my tray. The moment she was gone, Mr. Toldeck looked directly at me.

"You know," he said, "if you wanted to examine Lea's shoes, all you had to do was lean forward and look to your left from right here."

He was right. From our seats we could see her shoes. She was seated in the same row as we were, just across the aisle. We both burst out laughing, and just like that, my burden of conflict was removed.

Soon Brielle stopped by to take drink orders.

"Oh, Mr. Ouellet," she said. "I'm so sorry I was so insensitive with you earlier! Ms. HonoOpono explained why you were on the floor. I understand now. So your drinks are on me. How about a glass of champagne? Or if you prefer, we have a fine scotch on board."

"Thank you for your kind gesture," I said, "but alcoholic drinks are for grownups only."

Lea and Brielle both started laughing so loud that everyone was looking in my direction yet again. Lea looked at me, and I could tell she was embarrassed that I had caught her listening to our conversation. I smiled back at her, and after a brief moment of eye contact, she looked away. My heart skipped half a beat. Brielle interrupted this magical moment.

"So then," she said, "what kind of drink may I serve you?"

"I'll have green tea please," I said. "Just like before."

"Coming right up, Mr. Ouellet," she said.

I turned to Mr. Toldeck. "I'm sorry for my lack of consideration," I said. "Maybe you would have enjoyed a drink? I hear from Brielle the scotch on board is very good." We both laughed.

"I'm okay, Gaston," Mr. Toldeck said. "Thank you. But there is something you mentioned before that I'd like to hear more about. Could you describe the astral world?"

"Let me see," I said. "Where do I start? It's simply another dimension where you and I, all of us really, reside in a higher vibration with our astral bodies. Within the physical body is a starry, subtle body, the Light Body of the astral world. It sparkles with millions of shining particles like stars in the night sky. When the physical body dies, this Light Body continues as Soul's vehicle of expression on the astral world.

"In the astral world, you can find the same cities we know in the physical world, such as New York, Cairo, and Paris, for example. And you can meet with past lovers, friends, and relatives who have passed away.

"Within this astral realm there are many museums of inventions as well. That's where most inventors journey in the dream state to learn new information and bring back the inventions themselves. Besides the museums there are many different kinds of universities, what spiritual travelers call Wisdom Temples.

"The astral world is so big that comparing it to the physical realm would be like comparing our galaxy to the rest of the physical universe. Its size is almost unimaginable. That's why the beings residing there have developed the technology to travel faster than the speed of light, beyond anything we can conceive. In the physical world we refer to the spaceships we can sometimes glimpse as UFOs; in other periods of our history we believed them to be gods. These are entities from the astral world. I'm not saying that in our physical universe there are no civilizations with such advanced technology; rather, that this technology originates from the astral world."

Then, suddenly, my train of thought was entirely derailed. I was unable to continue talking. My focus was pulled irresistibly to my left.

ON THE MOVE

III

Lea shifted her slender legs, then rose and walked toward the bathrooms. The moment she stood up, my attention was no longer involved in what I was saying or doing. Now it focused on how good her silk dress looked on her. She was breathtaking, the incarnation of divine femininity itself. After a moment I started breathing again. How could anyone not stare? How could I not long to behold such beauty? Somehow Mr. Toldeck managed to pull my attention back to our conversation.

"It's obvious by the way you looked at Lea that you really like her," Mr. Toldeck said. "And that's okay, you know. It is always the right thing to do, to be honest with your feelings, and with yourself, of course. Women can be a great inspiration to a man's heart—you realize that, right, Gaston? I assume you have the highest respect for your mother as well; just by the way you spoke about her earlier. Mothers are usually the first to inspire Love."

My heart was touched by his statement, as if I had just taken a conscious step forward in my capacity to accept Love. Then, though I didn't really know where it was coming from, a disquieting sensation began to come over me. I marshaled all my inner strength to dislodge this feeling which seemed to gather greater momentum with each passing second.

"Well, as for myself," I said with a little hesitation, "there were countless women in my youth who inspired my heart to love."

I was trying to contain my emotions. This subject of women and love had always troubled me in so many ways. I saw that Mr. Toldeck realized he had struck a tender spot.

"Alright," he said. "So you were a womanizer in your earlier years." We both laughed at his remark. "Tell me then, Gaston," he said. "What was your most memorable moment with your mom?"

He paused and looked at me as if he knew his question was going to overload my heart once again. As soon as he brought the subject of my mother into our conversation, he could perceive a change in my demeanor. I paused as well for a moment, realizing that I had told a complete stranger about some of the most private experiences in my life. But I knew in that instant that I could fully trust this man. What, after all, did I have to lose?

"This moment is as clear to me as both of us sitting here right now," I said, my eyes seeing both present and past. "I was six months old. No one else was home. My two sisters and my older brother were out with my father. For weeks prior to this day, my mother would just hold me and cry for long periods of time. And only a few days before, I had begun to see my mother's beautiful face distinctly. Every time my gaze came into alignment with hers, she would smile back through her tears. Whenever I think of my mother's gentleness, I'm always reminded of her radiant face beaming Love back at me.

"Suddenly, the front door of our home opened. My father entered, accompanied by two police officers, a social worker, and two men dressed in white. They talked with my mother while she held me tight in her harms. She began to scream when the two men pried me from her arms. She screamed loudly and began to cry like no one I had ever heard cry before. And so did I. The more I was ripped away from her, the more a sensation of profound abandonment infused me. I felt completely lost for the first time in my short life. I tried to remember what Rebatarz had told me only one day earlier about the state of surrender. I concluded surrendering would be my only salvation. When I opened my eyes after crying for hours, I tried to find a familiar face. But none was there. In fact, I had lost my ability to see clearly. When I awoke the following day, my sense of abandonment was stronger than ever; my deep longing for the communion of love I shared with my mother continued. And my vision still had not returned. After that, I was moved every three to four weeks among family members. This lasted for a year and half.

"My mom had experienced a deep depression for many months prior to giving birth to me. In 1960, women struck with such afflictions were committed to asylums. Such facilities back then administered massive electric shocks to the crown area of the head and prescribed strong medication.

"My mother remained in that institution for most of her adult years. Hardly anyone ever recovers from such treatment, you know, no matter how many spiritual guides they have. Her karmic debt was being addressed. Each Soul, prior to entering into the lower worlds, is given a karmic curriculum in order to balance its own karmic debts one lifetime at a time. This curriculum is administered by the Lords of Karma."

Suddenly, I noticed Lea walking back toward her seat. I was instantly nervous. Mr. Toldeck glanced at me and shook his head, indicating that I should stop worrying. Lea stopped at my side; her brown eyes were filled with kindness and love. She spoke in a melodic, childlike tone. At that moment, all I wanted was to look into her eyes forever.

"I'm sorry to bother you, Mr. Ouellet," she said, "but would you be able to help me?"

"Yes," I responded. "For sure!" My tone was confident, but inside I was telling myself over and over, *don't mess it up now! Don't mess it up!* How could I not acquiesce to her request, even though I had no idea what she wanted?

"It's Ms. HonoOpono," she continued. "She's fallen asleep and is slipping sideways. I can't push her back into her seat. Could you help me with that?"

I turned my head and saw the large Hawaiian woman dead asleep and leaning across the aisle. Her left arm was extended with her gigantic, multi-colored handbag clutched in her fist. No one was able to pass. *This is certainly a man's job,* I thought to myself. *To push a four hundred pound woman back into her seat takes serious muscle.* I regarded Lea with an expression that said, "I thought you were going to ask something easy."

I proceeded to push and shove at Ms. HonoOpono's bulk, thrusting my whole body into the effort, but without success.

Lea was standing behind me, patiently observing my futile attempts. I felt like a high school kid trying desperately to impress the new girl in school with a task that exceeded my abilities. After a dozen or so tries from many angles, it was evident that I wouldn't be able to move that much weight by myself.

"It's okay if you can't push her into her seat," Lea said in a soothing voice.

Her comment only served to challenge my ego to new heights. I tried even harder, but by now I was completely exhausted.

"You could try to wake her up," Lea suggested. "She won't mind at all. She'll understand, you know."

"Really!" I said. "Well, you're probably right." Still trying to catch my breath, I began to move Ms. HonoOpono's arms and shake her left shoulder. Finally she awoke with a start.

"Oh, my God," she said. "Are we there already?" Her voice boomed like thunder through the compartment.

"No, Akina," Lea said gently. "There are a good six hours left before our arrival. Just lean back the other way and get some more sleep. It's all good."

She helped Ms. HonoOpono lean back and carefully tucked a blanket around her, caring for her as if she were her very own mother.

"Mahalo, Gaston," Lea said when she was done. With her distinctive accent, it was evident she spoke Hawaiian fluently. *Mahalo* means a heartfelt thank you.

"You're welcome," I said, my tone conveying the faint hope that we might continue our conversation. But she turned and walked to the circular staircase that lead to the bar upstairs. With a mental shrug I headed for my seat, but before I even reached it I was asking myself, *Why didn't you follow her?* Sighing, I sank into my seat with the overwhelming certainty that I had failed once more. More than ever I was confused over how I felt towards this woman whom I really knew nothing about.

"You did the right thing trying to help Lea," Mr. Toldeck said. "Now she knows she can ask you anything, even if it means attempting to move a four hundred pound woman out of the way if need be. That's quite impressive, you know."

Once again, Mr. Toldeck had found a way to make me laugh while dispelling all my doubts. Nevertheless, I kept quiet about my choice of returning to my seat. I certainly couldn't tell him that I didn't understand why I seemed to be more drawn to him than to Lea. That would probably create the wrong impression, which I had no intention of doing. However, I was drawn to his presence as if he were an old friend, a true ally.

"Tell me more about your family," Mr. Toldeck said. "You have a very interesting way of looking at the world."

"You know, Mr. Toldeck," I replied, "My father was only fulfilling his destiny by accepting what the medical professionals were telling him. Sometimes we would visit my mom on the weekends, but her instabilities were growing deeper roots under the influence of those treatments. After a while, we stopped going.

"Many days after I was torn from my mother, I regained my vision from the temporary blindness caused by the trauma of the separation. For a very long time after that, I looked for her face in everyone I met. Even though I had spent scarcely more than six months in her presence, our emotional ties were profound.

"During the months that followed this rupture, I visited every aunt from both my father's and my mother's side. Moving around like this led me to attach myself to each aunt as soon as I felt comfortable there, but then I'd move again and have to detach myself all over again. During each episode, I'd learn the value of detachment and recognize that my pain originated from my own emotional attachments. Some relatives loved me more than others. Over time I became aware that the more I focused on smiling back and loving them, the happier I got. I even learned that I could have others experience this with me. However, at times my ache to feel loved was so unbearable that I fell into a state of complete helplessness, a state of 'please pick me up, and never let me go.' Whenever this turmoil of emotions arose, I'd be on the lookout for contact with someone who would help me cope with it. This state amounted to a sort of emotional torture.

"By the time I'd traveled the entire family circuit, I'd learned how to walk, talk, and make a lot of people laugh. For emotional survival, I had become a one-year-old clown. Everywhere I was taken, I designed my actions to attract other people's attention. After many attempts to generate attention through crying, I'd learned that acting silly was far more effective. But my heart ached for a cradle without wheels, a permanent place of residence. Sometimes stability can be your only anchor to contentment.

"I remember one afternoon my father brought me home for the weekend. Whenever this happened, my older sisters, Jacqueline and Denise, would take care of me. Jacqueline was hanging clothes on the clothesline on our balcony over the backyard alley. Our family lived on the third floor of a triplex. I was helping Jacqueline by standing on a wooden stool and giving her pieces of clothing to hang. At one point in the process, I climbed too far out over the railing and tumbled over, falling from the third floor onto the second floor clothesline strung below. Caught by the line I bounced up and down for a moment, then fell onto the first floor clothesline farther down. After another bounce I hit the metal roof of the shed in the back alley. As I was falling I could hear my sisters screaming at the top of their lungs, and some of the watching neighbors as well. Jacqueline and Denise were devastated by what had happened. As for me, every part of my body was throbbing with pain and fear."

I paused for a moment, unable to continue. The break gave me the opportunity to admire Lea walking back to her seat from the staircase. I shook my head in amazement at the perfection of her beauty.

"It's okay if you want to go over to Lea and spend time with her," Mr. Toldeck said knowingly.

Lea looked our way. Noting my admiring gaze, she smiled invitingly. I hastily averted my eyes, pretending I hadn't been staring at her. Turning to Mr. Toldeck I said, "Why, Mr. Toldeck, don't you want to know what happened to me after my great fall from the sky?"

He regarded thoughtfully me and nodded, his expression telling me that I had the freedom to do whatever I chose.

"Go ahead," he said. "I'm listening."

"Well," I went on, "my sisters screamed unbelievably loud. I mean, the whole neighborhood heard them yelling as they ran down the metal staircase to the back alley. The other neighbors who had witnessed my fall as well called it a miracle. After that day I was known as the Miracle Kid, *L'enfant du Ciel*.

"That evening, my physical body still in excruciating pain, I cried out to be with Rebatarz. As soon as I lay in my little bed, I was once again out of my body. However, this time I was not with Rebatarz. Instead, I was in the presence of a tall man with long white hair and a long beard. He wore a robe similar to Rebatarz's, but his was white as snow. Its hood was pulled up over his head.

"He looked at me as if he had been patiently waiting for my arrival. His eyes held the most peaceful gaze, and within them rested Divine Love Itself.

"'I am Fubee,' he said, 'and I have assisted many travelers in fulfilling their missions such as the one you have undertaken. My duty, like Rebatarz's, is to assist you.'

"I was thinking to myself, *Why does it take two of them to assist me?* As if he had been reading my mind, and perhaps he had, Fubee answered my question.

"'On earth,' Fubee said, 'it has always taken a village to raise a child. The spiritual worlds are the same; the spiritual education of each Soul requires the involvement of the entire spiritual hierarchy to raise It to self-realization and God-realization.'

"I pleaded with Fubee to remove me from my unbearable situation. He only laughed kindly and shook his head. Despite my predicament, his gentle laughter made me laugh as well. Then he explained the truth of things to me.

"'The path you have agreed to undertake cannot be a selfish one,' he said.' Every time one individual attains an exalted state, the human race is lifted a little higher, just as a rising tide lifts all boats. Souls have infinite guidance, dear Gaston, and it shall always be thus. Practice patience in this situation you find so unbearable. Patience is the greatest discipline of all.'

"Then he waved his right hand and said 'Baraka Bashad.'

"At that moment I realized that he, too, was part of the ancient line of masters I was in spiritual contact with. Then I awoke in my little body; it was morning. Most of my physical pain had been removed. I was ready to re-conquer the world."

Suddenly Brielle caught my attention. She was walking down the aisle collecting trash and conversing with each passenger, asking if they needed anything else or if she could help them in any way. She stopped by our row and looked right at me.

"Lea told me upstairs that you tried the impossible task of moving Ms. HonoOpono out of the aisle. I saw her too, but decided to refrain from such an enormous undertaking. It's funny, because I was also planning on asking you for help. So I want to thank you. Mrs. Pearl in Honolulu had already told me that if I needed help with Ms. HonoOpono I could count on you. I never imagined that I might be asking you to move her out of the aisle. Well, she was right. I can count on you for anything." She laughed.

"Yes," I said, smiling. "You can continue to depend on my assistance if needed."

I was relieved she still didn't bother Mr. Toldeck, as he was not supposed to be in the First Class section. I knew it, and probably so did everyone else in the compartment.

"What's your final destination?" Brielle inquired, paying no attention to Mr. Toldeck. I tried to answer as quickly as possible so she could be on her way and not ask him to return to coach.

"I plan on staying in Bangkok for a few days," I said. "But I don't know where yet. I'll leave that to destiny. I need to recuperate from this long flight, then it's on to Koh Samui Island."

"Oh," Brielle said. "I was there just last year." She shrugged. "It's alright."

"What's your favorite vacation place?" I said.

"For me, it's Maui," she said. Her face took on a bit of a glow. "I just spent two whole days there."

"Why Maui?"

"I can't really explain it," Brielle answered. "Maybe it's something they put in the water. Whenever I spend a few days there, I feel completely rejuvenated. I feel at home on Maui."

"Alright, Brielle," I said. "Mrs. Pearl told you that I've live on Maui, right? Or was it Ms. HonoOpono?"

"No," Brielle said, her tone a little indignant. "No. No one told me."

"Okay, okay," I said. "I believe you. You know, Brielle, every time I return to Maui, and I mean the instant that I see the island from the plane, my heart experiences an instant feeling of happiness. It always feels like returning home. I've lived in many places, but Maui is my favorite, too."

"Where else have you lived?" she said.

"Well, let's see," I said. "In Canada—Vancouver and Montreal. In the US—the San Francisco Bay area and Minneapolis. And in Europe I lived in Geneva and Paris."

"Working with China Air Line, I've traveled all over the world in the past ten years. You've lived in three of my favorite places: Maui, Montreal, and Paris. What a coincidence. But I noticed you didn't seem to include Maui as part of the US. Am I wrong in making this assumption?"

"You're very perceptive," I said. "Hawaii may be governed by Washington, but it is certainly not an American culture. The Hawaiians are the best Americans of all, from my point of view, besides Minnesotans, of course." I paused to smile at the memories of these places. "I first visited Maui all by myself at the age of 18 in the fall of 1978. Then I moved there the fall of 1989. That year when we moved there during Thanksgiving, our entire neighborhood invited us over for a traditional Thanksgiving feast. It was a true miracle to see all of these happy people wanting to share so much together, all in the spirit of Love. Thanksgiving may be an American tradition, but the Hawaiians truly live the spirit of this holiday, being thankful and generous with their Aloha Spirit.

"And for them it's not just a one-day event either; it lasts all year round. Let's say you have a flat tire on Maui, or the hood of your car is open by the side of the road. You have to stand by the roadside and wave people away. If you don't, everyone passing by will stop to help you. Next time you're on Maui, just park your car on the side of the road, open your hood, and watch the magic unfold. The Spirit of Aloha will come alive right before your eyes. You'll be overwhelmed by their generosity. And I mean within seconds. How could you not feel at home in a place filled with so much goodwill? Maui is my favorite place, next to heaven."

We both laughed.

"Thank you Mr. Ouellet," Brielle said. "I'll try that next time I visit Maui. And I can assure you, I'll remember your story. I have to go and attend to others passengers now."

I watched her walk away, then turned to Mr. Toldeck. He was staring at me, smiling.

"Well, well, well," he mused. "You're quite passionate about Hawaiians, aren't you?"

"You can say that again," I replied emphatically. "So little is known of this great culture. Many ancient stories are hidden within these sacred lands. Like the legend of the Menehune people. Until the early 1900s, the Menehune were actually part of the US census records. Then one day they all vanished, never to be found or seen again. Many elders and Kahunas know of hundreds of their sacred sites throughout the islands. Stories tell how the Menehune would create great fish ponds for the Hawaiians within an astonishingly small time frame and with a reverence for nature. The Menehune were three or four feet high with a sturdy bodies and childlike spirits, always willing to play with the Hawaiians and to help them. But then one day they were just gone.

"Another legend tells about the Tall Brothers. They were twelve to fifteen feet tall, with very slim bodies and long arms and legs. They were one of the most evolved human forms on earth; their state of consciousness far exceeded anything we can currently conceive of. Many of the mysterious monuments around the globe are remnants of their ancient culture.

"North Americans are always proud to travel the world, trying to save countries like Tibet, or to provide assistance to the sick in Africa. I believe we're extremely presumptuous in assuming we can bring democracy to the tribal people of Afghanistan or to anyone else for that matter. Meanwhile, in our own heartland the cry to be heard is loud and clear, so we might begin by giving ourselves real democracy. We are trying to bring democracy to the world, when all along we haven't even honored our own agreements with the First Nation. And we've disgraced ourselves by what we have done to the Hawaiian Nation."

"Well," Mr. Toldeck said. "I said you were passionate about Hawaiians. May I ask you a question?"

"Of course you may." I said.

"Let me go back to some things you mentioned earlier that puzzle me, if that's okay with you."

'"Please," I said. "Go ahead!"

"You talked about regaining your sight as a small child," Mr. Toldeck said. "Could you tell me more about that?"

"Losing my sight was brief. Such occurrences are quite common when a traumatic event occurs. For some it's permanent. For others it affects the vision in different ways. Sometimes, they no longer want to see close up for fear of being hurt again. At times the pain inside them is so severe they choose to alter their visual capabilities for survival purposes. If we choose to, we can unlock these frozen emotions and regain balanced vision again. Emotional vibrations or energies are stored in our causal bodies, safely tucked away until we're ready to deal with them. The possibility of facing our pain overwhelms us most of the time. This is why we so often remain in a state of misery rather than confront horrible events from the past and set ourselves free. It requires monumental courage to revisit events that have created major impacts in our lives, and consequently, our psyches. In a way, due to our spiritual weaknesses, we have become attached to our pain, just as we sometimes remain attached to our favorite foods even when we know they're not good for us."

Abruptly I stopped talking and raised my right hand. Somewhere in the background noise of the plane, I heard a recurring sound. It increased in volume each time it was repeated, but I couldn't determine exactly what it was or where it was coming from. Then it suddenly became clear what the sound was.

"Psst! Psst! Psst! Psst!" Ms. HonoOpono was wide awake, frantically waving at me.

"Alas," I said to Mr. Toldeck. "I am being summoned once again to the humility chamber."

He smiled, and we shared another laugh. This time I was on my guard. I snuck a glance at Lea to see if she noticed me, but her attention was occupied by the movie she was watching on the screen in front of her. I reached Ms. HonoOpono unnoticed. She began talking before I even sat down.

"So," she said. "You and Lea have had the opportunity to get to know one another, right?"

"Well," I replied, "I wouldn't quite call it that."

"What are you talking about?" she said. "I woke up when you were moving my arm, and there she was, standing right behind you, watching your every move. When I saw the two of you standing there, I immediately told myself 'You can go back to sleep now, Akina. You've reached your goal to have them connect.' So, if that's not the case, what would you call it?"

"Well," I answered cautiously, "first she asked for help because she couldn't pass through the aisle. Then she left right away to go upstairs to the bar. If she were really interested in me, she would have…"

"Would have!" Ms. HonoOpono snorted, interrupting me. "Would have what? Come on! You're a man, right?"

"Ah…" I replied, taken aback by the bluntness of her question.

"Act like one, for God sake," she continued. "Don't go expecting gorgeous women to just throw themselves at you! You may be an attractive man, Gaston, but good women just don't do that. If you're expecting them to, you aren't respecting the true nature of women or honoring our traditional roles." She paused in her lecture long enough to catch her breath and smile sweetly at me. "In my opinion, of course."

It was plainly evident how invested she was in her point of view. I pondered her last remark. It made so much sense. Why hadn't I seen that before?

"I guess you're right," I said. "How did you know that Lea had asked me for help?"

"You guess I'm right!" Ms. HonoOpono huffed. "How long have you been blind to women being interesting in you?"

"Is it that obvious?" I said. "Most of my life, I guess. Since you've asked."

"Well, you're going to have to tell me what this is all about," she said. "I may choose to ignore any reasons why a handsome man such has yourself has been blind to women's' interest most of his life." She wagged her index finger at me. "But make it a good story. And no excuses now, because I won't let you get away with any." She crossed her arms with conviction. "Be prepared for a rebuttal."

She was genuinely interested in finding out all about me and my fear. She was truly concerned, just as a good friend would be, the kind who calls you on your issues right away and won't let you get away with anything.

"And don't you worry." She grinned and patted me on the shoulder. "Your secrets are safe with me. You can be sure of that, Gaston; especially after all we've been through together."

We both laughed at her exaggeration. Lea turned her head and looked at us over the back of her seat. I began to wonder what kind of situation I had gotten myself into again. Why didn't I just decline when she called me over? After all, I was in the middle of a conversation with Mr. Toldeck.

"Okay," I began. "Here it goes. It is my personal belief that our first intimate relationship has profound and lasting effects. My first intimate relationship was with an older woman. I was fifteen, and she was quite a bit older. She desired me—I didn't have to work to attract her. As a result, I didn't have the incentive to develop the necessary skills to conquer women."

The instance I spoke my last syllable, she was all over me.

"Conquer women?" she all but shouted. "We're not in the caveman days, you know, Gaston!"

Yet despite herself, she laughed with her usual battlefield voice. "Go on! Tell me more."

"Because this relationship lasted for over a year," I explained, "I picked up everything a young man can learn from an experienced woman about relationships. But of course she never taught me how to approach a woman in a traditional manner; she didn't want me to do that. What I subsequently internalized was that women initiate all the moves. I came to believe that I only need to watch and wait, and that she would come to me if I would just be patient.

"I was born and raised in Quebec, and let me tell you, it's a matriarchal culture. Women dominate; mothers are the head of the family and make the major decisions. And I'm not joking!

"If you visit Quebec, you'll see behavior in women that rarely exists in Anglo-Saxon communities. We're a product of where we're raised, just as you are a Hawaiian woman with your own traditions and social customs."

"What do you mean by women ruling a matriarchal society?" Ms. HonoOpono said. "I've heard of that, but I didn't know it existed in this day and age. The women over there must be very happy. I know I would be!" She made the Hawaiian "hang loose" sign.

"The women aren't necessarily happier, I don't think," I said. "In western culture, it's very much a man's world, as you know. There, the woman is the heart of the home, and the man is the head of the household. In Quebec, women through many generations have become the head of the home, and the men have moved to be more of the heart."

"Oh, come on!" she retorted. "How can a woman ever want to leave the throne of being the heart of her home? Anyway, that's impossible in a man's world."

"The women in my culture have had to do this through centuries of conditioning. Before the 19th century, when our French ancestors came to the New World, all they wanted after the ordeal of crossing the Atlantic for three months was to find companionship and intimacy as soon as possible. And guess what? Within a very short period the French settlers not only made contact with and befriended the local natives, they also married native women, unlike the British settlers.

"The culture that developed in Quebec was mostly half French and half Native American. Many of these mixed couples lived near native villages, which were mostly matriarchal societies. Most of the men became *coureurs des bois*, or "runners of the woods." The French Canadians lived for the most part in log cabins they built with their native wives. The women would stay at home while their men were out in the forest trapping animals. When the men returned they'd sell their furs and trade for other goods. This practice lasted from about 1650 to the late1850s.

"For over 200 years, French Canadian women learned to do everything by themselves because their partners were away from home for long periods of time. Usually, they were totally isolated from any communities as we know them today; a woman's creative skills became her survival tool kit. So she became a Super Woman. At least, that's what I call them.

"As a result of that independence, our women know what they want and how to get it. After ten generations of developing their survival skills, you can't expect women to just give up their independence, even if you give them dishwashers, clothes dryers, and home delivery services. I'm speaking from experience here. I've been married to both—an American woman at the age of 21, and a French Canadian woman at the age of 28. The differences between these two kinds of woman are vast. For example, an American woman whose light bulb is broken in her fifteen foot ceiling fixture will wait for her husband to come home and fix it. This, in turn, gives her man a sense that his role of assisting his mate is being fulfilled and honored. But for a French Canadian woman, none of that exists. When her man comes home, he'll discover that she has dragged the kitchen table into the middle of the living room floor, placed the highest chair she could find on top of the table, and is standing on tip toes on the chair replacing the bulb herself. Her man walks in wondering why she didn't ask him. Like an American man, he too would have been very happy to assist his beloved in fulfilling her needs. But two hundred years of *I can do it all by myself* is still pulsing through a French Canadian woman's veins. That's the culture I come from; those are my roots. For that reason, in my culture, a woman literally chooses her man, and the man waits patiently. And that's the reason I have not pursued Lea. God knows that every fiber of my being wants to. By the way, through this cultural facet I have learned to be patient, if that's ever possible for a man to learn."

I took a breath. Ms. HonoOpono just stared at me for a few seconds.

"So, if I understand you correctly," she said slowly, "your reason for not pursuing this beautiful, amazing woman sitting right here on this airplane, who is obviously interested in you, is that two hundred years ago women of your culture were driven to become Super Woman and you're still waiting for one of them to come pick you up. Did I get that right?"

I drew a breath but remained silent; I had no reasonable answer to that.

Ms. HonoOpono smiled, then laughed outright. I wasn't quite sure what to think of what she said, but I was on the edge of my seat waiting to see what she might come up with next.

"Well, Gaston," she said, shaking her head. "If you're waiting for a woman like Lea to pursue you like these French Canadian women, you'll probably be missing out on an opportunity to know a great woman. And let me tell you, French Canadian women might be Super Woman, but Lea is a Divine Goddess. She's learned the value of a man's role in her life. She's become skilled at honoring her own femininity, and that's truly rare in any culture today."

She stopped talking, and her face took on that mischievous expression I was coming to know so well. I couldn't help but wonder, *What now?* When she began to speak again, her tone of voice was much softer.

"Could you do me a favor?" she said "It would mean a lot to me."

"Yes," I said. "Of course I'd be honored."

"Could you go over to Lea and ask her to come over here, please? I need to talk with her."

I immediately became nervous. "You assured me earlier that my secrets are safe with you, right?"

She smiled and nodded affection clear in her eyes. "Yes," she said. "Very much so, Gaston."

Nevertheless, it was obvious she was up to something.

"Thank you for taking the time to listen to my stories," I said. "By the way, Ms. HonoOpono, why did you ask me over here? I am sure it wasn't to ask Lea to come over. So what was it for?"

Ms. HonoOpono waved her hand dismissively. "I can't remember right now," she smiled. "Your stories were so good that I forgot. As soon as I remember, I'll tell you, I promise."

"Alright." I made my way over to Lea's seat. "Hi, Lea," I said. "Ms. HonoOpono asked me to tell you that she needs to talk with you."

Lea got up right away. "So, now it's my turn to have some fun," she said with a twinkle in her eye. Her laughter rang like silver bells.

"Good luck back there," I offered.

Lea wandered the three rows back and sat down. When she moved, I couldn't help but notice her elegant figure dancing beneath the colorful silk of her dress. From my seat I could hear them giggling, like little girls do when they get together. I kept telling myself, *I hope she doesn't tell her my story.* Turning to Mr. Toldeck, I found him waiting with a patient smile. I looked away—the last encounter with Ms. HonoOpono still preoccupied me. Understanding, Mr. Toldeck shifted in his seat to gaze out the window.

It was still daytime, and the view outside was spectacular. Yet as we flew over a vast cloudscape, fears of betrayal resurfaced within me. Mr. Toldeck must have recognized the signs, for he allowed me a period of silence to regain my composure. After a while, he turned back to me.

As I looked into his eyes, the uncanny familiarity of his presence continued to grow within me. Just like before, when I tried to follow the thread of this strange feeling back to its source, my attention was pulled elsewhere. Lea was returning to her seat.

Again, I observed appreciatively the way her dress seemed to float around her body when she moved, graceful as an eagle soaring in the sky. This time I felt I was ready for her. I assembled all my courage and gathered as much determination as I could to cross the aisle and talk to her.

Quietly, I shifted my weight forward to stand but then I noticed Brielle had followed Lea to her seat and they had started a conversation. Dejected, I settled back and lowered my eyes. *Well,* I thought, *missed the boat again.* Mr. Toldeck waved his left hand trying to wrest my attention away from the moody state I had drifted into.

"Do you remember another time earlier in your youth," he began, "when you met with your friend, Fubee? Or perhaps I should call him Master Fubee?"

"Both descriptions are appropriate," I said. "As for another time? I definitely remember. I must have been about eighteen months old. The assault of the instability in my living conditions persisted for a very long time and caused me enormous sorrow. I had to constantly readjust to new family rules, settings, bedtime schedules, and cousins. Besides the presence of Fubee and Rebatarz, there seemed to be only two things that followed me on my journeys: my little brown teddy bear, Baba, and my little green suitcase.

"Several weeks before Fubee paid me visit, I had finally made peace with the fact that I was destined to be moved around within our family circle. For the moment I had found a comfortable nest at my aunt Marie-Anne's who loved me very much. At last I experienced a little of what being part of a family felt like. On the afternoon of Fubee's appearance, my father came to the house. He argued with Marie-Anne for over an hour. She never let him touch me that day. After my father left, she cried so hard I cried with her. When it was time for my nap, Aunt Marie-Anne wiped her tears and mine, and laid me down in my crib.

"As soon as she left the room, I stood up in the crib. I longed for her to return. I waited for the longest time for her to come back. Somewhere in the far distance, I heard her desperate sobs, but there was nothing I could do to comfort her. Eventually I grew tired and lay back down. As soon as I did, I slipped out of my body. Fubee was waiting to greet me. He often visited. Sometimes our conversations lasted for what felt like hours, sometimes they were shorter. But this visit would prove to be very different, indeed.

"He looked into my wide eyes. 'Soon, Little One,' he said, 'a great change will come into your life.'

"I looked quizzically at him, wondering what he meant. This was to be the shortest conversation we'd ever have. I'd learned from our previous discussions not to try to figure out the meaning of what he was saying, but just to be happy in his presence. Every time he visited me I would remember more about where I had journeyed from. The constant ache in my heart always vanished in his presence. Now I took my little Baba bear in my arms.

"Fubee continued to look into my eyes.' Remember what I told you, Little One,' he said.

'A great change is coming.'

"Fubee smiled and vanished as quickly has he had arrived. When I woke up the next morning, my aunt was kneeling on the floor beside me, filling my little green suitcase. I squeezed my Baba tight to my chest, knowing very well what this ritual indicated. I stood up in the crib and opened my arms wide for my aunt Marie-Anne to pick me up. Her eyes overflowed with tears; her heart was overwhelmed by the opportunity to hold me once more. That afternoon I was transferred to a new home."

MATERNAL LOVE

IV

As I told Mr. Toldeck about my childhood, conflicting emotions kept bubbling to the surface. Why was I disclosing the most intimate pain of my past to this complete stranger, no matter how comfortable I felt with him? And yet as I noticed the love emanating from Mr. Toldeck's eyes, his very presence comforted me in ways I could not understand. In the presence of his love my self-pity simply burned away like an insubstantial mist. I took a deep breath and let out a sigh.

"I think I'll go for a short walk," I said. "I'll be back soon."

Mr. Toldeck nodded. "I believe it'll do you some good."

When I stood, Lea looked up through her beautiful lashes and smiled, her eyes signaling an invitation to join her. But I had just told Mr. Toldeck I was going on a walk, so I felt I certainly couldn't just get up and then sit right back down with Lea. Instead I smiled quickly in return and kept walking. As I passed Ms. HonoOpono's seat, she called out to me in her usual foghorn voice.

"Hey Gaston," she said. "I remember now what I wanted to ask you! When you get back I want to talk with you some more."

"Sure," I nodded. "I'll see you after I finish my stroll."

I passed by the stainless steel spiral staircase to the lounge upstairs and parted the heavy curtain that led to the coach section. A group of people were gathered at the very back of the plane where I usually spent most of my time on long flights such has this one. Intending to join them I proceeded toward that area. Suddenly, out of nowhere, I heard a woman's voice.

"Gaston! Gaston!" she called. I turned to see who was calling my name and saw my friend Ellouise waving at me. Her six-year-old son, Nelo, was on the seat beside her, hugging his knees.

"Oh, it's so nice to see a familiar face," Ellouise said. "Especially after all the turbulence we went through at the beginning of the flight. Nelo still hasn't stopped being afraid since the storm."

Ellouise stepped into the aisle and hugged me. She always hugged everyone she cared about, no matter where they were or what situation they were in. But this time her hug felt different. I sensed she needed reassurance. Nelo was scrunched up in a tight, six-year-old ball of fear, his eyes still wide with remembered terror.

I leaned down to him. "Can I sit beside you?"

Nelo nodded and sat upright.

"Can you help me, Coach Gaston, like you did at Big Beach?"

"Everything's going to be fine, Nelo," Ellouise said, but the slight tremor in her voice betrayed the fear she still harbored deep down.

"I can certainly try to help you, Nelo," I added. "But only if you let me. Okay?"

"Yes, Coach Gaston," Nelo said. "Please."

I nodded reassuringly. "So, Nelo, tell me what's going on?"

As Nelo's soccer coach for the past two years, I had discovered he was a very determined young boy. He was one of my favorite players.

Ellouise asked me if I could slide over one more seat so she could sit at my side as well. Nelo and I scooted over to make room for her. Deep inside the boy, I could sense his great courage struggling to rise to the surface.

"Ever since the plane tried to fall from the sky," he began, "I've been afraid of..." His voice trailed off.

"What are you afraid of, Nelo?" I prompted, smiling to reassure him.

"Don't laugh at me," he shouted, tears brimming in his eyes.

"Gaston would never do that, Nelo," Ellouise soothed. "You know that."

I could tell she had tried to get him to open up about his fear before I got there. Like me, Ellouise was a single parent. I had been in her son's life for many years now, and she had confidence in my parenting skills. God knows she had witnessed them being put to the test many times by children on the soccer field and by their parents as well.

"To conquer the monsters of your fears," I said, "you have to first admit what it is you're afraid of. It's the only way. I know what it means to be afraid. I give you my word, Nelo, we'll both listen to you and we won't laugh."

Nelo searched my eyes. "You've been afraid, Coach Gaston?"

I met his wide six-year-old gaze and nodded. "Many times," I affirmed.

Nelo swallowed and took a deep breath, forcing his courage to the surface. "I'm afraid..." he said, looking at his hands, "...I'm afraid my mother will die if we fall into one of those air pockets again." He looked up to see if I knew what he meant. "That's what my mother calls them," he explained. Then he leaned forward and whispered, "I think they're big holes in the sky."

Ellouise was so touched by her son's concern she silently began to cry. Just at that moment, Lea walked by in the aisle. She smiled graciously at the three of us and continued walking. My answering smile remained outwardly invisible.

"Let me see," I said to the boy. "You're afraid, right?"

"Yes," Nelo said.

"Because you believe your mom might die if we fall into a hole in the sky?"

Ellouise reached across me to hold Nelo's little hand. More tears trickled down her face.

"Let's remove this fear," I said. "Are you ready?"

Nelo compressed his lips, narrowed his eyes, and nodded.

"Then close your eyes," I told him. Nelo clenched his little eyes shut. "Imagine this. You're in the pilot seat holding the controls." At this, Nelo's eyes and forehead relaxed a little. "Now you're the pilot," I continued. "You control the plane." He gasped, and his chin lifted a fraction. The corners of his mouth turned up just the slightest bit. "Keep your eyes closed," I reminded him. "Look, your mom is sitting beside you. She's your co-pilot. Now look out the big windshield in front of you and tell me what you see ahead?"

"I can't see anything," he said. "There are too many clouds."

"That's good," I said. "You're already seeing with your imagination. Now pull up on the controls so we can climb above the clouds. See all those clouds falling away beneath us as we fly higher and higher."

Nelo's breath caught in his throat. "The clouds are almost gone, Coach Gaston," he said, his voice filled with wonder.

"What do you see now?" I asked.

"Stars," he said. "The sky's filled with bright stars!"

"Great job!" I said approvingly. "You did it! You've conquered your imaginary monster. You're now a Celestial Warrior! From this moment on, you can pilot the rest of your life and never have to worry about falling from the sky."

Nelo's relieved smile told me he was back to his normal, joyful self. With his eyes closed he continued to navigate his inner skies.

"How did you do that?" Ellouise breathed. "I've tried to help him for more than three hours now."

"Nelo created his fears from his own, out-of-control imagination," I said. "It's true that experiences can cause fear, but we only remain stuck in it when we can't let go of what our imagination has created. For Nelo, his fear was about losing his precious mom."

Ellouise laughed and looked fondly at her son. "What do you see now, Nelo?"

I knew then that she understood, because now she was participating in Nelo's imaginary world.

"I see you, Mom," he responded. "You're looking at the stars through the side window of the cockpit. You're piloting the plane now, Mom!"

Ellouise snapped down the tray in front of her, making sure Nelo could hear the sound. She then gripped the tray like an imaginary steering wheel and clicked it back into place.

"That's right, Nelo," she said. "And now we can rest because I just put the plane on automatic pilot. Is that okay, Captain Nelo?"

"Oh yes, co-pilot," he said. "I mean, Mom."

"Do you think it would be okay if Coach Gaston returned to his seat now?" she said.

Nelo opened his eyes and regarded his mom, then me, assessing the situation with the gravity only six year-olds can muster. "Yes, Mom," he decided. "You'll be fine now."

When I rose to leave, Nelo jumped up on his seat and gave me a big hug, just like his mom had taught him. By this time Lea was passing by again. I shrugged imperceptibly and favored her with an expression that indicated, "What can I do?" Ellouise gave me a big hug as well. Her heart was now wide open, and when she sat down, Nelo rested his head in her lap.

When I re-entered First Class, I noticed Lea's head was turned towards the curtain where I would appear. I had completely forgotten my past discussion with Mr. Toldeck. At Ms. HonoOpono's seat I paused and leaned in close.

"Sorry, I'll have to come back later," I told her. "I need to sit down now."

She gestured with her hand and cocked her head sideways as if to say, "What's wrong with *this* seat?"

Lea stood up the moment I approached. As I sat down in my seat she turned to walk away, this time with her handbag in her hand. She stopped abruptly and turned back to me, disappointment darkening her beautiful eyes.

"Nice little family you have back there, Mr. Ouellet," she said.

"What?"

I blinked in confusion, then I understood. "Oh, no. They're not my family. They're friends of mine." But she turned away and was gone before I could be sure she heard me. I let out another frustrated sigh.

"Did you enjoy your stroll?" Mr. Toldeck inquired politely.

"I did," I said, forcing my attention to focus on him. "It was very short. I tried to walk to the back of the plane, but my friend Ellouise called me over. Her son, Nelo, was caught up in a web of fear and asked me to help him. So I did." I glanced along the aisle where Lea had disappeared.

"How did you accomplish that?" Mr. Toldeck said.

"I just helped him use his imagination, that's all."

"Ahhhh...imagination," he mused. He paused and took a deep breath. It was obvious this was a subject he was fond of. "What is imagination to you, Gaston?"

"Mr. Toldeck, you're one of the most interesting men I've ever met," I said to him. "I once heard from a wise man that you can always tell what kind of a person someone is by the questions they ask. During this flight, you've asked me the most interesting questions, this last one being no exception."

Mr. Toldeck smiled and nodded his thanks; he made a rolling gesture for me to go on.

"Imagination is simply one of the greatest gifts the Great Spirit has given Soul," I said. "It's maybe the best tool Soul has to reach Its true home. You can't find it in a book or acquire it in a class. It's only through practice and experience that anyone can reveal this reality as a tangible truth."

Mr. Toldeck's attentive eyes never left my face. His piercing, loving gaze continued to boost my confidence and my willingness to share my experiences with him.

"The most amazing thing about imagination is that our greatest leaps forward haven't yet occurred. As Albert Einstein once said, 'Imagination is more important than knowledge.'"

Mr. Toldeck held up his hand.

"Albert Einstein," he repeated, shaking his head. "Amazing, Gaston."

I beamed at him for a moment, then my attention was drawn to Brielle who was approaching from the galley carrying a round, silver tray full of drinks. Suddenly I realized I felt completely dehydrated.

"You must be thirsty by now," Mr. Toldeck ventured when I turned back to him.

"Very much so," I agreed. "I've spent most of my life listening to others, but with you I don't seem to ever stop talking."

Brielle reached our seats. I raised my eyebrows at Mr. Toldeck in question, but he once again declined with a shake of his head. I turned back to Brielle.

"A whole bottle of water, please, and not a drop less." I requested." I'm completely dehydrated."

Brielle opened a bottle of water, and as she was about to pass it to me Nelo peaked out from around her skirt.

"Thank you for showing me how to fly the plane," he said.

Startled by Nelo's sudden presence, Brielle jumped, spilling water onto his head.

"You are now blessed, Nelo," I quipped. "Holy water has fallen upon your head. That's a Hawaiian blessing, you know."

Brielle and Lea both laughed out loud, caught up in the delight of childhood innocence, although I had merely wanted to comfort Nelo to prevent him from being embarrassed. The boy simply wiped his forehead and looked at me with wise young eyes.

"If I'm blessed because water fell on me," he stated, "then I'll be blessed for the rest of my life."

"Why's that, Nelo?" I said.

"Because we live in Aio Valley," he confided with a huge smile, "and it rains every single morning on my head when I walk to school."

Now Lea and I were laughing together. We both knew the magical energy of Aio Valley, one of the most sacred sites in all of Hawaii. In the ringing echo of our laughter my eyes briefly met Lea's in a moment of profound connection. Then we broke eye contact and Lea tried to recompose herself, while Nelo, having accomplished his mission, ran down the aisle to his mother without another word.

"So," Brielle said, "now you have to tell me what's so funny about Aio Valley?"

"Aio Valley is in the heart of Maui," I said. "It rains there more than anywhere else in the whole world, except for Lalalau Valley on Kauai. The two compete every year to see who gets the most."

"I had no idea," Brielle said.

I nodded, glancing quickly at Lea. "In Hawaiian legends it's the most sacred valley in all Polynesia," I said. "Next time you're on Maui, go see for yourself. You'll see that the legend is real."

I drank down half the contents of my water bottle in one long gulp as if my throat were on fire.

"I'll check it out next time I get back there," Brielle said. Then her voice turned playful. "By the way Gaston. Is there anyone on this plane who doesn't know you?"

I waved my hand to sweep away the idea. "I doubt there's anyone who knows me, especially on this plane. I barely know myself."

"Oh, I get it," she said. "You're a philosopher, and a comedian, too!"

Brielle left to deliver the rest of her drinks to thirsty passengers. Lea had not stopped staring at me. Our eyes met once more in a connection like the sun piercing early morning clouds. Overwhelmed by the light in her eyes, I had to turn away. Mr. Toldeck, patient as ever, looked up and raised his eyebrows as if to say, "Well, are you going to go over there on your own, or will I have to walk you over?"

I shook my head the slightest bit—not yet. He nodded his understanding.

"Since you're not going to see Lea yet," he said out loud, "I guess I'm compelled to ask you more questions."

"Ask away," I replied, trying to relax my tense shoulders. Bending forward I continued in barely more than a whisper. "Because I'm not quite ready to..." I jerked my head slightly to indicate Lea.

Mr. Toldeck nodded again. "You mentioned earlier that you moved again when you were one-and-a-half. What was the new place like?"

I took a deep breath and sighed at the sweet memory. "It was the best place on earth and the best years of my childhood. As soon as we arrived my father placed me in the arms of an angel. She surrounded me in maternal love that stayed with me even after I left her.

"Her name was Amelie. Her husband was rarely home, or at least I have very little memory of him. I was received like a king. I had my own bedroom and toys of every imaginable color and shape. From my child perspective, I had died and gone to heaven. Did you see how fast I drank that water to quench my thirst? Amelie's love was like that: thirst-quenching to the love-starved Soul. I had never experienced this kind of love before. Most of my family had been caring for me out of duty. But Amelie had wanted so long to have children, and then I came along. For her, it was a miracle. I learned from Amelie that maternal love is the closest thing to Divine Love you can experience in the human condition. Mothers are the divine vehicles for the Creator to bring forth and nurture Soul in the lower worlds. The echoes of her love still ring in my heart today."

After these words my entire body was vibrating with the memory of Amelie's love, and it must have shone through my eyes. Mr. Toldeck continued to regard me with his piercing gaze and I realized that even though I was overflowing with love, his love for life far exceeded mine. I had to look away.

My attention turned inward. *Feelings like these occur only when you open your heart*, I thought to myself. *They rise when you share your most intimate self with another.* I knew that even if I had wanted to extricate myself from these feelings, this profound love would never leave me.

Beautiful memories of Amelie scrolled across my inner vision faster than the speed of thought. Gratitude swelled in my heart. In the midst of my reverie, as if from a great distance, I sensed Lea rising from her seat across the aisle. *This time you do it*, I told myself. *Now.*

I was prepared to bounce up like a jack-in-the-box, but before I could do so she walked down the aisle and sat down with Ms. HonoOpono. Soon I heard them laughing and sharing stories, so I closed my eyes and drifted back into my own daydreams. After some time, I sensed a presence hovering beside me. When I opened my eyes I found Lea standing in the aisle leaning in close, her hair like a lustrous black curtain. My breath caught in my throat and I tried to keep my mouth from gaping.

"Mr. Ouellet," she said. "Ms. HonoOpono really, really wants to talk with you. Could you please go see her? She asked me to come get you."

I cleared my throat to be sure I could talk. "For sure. But please call me Gaston, if that's okay with you." I glanced back toward Ms. HonoOpono. "Is she okay?"

Lea's brow was knit. "I'm not sure."

I got up and cast a glance at Mr. Toldeck to let him know I would be back soon. Ms. HonoOpono began to talk before I had even settled into the seat, her voice filled with sorrow.

"Mahalo, Gaston. I need to talk to someone, and Lea thought you might be the right person."

"In regards to what?" I inquired.

"It's about my granddaughter." Her voice shook. "Lulu is dying as we speak. *Right now* and I feel so helpless!"

Torment gripped her tender grandma's heart—she needed to confide in someone. She needed someone to listen to her and share her feelings. I was ready, even though I had been talking for almost three hours straight by now.

I put my hand on her arm. "You gave me your word earlier that my secrets were safe with you, Ms. HonoOpono, and now I offer you the same sanctuary. Besides," I added, spreading my hands, palms up, "after everything we've been through together."

She laughed, despite herself, but then her laughter gave way once more to anguish. Her wails were so intense every passenger turned to look at us. I held her soft hand and let her sob until she had cried herself out. She rested her head on my shoulder, and I closed my eyes. A reverent silence reigned in the entire section. The Holy Sound Current was rushing through me in waves; my heartbeat kept time with Its pulsing rhythm.

We held hands for quite some time until Ms. HonoOpono noticed Brielle was preparing snacks in the galley ahead. With an effort she pulled herself together, raised her head from my shoulder, and began to come back to life.

"I am so sorry, Gaston," she apologized. "I…"

I held up my hand to cut her off. "You never need to apologize for expressing what's in your heart. Do you feel comfortable telling me what's really bothering you?"

She nodded and looked intently into my eyes. "I feel very comfortable talking with you. I just don't know where to start."

"That's easy," I said. "Always start with the hardest part. The rest comes more easily after that."

She smiled. "That's exactly what I used to tell Lulu." She squeezed my hand in both of hers.

"The hardest part?" she continued. "That would be the thought of my granddaughter dying before I do." She stopped for a moment, took a deep breath, and blew out the air between pursed lips. *"That's it!* Wow! I said it! But I still feel so helpless! It's just not fair for her to die so young. And I feel so guilty for not visiting her sooner. I just kept believing she could beat this thing, but as the months went by and her condition deteriorated, my guilt got worse and worse, preventing me from being there with her. Oh, don't get the wrong idea. I'm on the phone with her all the time!"

"Don't worry, Ms. HonoOpono," I assured her. "I hold no judgment. Only both of your hands."

The old trick of mine, trying to make her laugh again. But this time it didn't work. She pulled her hands away and folded them in her lap, avoiding my eyes.

"I hadn't even noticed we were still holding hands."

"Hey, that's alright," I smiled. "After everything we've been through together."

This time it did work. She guffawed with her usual thunder, showing her heart was beginning to open once again. Soon her laughter subsided, though, just as her tears had before.

"How do you do that?" she marveled. "How do you remove my tears and replace them with laughter?"

"I don't do anything. I just listen to my inner voice, my intuition—the Mana, as you call it in Hawaiian culture. I've devoted my entire life to learning to listen."

"Really!" Ms. HonoOpono said, perking up a bit. "How so? Do you have an example?"

"Let's see…I'll try my best." I pondered for a moment. "Okay, I know. Today for instance, I was going to be late for this flight. I had so much to do before leaving. Then I got a call from one of the realtors in our office asking if she could do some open houses at one of my listings while I was on vacation. I knew if I said yes I'd have even more to do before my departure. But my inner voice spoke loud and clear: *Say yes*.

"She was so grateful she helped me finish my errands and drove me to the airport in perfect time to arrive behind you in line. If I hadn't listened, you and I probably would have never met. Certainly I wouldn't be sitting in First Class talking with you. Everything is interconnected, but we usually never notice.

"I've learned that whenever someone asks me for something that requires a selfless act on my part, there's always a blessing waiting for me on the other side. When I woke up this morning I wasn't sure how to accomplish everything I needed to do. But the Mana, the Holy Spirit, knows what's best for us at all times. All we have to do is learn to listen and follow Its guidance."

I stopped talking and looked sideways at Ms. HonoOpono. She was completely engrossed in my story, so I decided to ask her a question.

"So tell me, Ms. HonoOpono. In your innermost heart, what did the Mana tell you about Lulu when you first heard of her cancer situation?"

The question had barely left my mouth when tears again cascaded down her face. Lea turned in her seat, her eyes wondering if I needed help. I shook my head slightly, not quite sure what to do. Ms. HonoOpono wiped her face with the cloth napkin she still had from her dinner. Slowly her breathing returned to normal.

"Did I tell you that my great grandfather was a Kahuna?"

"Yes, you did," I said.

"When I was a little girl, he told me all about the Mana and how It even uses nature to talk to us, and how important it is to learn to listen. Every time we went fishing he'd drill that into me over and over again, so I learned very early to listen to the Mana. But the first time my son, Kimo, called to tell me about Lulu, I didn't listen. My fear of losing her made me deaf to the Mana. I'm sure you can understand that, Gaston."

"Very much so, Ms. HonoOpono."

"But that same night, before I went to sleep, I did listen," she went on. "I was told to go see her as soon as possible and that everything would be fine. But after that every time I talked with my son, his desperation blotted out my intuition." She stopped for a moment, then smiled to herself. "Wow, Gaston! Thank you! This is the most inspiring conversation I've had in a long time. Since this ordeal started, actually. Just having you listen helps me remember that Lulu will be okay. I mean, she'll be fine. I just have to be ready for Kimo. He'll need me more than Lulu."

I could see from the sparkle in her eyes that she had passed beyond the shadow of fear and was once more listening to her heart. She squeezed my hand again with both of hers and looked deeply into my eyes.

"Knowing you has made this journey more bearable. You've given me the incentive to listen again, just as my grandfather did. And for that I am forever grateful. Now I'm filled with renewed purpose for all of my *keikis*. You know what *keiki* means, right?"

I nodded with a smile. "Child...kid, baby, toddler, youngster. The most precious beings in the entire world." Seeing her equilibrium restored, I ventured a question. "By the way, what was the original reason you asked me over here?"

She bowed her head for a moment, then faced towards me again. Her mischievous smile reappeared, and her wise eyes twinkled.

"All I wanted was to know if you knew what *keiki* means," she stated.

At this little white lie we both started laughing. She pulled her hands back and placed them in her lap.

"Honestly, I don't remember why, Gaston. But I think I really need to take a nap now."

I understood her need for solitude. Spreading the blanket across her lap I got up and returned to my seat.

Mr. Toldeck was awaited me there, but as soon as I sat down Lea waved to me. I moved to cross the aisle to sit next to her, but she slid over from her seat so that only the aisle separated us. In her delicate voice she told me that Ms. HonoOpono was a very special Hawaiian woman in the Maui hula community. Pausing, she looked into my eyes. Time briefly stood still, and I was lost in the most pleasant kind of way.

"Did you know that when I was a young girl Ms. HonoOpono was my hula teacher?" she said.

"No, I didn't."

"To hear her crying earlier was very difficult for me. I'm very proud of her, as you probably already know. Not long after she started crying, you had her laughing again. Thank you, Gaston. On this trip you've been of great assistance from the very beginning. So, tell me, what brings you to Asia?"

"I'm heading to a small island in the southern part of Thailand, called Koh Samui. I'm scheduled to undergo a three week fast and rest as much as possible."

"Fasting," Lea said, shaking her head. "I tried fasting once, but because I only weighed 117 lbs. I stopped after three days. Or, I should say, my boyfriend stopped me. To him it appeared as if I was going to die. I certainly wasn't fasting to lose weight, you know, but to improve my health. I had read a few books on the subject. Why are you fasting?"

"First, I love it," I said. "Second, the way I view my body is like this: It's a temple for the Aloha Spirit to dance within me."

She laughed and leaned closer. Her eyes glowed with what I hoped was affection.

"Fasting to me is like cleaning house," I went on. "I usually fast every Friday. But this fast is a very special occasion for me."

"Why's that?" she asked.

"I've been telling my whole family and friends that after this experience I'm never going to be the same again. That there will be a great transformation within me. I don't know yet what it will be, but deep down I'm prepared for whatever happens."

"It'll take a lot of discipline to fast for so long, I think."

"Maybe," I said. "But to me discipline is only difficult when I do something I dislike. It's different when I love what I'm doing. Look at artists, for instance. An artist can spend 15 to 18 hours a day creating his art and still be rejuvenated at the end. On the other hand, if you do something you dislike for only two hours you could be completely drained. Over the years I've disciplined myself to choose to do only things I love, and I've learned to love everything I do. And that includes washing the dishes. Just as you've learned to love hula dancing, I've learned to dance through life by simply choosing to love what I do and do what I love."

"Ms. HonoOpono told me you were a different kind of person," Lea chuckled. "She wasn't kidding!"

Out of nowhere, Nelo appeared between us in the aisle. He grabbed my hand with both of his and pulled at it with all his strength.

"Coach Gaston," he urged me. "Come and see. Please, Coach Gaston? Please? I want to show you something. Please?"

I looked at Lea, the disappointment of having to break off our conversation clear on my face.

"Go ahead, Coach Gaston." Lea's eyes were twinkling. "Go with him." She smiled her beautiful smile and the whole First Class section seemed to light up. "He wants to show you something." She slid back over to her window seat.

I gently turned Nelo's towards her. "Nelo, before I go with you, I'd like to introduce you to Ms. Lea. She's a great hula dancer."

"A hula dancer?" he exclaimed. "Wow! That's cool."

But the concept held his attention for only a moment. "Please, Coach Gaston? Come with me? I want to show you something."

"Okay, I will," I said. "Go back to your seat and I'll there in a few seconds."

"Promise?"

"Yes, Nelo, I promise."

Nelo dashed away as fast has he had arrived. I turned to Lea.

"I would really like to continue our conversation later, if that's okay with you."

"I would like that, Gaston."

As I walked toward the coach section, I couldn't help but feel I had lost a great opportunity. Already, after such a short time, I was besieged by a powerful longing for her presence. On my way to Nelo's seat, I kept running the same questions through my mind. *How can this be? I hardly know her. Is this love at first sight? Are we Soul Mates?* I had never accepted the belief that there could be one single woman created from the essence of God just for me. How foolish of anyone to limit God's creation this way. Still, the thought of this possibility brought me great joy, even though went against the grain of my understanding of life.

When I reached Nelo's seat, he was there all by himself with his crayons and drawings. I sat down next to him. He handed some of the papers to me.

"Here are the drawings of me and my mom flying the plane," he said proudly.

It was evident from his drawings that the Light was shining again in his life. Each drawing showed a big orange sun, and all his planes were four times smaller than the sun itself. By the time Nelo had finished explaining each picture and the story behind it, Ellouise made her way back. I stood up to vacate her seat. Once Nelo finished thanking me for coming over, he promptly began a conversation with his mother, giving me the opportunity to excuse myself. I hurried forward toward first class with the burning anticipation of being with Lea. With each step, my heartbeat increased. My palms were sweating.

For every second that went by, my mind ran thousands of potential scenarios of what I could do and say. At last I reached Lea's seat. She was curled up under a blue airline blanket, her eyes covered with a mask, thoroughly asleep.

I sank into my seat, my own face covered with a mask of disappointment. It had only been ten minutes since I left.

"Not what you were expecting?"

I turned to find Mr. Toldeck smiling at me.

"Life is always full of surprises," I sighed, returning his smile.

"Isn't that the truth," he concurred. "That being said, Gaston, I want to hear more about your childhood."

"Go ahead and ask."

"Besides discovering maternal love with Amelie," he said, "were there other surprises you can recall?"

"Other than being taken out of the body night after night by Rebatarz and constantly having to readjust to my small physical body afterward?" I smiled. But, in truth, there were many more.

"It was in early spring of 1963. I had just turned three. I was playing in the backyard sandbox, which had been built especially for me just a few weeks prior. I was playing with my fleet of yellow trucks when a tall, imposing figure appeared right in front of me. He sat down in the sand box and said his name was Gopal. His eyes were the clearest blue you could ever imagine. He had shoulder-length, yellow-golden hair and a snow-white robe similar to the one Fubee wore, except without a hood.

"Gopal looked deeply into me with compassionate, luminous eyes. He told me Amelie's home would only be a temporary resting place, and that my next destination would require all my inner strength to endure. At that time in my life I wasn't afraid of anything any longer. I had been reunited with love; pure, maternal love. The Holy Spirit was roaring within me. Due to my newfound 3-year-old confidence, I chose not to believe a word he said about the next journey requiring all my inner strength. I just kept thinking, 'How could the next journey be any worse than where I've already been?'

"Gopal and I talked while I played with my trucks. Just before he left, he said something to me that marked my life forever. I still use it to this day.

"'Know and remember,' Gopal said, 'that God's love is all there is.'

His statement reverberated strangely through me. I got up and ran as fast as I could from my little sand box into Amelie's arms, crying. In my heart I knew very well that each time a Master visited me, his words contained the truth, no matter how much I might try to deny it. I spent the rest of that afternoon glued to Amelie's side as much she let me. Her love was like a nostalgic perfume to me; no matter where I was I could sense it. Later that afternoon my father arrived with a big smile on his face. His joy at the mere sight of me was clearly evident, even though there was also fear in his eyes. I thought to myself, n*ow there's a familiar face, finally.* I hadn't seen anyone from my family for over a year and a half, so my heart rejoiced at my father's presence. Amelie asked me to go into the back yard to play. Not long afterward, I heard her devastating cry. She was screaming the same word over and over at my father.

"'No! No! No!'

"I ran to Amelie as fast as I could to comfort her. My father lowered himself down on one knee to embrace me, but I ran right past him. I was screaming too by now, crying and repeating the same word as Amelie.

"'No! No! No!'

"We sought comfort in each other's' arms and held on tight for what seemed like an eternity. When we finally separated, Amelie went upstairs and began to pack my green suitcase while my father tried to convince me it was best for me to go where my brother, Jean, lived. At the mention of my brother, I began to imagine going home. I ran around in joyful circles shouting 'Home! Home! Home!' over and over.

"'Yes,' my father replied several times. 'A big home with Jean.'

"By the time Amelie made it downstairs with the suitcase, I was completely overjoyed. I was going to see my brother! I was going home! She held my little hand in hers and walked me to my dad's car. I sat in the front seat and watched her walk back to her porch. Amelie waved at me as we pulled away, her face drawn in sadness. We drove for a very long time. The farther we drove, the more I could sense Amelie crying across the distance. In response I began to cry in a deep, gut-wrenching way I had never done before. The longing for someone who loved me unconditionally was physically painful. The torment would last for many months, but for the moment, I was overwhelmed by mixed feelings. I couldn't wait to be with my brother and my family, but I ached for Amelie.

"As my father drove, his eyes filled with tears as well. Every once in a while he would dry my cheeks and tell me again, 'Yes, a big home with Jean,' and 'everything will be all right.'

"But hidden in his voice I heard a different message. All I could do to stop myself from crying was to remind myself that we were going to see Jean. It had been a long time since I had played with Jean or even seen the rest of my family.

Given that I was the straggler in the family, I never got to play much with other children. So the thought of playing with my older brother and being at home brought me a great sense of happiness.

Truly, I had no idea what was really in store for me.

THE VISIONS OF SAINTS

V

"After a while I fell asleep like I always did on car trips. When we arrived, my father shook me gently. I awoke filled with joy and excitement. Finally I was coming home! Dad parked his blue '55 Ford in front of a huge brick mansion I had never been to before. I noticed right away that my father's expression wasn't happy anymore. Looking out the passenger's side window, I saw the biggest home a child could ever imagine—my first look at my father's house, I thought. The building reminded me of one of the temples I had visited with Rebatarz and Fubee in my inner travels, except this place seemed much darker.

"As we walked up the long, black marble staircase to the entrance, I noticed how many other children were playing in the yard around us. There were quite a lot of them, all boys. And suddenly I understood why my dad couldn't take care of me before: he simply had too many children! Boys of all ages ran up to greet him, all offering to help him or wanting to strike up a conversation. *That's my dad*, I thought happily. *He's very welcome at home.*

"Then, from behind one of the biggest double doors I had ever seen in my life, we all heard the boom of heavy shoes pounding on the wooden floor. In a flash, every single child disappeared. My dad opened one of the door halves, and the most frightening figure a child could ever imagine was standing there, framed in the twelve foot doorway.

"She was dressed in a dark gray robe and wore a white bonnet on her head. I was used to seeing people in robes after all the visits from Fubee, Rebatarz, and Gopal, but her robe was not like theirs at all. Besides that, the love I felt when the Masters visited me was barely discernible in this person. A sense of oppressive power occupied each square inch of this house, and she was the personification of it. To me, she seemed like the incarnation of the darkness itself. Her very posture demanded complete obedience. Her perfume was the awful scent of fear.

"*I hope this isn't my mother,* I thought. *She dresses funny.*

"Then I noticed many other women in similar gray habits walking towards us in the grand foyer. Their sight brought relief, since now I knew for sure the woman in the door wasn't my mother. She instructed us to follow her and ordered us to take a seat in a spacious office. My dad placed my little green suitcase by my side. He introduced himself to her and asked me to shake her hand. She was so terrifying I couldn't even look at her, and I shrank back in my chair. She introduced herself as Mother Superior Diane. She was in her late 50s, with a sturdy frame and a habitual frown.

"From her giant, creaking armchair behind a colossal wooden desk, she asked my father question after pointed question. The Mother Superior drilled my dad until his self-assurance caved in and he seemed close to tears. She finally noticed his fragile emotional state and softened her interrogation. I held on to my father's hand as if my life depended on it, feeling as if we were crossing a rushing river and I might be swept away at any moment. My breath became labored. I was trembling, barely able to control myself in the overwhelming presence of fear and darkness. All I could think was, *When do we get the hell out of here?* I'd heard more than enough already.

"Suddenly the ringing of a bell boomed over the PA system into every corner of the facility. In the distance I began hearing hundreds of muffled little footsteps scurrying up and down huge staircases. It seemed obvious to me the bell was announcing a great moment for everyone. Once the deafening sound echoed to silence, Mother Superior stood and indicated to my father it was time for him to leave. She took my little suitcase in one of her bony claws and captured my left hand in the other. Without a further word she walked me away from my father.

"'It's suppertime,' she said, 'and these little ones need to eat like everyone else.'

"As I was being dragged away towards the supper line where several hundred boys of all ages were lined up, I could hear my father sobbing behind us in the hallway. Once the cafeteria doors closed behind me I couldn't hear him any longer.

"Desperation and anxiety churned my stomach. I was terrified. When we reached the line, the Mother Superior asked one of the other boys to assist me with my meal. She continued on with my little suitcase in her hand. I sat down at a table with my meal tray, which was overflowing with food as if I were to fortify myself for battle.

"I addressed the kid sitting across from me. 'Where am I?'

"'You're at an orphanage!' all the boys at our table replied in unison,

"'An orphanage? What's an orphanage?'

"Everyone laughed. Then each boy tried to tell me about the place to the best of his abilities, describing it the way they themselves were experiencing it. Soon I began to cry, and from then on everyone left me alone. The rest of the boys finished their meal and ran outside to play. I sat forlornly where I was and watched the staff clean up the dining hall. Then, out of nowhere I sensed a loving presence amid all the darkness. She approached me and sat down by my side.

"'Hi,' she said. 'My name is Sister Michelle. I'm going to show you where to play and where you're going to sleep.'

"Sister Michelle was perhaps in her late twenties. The light that shone from her brown eyes was like a serenade to life. The love in her heart was as apparent as if it were dripping from her fingertips. Being with her instantly comforted me. She took me by the hand and led me to a balcony overlooking the yard. There I saw rows and rows of swing sets, sandboxes, and slides. Among them children from the ages of three to their late teens were gathered in distinct cliques all over the yard.

"Farther out I beheld the most horrible sight of all: a twelve foot fence surrounding the perimeter of the yard. So this was really a prison; they only *called* it an orphanage. Sister Michelle encouraged me to go and play, but I refused with a determination that almost equaled her persistence. Eventually I took a couple of tentative steps forward, sat down on one of the stairs that led to the playground, and cried some more. I thought of Amelie and how much I missed her. I could still smell her perfume, feel her tender touch, and remember the comfort of her love. But those sweet days were gone for good now."

Mr. Toldeck watched the tears roll down my face. My emotions had gotten the better of me once again. I'd assumed

I had them under control, convinced myself I'd made peace with my past, but apparently not so.

My throat was choking up, cutting off any further words. Mr. Toldeck allowed me time to compose myself and wipe away my tears. Furtively, I looked around to see if Lea or anyone else had seen my emotional display. I was relieved to discover that no one seemed to have noticed. Mr. Toldeck continued to regard me with profound love. It was clear that his inner state remained balanced; no matter what I shared, he was able to be fully present with me. His eyes revealed an understanding, not just of my words, but of the deepest feelings behind them. He could even tell I was unable to continue looking him in the eye, so he shifted his glance to the window when he next spoke.

"Your story is filled with the light of truth, Gaston. Remember that." He paused for a moment, then turned away from the window to look at me again. "Sometimes when you cry it means your heart is being heard. I wish to assure you that your heart is being listened to. But you can stop sharing your life story with me whenever you wish if telling it becomes too much to bear."

I nodded and wiped my face with the back of my hand. "The truth is, I didn't expect to re-experience so many emotions. They definitely took me by surprise." I paused to swallow and take a deep breath. "But there is a strong voice within me that urges me to continue this story."

He smiled. "When you're ready, I shall be eager to listen."

"Thank you," I said sincerely. "I've always told everyone in my life that to love is to listen and to listen is to love. In that light I wish to express my heartfelt gratitude for your listening. For the moment, though, it's time for me to make a trip to the bathroom."

I practically sprinted to the lavatory. Inside I gripped the sink with tight hands and stared for a long time at myself in the mirror. My breath rasped in and out in short gasps.

I am blessed to have experienced these challenges in my life, I told myself, over and over.

Strangely, it felt okay to share them with someone now. More than okay, really. It felt good to share them. Mr. Toldeck was probably the best listener I had ever met. And I was pretty sure no one would ever hear these stories again.

Soon my breathing returned to normal. I favored my reflection with a soft smile and ran my fingers through my hair. When I opened the door, Brielle was standing nearby.

"Hey, Gaston, you okay?"

"Of course. Why do you ask?"

Brielle gave me a warm smile. "Never mind. Would you like me to bring you some more tea?"

Who was I kidding? Of course her eyes took in the two big spots where my tears had darkened my light blue shirt. I've never been able to hide my emotions very well.

"Yes, please," I answered. "Some hot tea would be wonderful right now. Thank you, Brielle."

Brielle placed a comforting hand on my shoulder. She may not have known what was really going on, but she was ready to offer her support nonetheless.

As I was about to reach my seat, Ms. HonoOpono called me over. I turned around and sat by her.

"Thank you for coming over earlier," she said, patting me on the forearm. "You're such a good listener."

We talked for quite some time; mostly about her children and her many years has a hula dancer. Then she stopped abruptly and fixed me speculatively with her eyes. The moment stretched out to nearly a minute.

"I want to ask…" she began hesitantly.

It seemed like she began to think out loud, rambling in starts and stops from one ragged thought fragment to the next. For a few awkward moments, nothing she said made any sense to me. Then she took a big breath, recomposed herself, and nodded decisively.

"So here's what I wanted to ask you, Gaston. Earlier, you talked about intuition. How do you remain open to it?"

I whistled softly and raised my eyebrows. "Well, that can be a tricky question. But, really, the ways are limitless. I remain open to intuition by practicing my spiritual exercises every day."

"What the heck are spiritual exercises?" Ms. HonoOpono demanded. "Are they one of your inventions?"

"Don't I wish," I demurred. "No, spiritual exercises have been taught for thousands of years, until recently mostly by word of mouth. Simply said, they teach the oldest creative art form ever devised: it's the ancient art of listening within."

Ms. HonoOpono's eyes were so bright they shone like stars.

"Can anybody learn it? Can you teach me? Then I can share them with Lulu I when I visit her."

I nodded in agreement. "There are as many spiritual exercises as you can think of. The easiest one is called 'The Love Song to God.'

"You know how in the ancient Hawaiian tradition the day began at sunset? Every day, a young Kahuna in training would go to the beach or to a mountain ridge to blow the conch shell. While singing into it, within his heart that person would express the highest gratitude towards the Aloha Spirit and all It brings forth."

Ms. HonoOpono nodded. She was well versed in her culture.

I continued, "Well, that's just one version of The Love Song to God. Other cultures around the world have similar practices. Tibetan monks use a conch shell too. In Africa they use their voices. The sound all these practices have in common is HU, an ancient name for God. All Souls hold this song in their heart. All you have to do is sing HU with an open heart to reunite with the Divine Melody within and experience God's Love."

Ms. HonoOpono scribbled furiously in a tattered, blue spiral notebook she dug from the depths of her gigantic bag. After a moment she paused, waiting for me to go on.

I continued, "You can simply sit on a chair, or lie down in a comfortable position and fill your heart with love while you sing the HU. You can also write a letter to God, our true Beloved, about your spiritual concerns. You could even create a journal entitled 'Letters to God, My True Beloved.' Or you can put your attention on something or someone you can love easily, and then just love it a lot. There are so many spiritual exercises, I could go on forever. What matters most really is that you practice them with an open heart, and that you do them consistently every day."

I waited for her writing to catch up.

"Right now, though, my legs are begging me to take them for a walk, and the rest of my body needs to stretch out. So I'm going to listen to the intuition of my body. It wouldn't be wise not to."

She smiled with understanding.

"Go ahead, Gaston. We'll see each other later. Thank you for your special gifts. I'll certainly practice one or two of the spiritual exercises with Lulu when the time is right."

"I am very glad to hear that. I hope they'll serve Lulu and you as well as they have me."

I stood and stretched. What I really wanted to do was collapse in my seat and rest, but instead I felt drawn to the back of the plane without really knowing why. So I decided to take that walk. This time when I arrived there was no one there. I spent some time looking out the small circular window of the exit doorway. The beauty of the night sky filled my vision. Soon a majestic presence began to make itself felt within me, conveying Its infinite love. Then someone emerged from the lavatory and the noble silence was shattered. Not long thereafter, Brielle came up behind me.

"I thought you should know, Gaston that first class passengers aren't allowed back here, just as coach passengers aren't allowed in the first class section."

Brielle was only kidding, of course, and it was obvious she was just trying to make conversation. I played along with her joke. "I tried to go as far forward as I could, but the captain told me all the seats in his cabin were taken."

Brielle laughed and walked away shaking her head. I remained where I was, peering through the circular window again. By now the sky was shading towards a darker purple and the view was even more magnificent. Yet inside me, all kinds of emotions were bouncing around with a burning desire to burst from my chest.

I entered the galley where another flight attendant was preparing drinks and asked for a glass of water. My heart was being pulled in two directions: one part of me wanted to hurry back to Mr. Toldeck to relate one of the most frightening moments of my life. Another part was terrified that I would be unable to tell my story without being overcome by emotion again.

As I stood undecided, I began to understand that sharing my story with Mr. Toldeck had initiated a healing mechanism within me that reached deep into the shadowy corners I had avoided for years. I had never previously told so many aspects of my youth to anyone.

Before I came to a decision, Brielle quickly made her way back towards me.

"You need to return to your seat right away! The captain just told me we'll be hitting major turbulence again soon."

Echoing her words, the captain's voice came over the intercom with the same message. As I walked back towards first class, I noticed many of the passengers were becoming agitated again. When I passed by Nelo's seat he looked up at me, his body language crying out as if to say, "What do I do now?" I leaned close to him for a moment.

"Everything will be okay, Nelo," I said. "I trust you. You're a very good pilot." He smiled up at me gratefully.

By the time I reached first class, I had somehow gained a grand sense of confidence. *Yes,* I thought. *I will continue to share my story with Mr. Toldeck.* Even so, I was more than a little nervous when I sat down next to him.

Taking a deep breath, feeling as if I were about to jump off a cliff, I began, "Mr. Toldeck, I'm ready to share more of my story." My voice carried conviction but fear still very much lurked in the background.

Mr. Toldeck nodded approval. "All right then, tell me what happened at the orphanage?"

"You're asking what happened at the orphanage," I returned. "But the question really should be, what didn't happen?"

He chuckled, his good humor contagious. My inner tension flitted away, removing the last sliver of doubt. Replenished by the light of our laughter, I was ready to re-enter the trenches of my inner battleground.

"I lived in the orphanage for three years, until I was six. Over four hundred children were housed in that six-story brick building, with a different age group on each floor. I was on the second floor where the three to six year-olds lived. On our floor there were close to ninety children, forty-five or so against each wall of the dorm. Our white metal beds were lined up like in a hospital scene in an old war movie."

I stopped for a moment and searched Mr. Toldeck's eyes. His compassion and the full presence of his attention were as evident as ever.

"I was wondering earlier where I'd find the courage to talk about what happened during my first night at the orphanage. I guess I found it."

Mr. Toldeck nodded almost imperceptibly, as if to tell me he always knew I'd be able to tell this story.

I continued, "That first day, after sitting on the outside staircase for some time, the bell rang again over the PA system. The children rushed past me up the steps while Sister Michele remained standing behind me. She told me that it was time to show me where I'd sleep. Up on the second floor I sat on the white iron bed assigned to me, watching and listening to all the commotion. Suddenly, the dark figure loomed near again: Mother Superior Diane.

"The other children stopped whatever they were doing and scurried to their beds. Mother Superior announced it was time to pray. One of the sisters lowered the lights. Every child in the room dropped to his knees facing an impressive, six foot tall statue of Jesus at the far end of the room. Everyone except me. The intercom blasted a loud broadcast of the Rosary Recitation, which, I learned later, lasted for over thirty minutes every night.

"For the longest time I remained seated on my bed. Then Mother Superior came over and instructed me to kneel. I did as I was told, of course. As soon as the recitation ended, we were instructed to go to the bathroom and then return to our beds at once. Mother Superior Diane turned off the lights as she left. Sister Michele and Sister Roselyn came in and sat at opposite ends of the dorm to watch over us while we slept. Each held a Bible.

"Then the most horrifying wailing filled the dorm, as if hell itself had cracked open. It seemed more than a third of the children were moaning, screaming, or crying out for their mothers. Their bodies writhed in ways I had never imagined. The pervasive darkness was overwhelming. Most anyone hearing these agonizing cries of loneliness and despair would be compelled to join in. I struggled to keep the dark despair from sucking me in. I squeezed my eyes shut, placed my pillow over my head, plugged my fingers into my ears. When you hear young children crying together like this, and no one is there to comfort them, you can't help but be deeply touched by their desperate call for love.

"After a while I could no longer hold it in. My heart ached for the sweet bedtime ritual Amelie and I had shared every night before I went to sleep. My inner fortifications fell, and I cried out for God in the most profound way I could manage. Several moments later, a small, white light appeared at the end of my bed and grew until it seemed to light up the entire dorm. At the very center stood Master Fubee.

"The deafening cries of the children receded, and in the soft voice I had come to know so well, Fubee said, 'Remember that you are loved.'

"As soon as I heard those words, the anguish in my heart vanished. I felt like an infant who had just been breastfed by the divine mother herself. Every cell of my being rejoiced. After that night, the crying of the children no longer had any effect on me. Fubee had placed an aura of love around me. I was protected; safe in the sacred space Fubee's words had created in the core of my being. *Remember that you are loved.* The impact of his statement remained with me for a very long time. For that reason, night after night when the horrible cries began, I would recite aloud to myself, 'Remember that you are loved.'

"After several months, I learned to create a rapport with most of the nuns. I never fell asleep right away like the other children, so I developed different strategies to engage the nuns during nighttime. One of the ways I had learned was to hold my urine so I could get out of bed later and go to the bathroom. This would allow me to walk along the grand hallways where paintings of many saints hung on the walls. During those times, when all four hundred children were asleep, the orphanage seemed quite mystical, especially after the rosary had been broadcast and the children were crying in the dorm rooms. Silence was precious for the sisters as well as for me, yet silence was a rare commodity in that place."

I felt a comforting peace descend over Mr. Toldeck and myself. It was as if he had crossed with me the bridge of one of the most evil moments of my life. We remained suspended in this still point of trust and inner silence until I realized that everyone around us was caught up in panic. Again the plane was being tossed up and down, just like when we first left Honolulu.

The only difference for me was that this time I didn't feel anything resembling fear. I hadn't even noticed the turbulence until my attention had abruptly been pulled back to my body. My hands were clutching the armrests with white knuckles.

Then the captain's voice came again over the intercom. Sighing with relief, he explained that we were almost out of the storm. I loosened my grip and closed my eyes to find peace, but in my inner vision I saw Mr. Toldeck's deep blue eyes staring directly at me. My eyes flew open; to my amazement, he began to speak as if nothing unusual was going on.

"Did you see anything?" he said with a hint of laughter beneath his words.

At this point I didn't feel comfortable telling him how much I was drowning in his magnetic presence. I was even beginning to see his eyes when I closed mine! How strange would it have sounded if I mentioned that? *There is a limit*, I thought to myself, *to how close you can let yourself become with someone, especially with a stranger on a plane.*

"Only my own fears," I replied to his question. But what I was really saying was, 'Please don't ask me anything else about this.'

"Well, if that's so, then you've seen a lot," he said. "Tell me, Gaston, was your brother really at the orphanage with you?"

"Oh, yes! Yes, he was! But because he was five years older than me, he lived on a different floor and had a different schedule and school program.

"Truthfully, I hardly ever saw him, but I distinctly remember an incident where my brother came to my rescue. By then I was almost five. All the children were on the playground, and there was a circle of much older boys surrounding me who were yelling at me and calling me names. A soccer ball came bouncing towards us from another group, and a twelve-year-old boy ran over and kicked it back. As he was returning to his group he called out, 'Hey, Jean! Your brother's in trouble over there.' We'd barely ever spoken, this boy and I. Jean was ten at the time and his friends were much older than me, so we rarely interacted. Jean walked right into the circle of boys around me.

"'What's going on here, Gaston?' he demanded.

"'They're calling me crazy,' I said, struggling to keep my voice steady.

"'Who says that?' Jean asked ominously. He turned slowly, taking the time to look at each of the boys. My brother's reputation as a tough customer was well known. The other boys pointed to the tall kid who had been the main cause of my anguish.

"'Gaston is crazy,' the tall bully said defiantly. 'He told the sisters he met a saint in the hallway last night.'

"Jean turned to me. 'Was that you, Gaston?'

"He waited expectantly, hoping to hear an answer to the contrary. It was apparent from his tone that he certainly didn't condone such claims, even though the nuns often invoked the saints when they wanted to inspire us to higher moral and ethical behavior. The nuns spoke of the saints as if they lived in a penthouse atop of the orphanage. Not a day went by without one of the sisters glancing reverently towards the ceiling and telling us how Saint-This or Saint-That would have handled a situation differently. They probably figured managing four hundred children from broken homes required higher intervention, no matter how they got it.

"Jean continued to probe.

"'I heard the story this morning, but I didn't know it was you, Gaston. Is it true?'

"I was already surrounded by ten angry boys, at least one of whom was ready to beat me up. Now my brother was interrogating me too. Should I cave in or speak the truth? I knew Jean could very well turn on me, just as the others had done so many times.

"Jean repeated the question, this time louder.' Is it true, Gaston?'

Everyone in the circle was afraid of my older brother by then. He was ten, and the rest of us were five or six.

"I hung my head. 'Yes, it's true.'

Staring at my feet I prepared myself for the worst. I was exhausted from what I had gone through the night before, but a beating would make things infinitely worse.

"To my immense relief, my brother shoved the tall bully to the ground and pointed his finger at him. 'Hey! If my brother says he spoke with a saint last night, it's because it happened!'

"In the blink of an eye, the other boys disappeared. The Mother Superior came rushing towards us because my brother had pushed a younger boy down. She began smacking Jean's right hand with a yardstick, hard enough to make his wristwatch fall off. He yanked his hand away and yelled,

"'Hey! You broke the watch my father gave me!'

"'Don't you dare talk to me in that manner, young man!' she said sternly.' Hold your hands out again!'

"Jean extended his hands purposefully. 'You better watch this!' he warned the nun. She swung the thick yardstick again, but Jean caught it in his right hand, jerked it away from her, and held it up to the sky. 'Enough!' he shouted and broke the stick over his knee into four pieces. He ran to the twelve foot fence and threw the pieces over the top.

"Mother Superior watched my brother, knowing she couldn't catch him. Instead she dragged me away by the ear and hissed, 'This is your entire fault, isn't it?'

Thankfully the gonging of bell came to my rescue, announcing lunchtime. The Mother Superior released my ear, freeing me to run as fast as I could to get in line."

Mr. Toldeck's lips turned up in a wry smile. "Sounds like your brother was as courageous as you were. Was that story true? About seeing the saint?"

"Oh, yes. Every night I'd wait patiently and then get out of bed to go to the bathroom. My real intent was to talk with Sister Roselyn. Whenever I went to the bathroom, one of the sisters had to escort me there and then walk me back to my bed. Over the years I'd learned to ask questions about the paintings of the saints while we strolled along the hallway. The sisters found great pleasure in describing in eloquent detail all the saints' purposes and what they had accomplished in their lives. These conversations would have inspired anyone, but especially an impressionable five-year-old. During these nightly strolls, I was learning about all the different virtues, which my heart and Soul already knew very well, but the true meaning of which I had not yet discovered. These nights provided the most uplifting conversations I had while at the orphanage.

"Sometimes our conversation would last for hours, and in those precious moments I felt privileged. These one-on-one conversations provided me great comfort, something I had lost when I was taken from Amelie.

"Each nun's interpretation of the saints and the Bible varied so greatly that I had to wonder how they could be reading from the same Bible or talking about the same saints. The more I tried to comprehend what they were saying, the more I got confused.

"The day I saw the saint, there had been an outbreak of small pox among the older children on one of the upper floors.

That evening, the rest of us heard a lot of commotion as the nuns ran up and down the stairs to attend to the sick. As usual, I patiently waited to make my nightly excursion. This evening when I reached the corridor, Sister Roselyn's chair was empty. I headed for the opposite end, but Sister Michele wasn't there either.

"The corridor was barely lit except for two red exit lights and the soft glow spilling from under the bathroom door. Standing in the middle of the hallway, I saw a tall man with shoulder-length blond hair and piercing blue eyes. He was clad in a white robe similar to the one Fubee wore. He fixed me with his eyes as if he'd been waiting for me for a long time.

"We never saw men at the orphanage except on Sundays at church, or when Father Peter came around. The facility was operated exclusively by nuns. We'd occasionally see a man during visits of prospective parents, during the special events we had come to call "Adopt a Parent Day." That's when families would come by to adopt children. It was a very stressful time for everyone.

"But the tall man just stood there in the hallway, not looking at all like the priests who sometimes visited from different parishes. Priests wore black robes, not white ones. Cautiously I walked toward him, studying the paintings of the saints in the hope I might recognize his face in one of them. After all, my understanding of an encounter like this was founded on the reality the nuns had created for me with their stories. I'd heard so many tales of saints and their miracles they were as real to me as the nuns.

"As I got closer, joy started coursing through my body. I was intoxicated by Divine Love in the presence of this man.

Time and the world seemed to stop. Even my thoughts came to a halt.

"He gazed straight into my eyes, smiling gently.

"'Do you remember?' he asked me.

"'No, sir,' I managed to respond. I cocked my head sideways and studied his face. Should I know him? I couldn't place him, no matter how hard I tried.

"Still, I was happy for the first time in a very long while. His presence emanated the same Divine Love Fubee and Rebatarz brought when they visited. I walked past him and continued towards the opposite end of the corridor. The farther I walked away from him, the more I was seized by an immense desire to turn around and sprint into his arms. At the end of the hallway, I turned and looked back. He was still standing there, waiting, and still smiling at me.

"'Do you remember?' he asked again.

I shook my head and shrugged my shoulders in apology. I cast about to see if any of the nuns were around, but they were still absent. How strange that they weren't at their posts. They were there every night like sentries in an army camp; you could always count on their vigilance. When I turned back towards the tall man, he had vanished completely.

"I was a very fast runner, even as a small child; whenever I got in trouble the nuns could never catch me. Eventually I'd surrender, of course, because the consequences would be more severe if I didn't. So I had a pretty good idea how fast someone would have to move to leave the corridor. It was simply not humanly possible for the stranger to have gotten away so quickly. No one could run that fast, and even if he had I would have heard the pounding of his footsteps. I'd heard nothing of the sort in the silence of the night. How could this be?

"This realization excited me so much I was overcome with joy once more. The feeling grew and grew within me until I was lifted into a state of euphoria. I took off as fast as I could to find and talk with this strange man. My desire to find him grew with each step I took. By the time I reached the opposite end of the hallway, I heard the two sentry nuns returning from the upper floor. Frightened, I raced toward my bed at the far end of the dorm.

"I had almost made it when the nuns appeared in the door. I was startled by Sister Michele's voice, and even more by what she said.

"'Do you remember?' she called out.' Don't run!'

"Her words stopped me in my tracks. I spun around and ran as fast as I could back to the nuns."

Mr. Toldeck fixed me with his penetrating gaze, which I had become comfortable with by now.

"'Do you remember?'" Mr. Toldeck repeated and shook his head in wonder. He paused for a few seconds, looking inward. "Did you know what it meant when the stranger said to you, 'Do you remember?'"

I issued a deep sigh and shook my head. "Not at the time. I was caught up in his presence and in the mystery of the moment. But ever since that night, I remind myself to remember every day that my mission is to learn about Divine Love in ways I've never known before."

Mr. Toldeck said. "To choose to remember is, in my view, a conscious act. If people remembered that we're all children of God that alone would set the stage for us to cross the bridge to unity. To know that we're all part of the same spiritual family—what an awakening that would be! You've heard of the hundredth-monkey effect? This is where a group of monkeys discovers, for example, a new way to crack open up a coconut using a rock. Once one of them has learned it, the rest of the monkeys all over the world know the same technique. Who knows, Gaston? Maybe you could do the same with your stories by sharing them with the world. You could start your own hundredth-monkey effect so people remember we're all children of God. It only takes one person to make that first step so others can follow, even if they're thousands of miles away. You could be the initiator of a Divine Awakening. What do you think of that?"

After listening to Mr. Toldeck's little speech, I suddenly realized I had hardly heard him talk during the entire flight. What he said puzzled me very much. On the one hand, the possibility of me initiating a global awakening seemed farfetched. On the other hand, I had witnessed so many unusual phenomena in my life that I had come to believe everything was possible. How probable it actually was, however, was another matter entirely.

"I see that you have high aspirations for me," I said, half-jokingly. This made him chuckle but didn't appear to merit a verbal response. So I continued with my story.

"I know with certainty that whatever the Great Spirit has in store for both of us, there is nothing we can do to prevent it from happening. Divine Will supersedes all. Even if we've forgotten It, we are still Its children, Its creations. We do Its will knowingly or unknowingly. God's Love is around us all the time, although most people are unaware of It. We've taken God's presence and Its Love for granted because It's as commonplace as the clouds, the sun, and the ground we walk upon each day."

To this Mr. Toldeck replied, "You see, Gaston, I told you you might just be the right kid for this job! You could be the one to inspire us all to rediscover who we are. You might very well serve as a spiritual pioneer. Sometimes a person can share his own experiences in a story and change others in ways they never imagined. Just the simple act of sharing a story can set into motion a birth of awareness beyond one's control."

He fell silent, allowing me to consider his statement.

In my mind, I repeated to myself, *Just the simple act of sharing a story can set into motion a birth of awareness beyond one's control.*

I felt I was a living witness to the truth of that statement. Our conversation was transforming me, healing me in ways I hadn't even known I needed.

Mr. Toldeck interrupted my train of thought. "So, what happened when you reached the nuns?"

Just as I opened my mouth to respond, Ellouise appeared at my side.

"Please forgive me, Gaston," she pleaded, "but Nelo has been asking me to come get you ever since the last turbulence. Could you come, please?"

Without a moment's hesitation I rose from my seat. Lea looked up as I stepped into the aisle. Intending to introduce Mr. Toldeck to Ellouise, I realized that in the moment I had taken to make eye contact with Lea, my friend had already started heading back to her seat. I smiled apologetically at Mr. Toldeck.

"Go on," he said. "I'll be here when you get back."

As I was making my way out of the First Class, Ms. HonoOpono caught my hand and boomed up at me, "Hey, Gaston, I'm ready to hear more about your stories and those spiritual exercises you promised me."

Inwardly I thought, *why does she have to be so loud*? Outwardly I leaned close to her ear and whispered softly,

"We'll talk soon, I promise." I hoped she would get the unspoken message.

On my way to Nelo's seat, I passed Brielle coming up the aisle.

"Some of the passengers are still having problems adjusting after our last turbulence episode. Are you okay, Gaston?"

"I am. Thanks for asking. How about you, Brielle?"

"Oh, I am now. I was truly shaken a little earlier. That was a pretty rough patch. But now I'm okay." She shrugged. "Besides, it's part of my job."

"Well, it's obvious you're devoted to your job," I said. "Oh, by the way, do you think you could help me with something?"

"Name it and I'll do my best to help."

"I'm on my way to see Nelo, a six-year-old boy who's still very much shaken by our last…episode, as you called it. I was hoping you had one of those small plastic China Airline planes for my young friend."

Brielle brightened. "Indeed I do. Come with me."

I followed her to the front galley where she pulled open a metal drawer and handed me two perfect replicas of a China Airlines jet. "One for Nelo and one for you," she said with a big smile. I thanked her and concealed one of the small treasures in each jacket pocket. When I reached Nelo's seat, I found him curled up on his mother's lap.

"Nelo, I have a gift for you! Well…it's more like a surprise."

Nelo turned his face up and knuckled his eyes to wipe away the remnants of tears.

"What is it, Coach Gaston?" he asked timidly.

"I can't tell you. You have to get it yourself." I patted both of my jacket pockets. "You have to choose, left or right."

Nelo looked doubtful. "Coach Gaston, which is it? A surprise or a gift?"

I glanced at Ellouise for some guidance, but she seemed at a loss for words.

"Get up, young man, and choose for yourself," I instructed the boy. "There is a surprise in one pocket and a possibly gift in the other."

"How can that be?" Nelo sat halfway up and craned his neck from side to side, trying to see each pocket from every angle.

"Come on Nelo," I insisted. "You can do it. Get up and make a choice."

Nelo stood shakily on his seat.

"All right, I want the gift instead of the surprise. Which pocket is the gift in?"

I wagged my finger. "Oh no, you have to make your own decision."

Nelo sighed with his whole body, as only young children can do. "All right, the left pocket then."

Turning the left side of my jacket toward him, I said, "Go on, and pull it out yourself."

He fumbled awkwardly in my pocket and became frustrated when the wings caught on the lining.

"It is okay, Nelo," I said. "Here, let me help you."

I spread the pocket so that it was more easily accessible, and Nelo's hand emerged with the miniature airplane. He was so filled with joy that he jumped up and wrapped his arms around me.

"What would have happened if I picked up the other pocket, Coach Gaston?"

"See for yourself, Nelo."

The boy released me and quickly reached into my right pocket. Out came the second airplane. Triumphantly he held it up, hooting with pleasure. He sat down immediately and began playing with them.

"You see, Nelo," I said. "Today you received a gift and a surprise. All I ask is that you share them."

"Oh, yes, Coach Gaston, I will! Just like when you taught us not to be ball hogs." He placed one of the planes on his mom's lap and continued playing with the other.

Ellouise beamed. "Thank you again, Gaston! Nelo, say thank you to Coach Gaston."

Nelo jumped up in his seat again to give me a big hug and a kiss on the cheek. Ellouise's mouth fell open and her eyes widened in surprise. This behavior was way out of character for Nelo.

"My pleasure, Nelo," I said warmly. And it truly was my pleasure. My heart tingled with the joy of helping Nelo, even with something so simple.

I found Brielle to give her the good news. After all, the love I shared with Nelo came in part thanks to her.

"Your generosity has been well received in the six-year-old section. Thank you very much for your help, Brielle."

"You're welcome, Mr. Ouellet."

She continued to prepare the next snack while I returned to my seat.

WE ARE NEVER ALONE

VI

Back in First Class I found Mr. Toldeck contemplating the moon's reflection off the ocean miles below. The story of this trip was unfolding in marvelous ways. So far, I had made two friends, Mr. Toldeck and Ms. HonoOpono, and I was excited to discover how this Hawaiian goddess, Lea, related to my world. Life was proving to me again that there are no coincidences. The hand of the Creator orchestrates every event as precisely as the migration of a monarch butterfly in the spring and fall. We are so inundated with divine encounters that we've come to view them as incidental happenings instead of divine aspirations of Soul. I knew in the depths of my heart that as long as I remembered to pay attention, one day this Grand Reality would reveal Itself to me, just as it has for countless other Souls.

Brielle came by and asked if we wanted some snacks. I declined and turned to Mr. Toldeck, but by the time I made eye contact with him, Brielle had already moved on to the passengers in the next row. Mr. Toldeck held my gaze, giving the impression he had been waiting patiently for me to find the courage to reconnect.

His genuine and sincere interest in my story was making this journey and this encounter a defining moment in my life. I still hadn't quite gotten over how I was managing to share so much with a man I barely knew. Yet each time I opened up to him, I felt that I was exposing another dark corner of my life to the brilliance of the sun. Imaginary walls were being razed to reveal a panorama that allowed me to observe key moments of my life from new perspectives.

As I was about to break the silence with a trivial comment, Mr. Toldeck spoke with the perfect timing I had come to recognize.

"You were about to tell me what happened when you ran into the nuns after you saw this saint in the hallway?"

In my mind I gazed for a moment into the past I had so recently revisited. I could still see the events as clearly as when they first occurred. Taking a sip of my now-cold tea to wet my lips, I picked up where I had left off.

"The instant I reached the nuns, Sister Roselyn caught my arm with fingers that felt like iron talons."

"'We just told you not to run,' she snapped. Her words hurt as much as her grip.

"'I know! I know!' I cried. My voice was shaking with excitement and wonder. 'But I've just been visited by a saint! Right now! Right in the middle of the hallway! A few second ago just before you came down the stairs.'

"Sister Roselyn's talons tightened on my arm. Both nuns began to interrogate me at the same time. 'Tell us the truth Gaston. Who did you see? Who was it?'

"I squirmed to escape from Sister Roselyn's grip, but her strength was far greater than mine. Over and over she hammered the same question at me, hoping that under the pressure of her intimidation I would recant my story. Sister

Michele wrung her hands in frustration. Yet no matter what they did or said, I wouldn't change my story. There was something very bizarre and mysterious about my encounter and it scared them.

"Sister Roselyn continued to repeat her question with stern insistence. 'Tell us the truth, Gaston! Who did you see?'

"Eventually Sister Michele placed a gentle hand on Sister Roselyn's arm.

"'Sister Roselyn, let me try and talk to him.' Sister Roselyn's grip on my poor forearm loosened just a bit. 'Gaston,' Sister Michele addressed me in a much softer voice. 'Tell me exactly what you saw.'

"Gathering all the five-year-old courage I could muster, I tried to pull my arm from Sister Roselyn's clutches, but she still wouldn't let go. 'I saw him just as I see both of you standing right here in the middle of the hallway. He was a beautiful man with long blond hair wearing a white robe. I think he was about your age, Sister Michele.'

"Sister Roselyn finally released my arm and lowered herself to be at eye level with me. Her tone of voice shifted just a little, as if she were beginning to think my tale might possibly be true.

"'Did you talk with him?'

"'No, I didn't.'

"At this Roselyn clutched my arm again in her vise grip. Both nuns knew me as the kind of kid you just couldn't shut up, always asking question after question. To them it had to seem very unlikely I wouldn't have said anything to the stranger in the hall.

"For a moment their disbelief made me doubt my own experience. But I'd had many other out-of-body experiences far more unusual than this one, and I was certain the encounter with the strange man had really happened. They were just trying to make me believe it didn't because they had never had a similar experience themselves. Frustrated and humiliated, I began to cry and let myself fall to the floor.

"'No! No! No!' I cried. 'He talked to me! He talked to me, but I didn't talk to him!"

Knowing that I didn't cry very easily anymore, Sister Michele placed her palm on my back to calm me down a little.

"'What did he say to you?'

"Her expression and tone of voice implied I should just tell them my lie so we could all get on with our business. I got up from the floor with the certainty of conviction that comes with knowing the truth. An intoxicating excitement filled my heart.

"He said, 'Do you remember?'

"Pausing to gauge their reaction, I remembered one more word of the strange man's question. My voice took on an even greater tone of wonder when I added that final word.

"'Me,' I said, not entirely sure why or how I recalled it. 'He said "Do you remember *me?*"'

"The sisters spent the next three or four hours bombarding me with questions. 'What did he look like? Where did he come from? What was his robe like?' There were too many questions to remember. After they had exhausted me by asking the same questions over and over, their demeanor finally softened. They went downstairs to rest and two other sisters replaced them at the guard posts. Of course the new sentries had been told about my claim and began renewed questioning which continued throughout the rest of the night.

"By dawn I could barely stand up. They took me downstairs to an office that was more like a living room. None of the children had ever set foot in this room as far as I knew. Several plush armchairs were decorated with crocheted doilies on the back and arms. Knitted blankets lay folded on the seats, just waiting to comfort their inhabitants. Some even had pillows with the sisters' names embroidered on them. This space was the essence of serenity. Statues of Jesus and the Virgin Mary, photos of different popes, and pictures of saints were displayed throughout the room. Gregorian chants played in the background.

"After sitting me down in a hard, wooden chair, Sisters Roselyn and Michele spent a long time studying book after book. Eventually they came to a conclusion and called me over. With radiant smiles they opened their arms to draw me into their embrace.

"'We believe you,' Sister Roselyn proclaimed. 'And we know who visited you.'

"'Really? Who was it?'

"'Jesus Christ, himself!' they chanted together.

"They had come to the conclusion that best fit their religious beliefs. Just about bursting with excitement, they asked me to recount my experience one more time. After I was finished, I mustered as much inner strength and courage as I could to respond to their belief that Jesus had been my visitor.

"'No, it wasn't Jesus Christ at all.'

"Sister Michele, the gentler of the two, grabbed my arm. 'Tell us why it wasn't Jesus, Gaston,' she demanded.

"'I've met him before,' I said with a little shrug. 'This was someone different.'

"That was the last straw for the nuns. Each of them now gripped one of my arms, immobilizing me between them.

"'Tell us the truth, Gaston,' they insisted over and over. 'It was Jesus you met last night.'

"I shook my head like a rebellious two year-old and kept saying 'no' each time. They dragged me over to the table and showed me paintings of Jesus, hoping that I would identify the man who had visited me the night before on one of them.

"Roselyn pointed at the paintings. 'How do you know it wasn't Jesus you met?'

"'I told you,' I repeated. 'I've met him before, and it wasn't him.'

"Exasperated, the sisters hauled me out of the room and marched me to the dorm, ignoring me as they talked to each other over my head.

"'From what he described, it could only be Jesus,' said Sister Michele.

"'Or it could be a saint,' suggested Sister Roselyn.

"Sister Michele told Sister Roselyn that in the early morning we should meet with Father Peter to further investigate this incident.

"As soon as I climbed into my bed I fell asleep. In the dream state, the strange blond man came to me again and reminded me his name was Gopal. A short man with eyes as blue as the sky accompanied him.

"'This is Peddar Z,' Gopal introduced him. His tone indicated great affection and the highest respect for this man. Gopal continued, 'His close friends call him Paulji. He is the Vi-Guru now.'

"I looked the new man over. He wore a dark blue business suit and a baseball cap. What a contrast to the tall man in the white robe, I thought. From my previous conversations with Fubee and Rebatarz I remembered what *Vi-Guru* stood for. I was finally meeting my inner teacher!

"In the back of my mind I wondered why they didn't let Paulji wear a robe, too, especially if he was the Vi-Guru himself. But as I inspected his suit a little closer, I realized it was sewn from fabric like none I had ever seen. A dynamic pulsation of energy literally emanated from him and his attire. I had to drag my eyes away from the suit to meet his. Even though I was unable to look into them for very long, I realized this was the moment I received my first *Darshan*.

"There are two elements of the *Darshan*. One is meeting one's Spiritual Master outwardly and being recognized by him. The other is meeting him inwardly, traveling with him in the inner worlds, and experiencing the enlightenment which comes with this encounter. The *Darshan* is given to those whom the Master has carefully selected. However, it is always up to the student to make the decision to honor the gift. As the saying goes, 'When the student is ready the Master appears.'

"After that night, I began to have regular out-of-body experiences with Paulji in the role of my spiritual teacher. As someone used to priestly vestments and robes, it initially felt funny for me to admit that a man in a blue business suit could hold the divine wisdom of God-Realization."

I paused to take a sip of cold tea, remembering the boundless love I felt in Paulji's presence.

Mr. Toldeck said, "At some point I'd like to hear more about God-Realization, but since you seem to be on a roll with your story at the orphanage, tell me, did you meet with the priest the following morning?"

"Oh, yes indeed. Sister Annabelle woke me up before everyone else that morning. She was the youngest sister at the orphanage, only eighteen years old and beautiful in so many ways. Whenever she watched over the playground, thirty to forty children would hover around her at all times. We were like bees buzzing around a honeycomb, and she was our queen bee. She was the most popular sister among the children, even more than the one in the kitchen who plied us with treats.

Sister Annabelle was the type of woman every child dreamed of having as their mother.

"You know, Mr. Toldeck, the heart is never deceitful, it only knows truth. We simply choose at times to deny our spiritual vulnerability. Why? Because, we know as Soul that vulnerability leads us to open up to our creator, the Great Spirit. When we let our hearts take the lead, we're like flowers opening their petals to receive the rays of the sun. In that moment, we become defenseless against any influences, be they good or bad. But it's always worth the risk.

"Interesting view point, Gaston: we are like flowers opening ourselves to our creator. Could you tell me what Sister Annabelle did that morning?"

"Sister Annabelle told me to dress as I would for Sunday Mass and took me to the Mother Superior who walked me over to Father Peter's office for questioning, or, as I've come to refer to it in hindsight, the Inquisition.

"On the way to the office I noticed that for the first time in two and a half years, Mother Superior Diane was polite to me, even kind, and nervous. Displaying any signs of insecurity was highly unusual for this frightening woman. We walked hand in hand, as if suddenly I had become precious to her. At every window we passed in the hallways, the curious and puzzled faces of children pressed against the glass. Clearly, nothing like this had ever happened here before.

"By the time breakfast was over, the entire orphanage had heard several versions of the event. One was the vision of the saint; another was that I had met Jesus Christ, himself; still another was that I was being adopted. These stories followed me for a very long time.

"We took a seat in the lobby of Father Peter's residence. From far away we heard multiple footsteps, then the big double door opened and three men walked in: Father Peter, Father Gabriel, our local Bishop, and the Archbishop of Montreal himself, Father André.

"All three priests were draped in nearly identical black robes, the only differences evident in the color of their buttons, skull caps, and wide belts. The Archbishop sported vivid red. The local Bishop displayed beautiful violet. Father Peter wore plain black only.

"Mother Superior was in a near state of ecstasy just being in their presence. Archbishop Andre asked her to recount the sisters' experiences with me from the night before. She told the story with frenzied eloquence, her voice rich with enthusiasm as she recounted each precious detail. Throughout their conversation, the adults ignored me.

"After the Mother Superior had finished, the priests instructed her to return to the orphanage. She departed with beatific contentment on her face. The rest of us entered Father Peter's study, where carefully arranged, red velvet chairs awaited. It was then that I experienced the strongest, most invasive psychic attack of my young life. For more than three hours straight, the clerics tried to convince me that the night before I had been visited by Jesus Christ. Each time I recounted my experiences, they would repeat the same thing afterward. "It's certain this was Jesus."

"The more persistent they were in asserting their own interpretation of my experience, the more I felt assaulted by their dark powers. It's said when faced by great adversity; people are able to see how strongly they're rooted in their own faith. The true conviction of their beliefs comes to surface.

"To be honest, Mr. Toldeck, I've wondered many times what my life would have been like if I'd given in to their interpretation of my encounter with Gopal. Almost certainly

I would have been adopted within the next few days, or a few weeks at most. In the overwhelmingly Catholic community we lived in, who wouldn't want to adopt a boy who had just been visited by Jesus Christ? Especially when the Archbishop himself had confirmed the miracle? And the entire parish fell in behind him?

"As it happened, of course, I didn't give in.

"The clerics continued their badgering until finally the Archbishop frowned in frustration and asked the question no one had ever asked me before.

"'Does anyone else come to visit you?'

"I told them about my experience with Fubee on my first night at the orphanage, and of the many other out-of-body travels I'd had with Rebatarz, Gopal, and now Paulji. The Archbishop leaned back in amazement. The more I talked, the more the priests were captivated, and the more I became aware of the truth resonating in my voice. It was an instance, I have since learned, of the Holy Spirit taking over and speaking through a person.

"Then I said something that baffled them all, even myself.

"'We are never alone.'

"Everyone in the room fell silent.

"'How so?' Father Peter finally asked.

"'God, Jesus, the Holy Spirit, God's helpers, the Saints… they're always with us,' I said.

"For a long moment after my statement, a statement that had come directly through my heart, silence prevailed in Father Peter's study. Our hearts were struck by this crystal-clear truth, mine as much as theirs. It brought us face to face with our faith because the most troubling thought that occupies a man's heart is his certainty that he is always alone. He believes this subconsciously, even though even deeper down he knows God created him and that he dwells among remarkable beings for eternity."

I stopped talking and let my last statement linger in the air. Mr. Toldeck turned his head to look out the window where he seemed to find solace in the clouds.

I closed my eyes, my thoughts drifting to Thailand. Soon my adventures there would begin. I had planned this pilgrimage, this great quest that would give birth to the new me, for a long time.

I opened my eyes just as Lea returned to her seat.

"You want to come over?" she invited.

"I would love to." I crossed the aisle and settled in the seat next to her.

"I've been sitting with Ms. HonoOpono," Lea said. "She's become very fond of you,

you know. During the thirty minutes I spent with her, all she talked about were the things you told her."

"Uh oh," I said in mock alarm. "She didn't talk to you about my views on women and relationships did she?"

Lea laughed. "No she didn't. But, since you brought it up, perhaps we should talk about that. You must know that relationships are the most common subject of women's conversations."

Wisely, I chose not to comment on that. Instead, I let myself bathe in the sound of Lea's sweet voice and listened to her contagious laughter ringing in my ears. Her happiness brought magical joy to my heart, although I tried not to wear my feelings too conspicuously on my sleeve.

Lea went on, "You two discussed other subjects dear to my heart too. Like the Aloha Spirit."

A secretive smile spread over her face. She looked down at her lap for a moment while she spoke. "Dreams—the

Menehune. And..." She raised her gaze to meet mine, the same mischievous twinkle in her eyes as Ms. HonoOpono. "And how you are intimidated by beautiful women."

"Oh no, she didn't!" I protested, feeling my face redden.

"Oh yes, she did."

This time I was going to try to emphatically discredit this false perception by stating the facts, thereby unknowingly setting myself a trap.

"How can I be intimidated by beautiful women when I am sitting calmly with one right now?"

"So you believe that I'm a beautiful woman?" She cocked a playful eyebrow.

I could feel my face turn lobster red. My fingers twisted around each other in my lap. It took all the will I had to even speak.

"In all honesty, Lea, how could I not be intimidated, when you are so stunningly gorgeous? Men have always been intimidated by very attractive women—even more so when they are highly intelligent."

She laughed, knowing how truly intimidated I was. Waving her hand as if to sweep all my worries away, she took the conversation in a new direction.

"Forget all that. Tell me your viewpoint on relationships."

"Between women and men?"

Lea rolled her eyes. "No—between whales. Of course between men and women!"

"You're sure Ms. HonoOpono didn't say anything about what we discussed?"

Smiling, Lea placed her hand over her heart. "I give you my word."

"All right, let's start. Are you married? Or involved in a relationship?"

Lea laughed. "Well, actually not, but I thought we were speaking in the abstract. Since you asked me, though, are you married? Or in a committed relationship yourself?"

"I'm not married any longer," I confessed. "But I am in a committed relationship with my four children for the rest of my life." The memory of each of their beautiful faces brought a smile to my lips.

"Wow," Lea said. "You may be the most direct man I've ever meet. Most single men try to hide the fact that they have children. You speak like it's the most important commitment in your life."

"That's true, it is. But because I'm French, my first commitment will always be to my beloved. Future beloved, I mean. That way, the children can benefit from a demonstration of true devotion."

Now Lea's face was turning red, her emotions for some reason catching her off guard. In an attempt to compose herself, she asked another question.

"Tell me why a handsome man such as yourself is not involved in a committed relationship."

"Probably for the same reason that you aren't, Lea. I haven't chosen the right partner yet. Besides, I think we've lost the art of courtship. The values that surround the sacred ceremony of courtship have fallen by the wayside. This is causing great sorrow for women, at least the ones I know." I raised my shoulder in a half shrug. "How can you value something when you haven't earned it?

"These days people meet and become intimately involved right away without really knowing each other. They don't give themselves a chance to learn each other's' values and gifts—each person's inner treasures. All that remains is lust, which they interpret as love."

"Wow, I wasn't kidding when I said you were the most direct man I've ever met." Lea shifted in her seat, tucking her left leg up under her right so she could turn to face me. "I have to tell you, Gaston. I'm not used to conversations filled with such blunt truth. Most people hide who they really are. I'm beginning to like this very much about you. You know, most of my girlfriends are single."

"Why is that?"

"Probably because of the reasons you mentioned earlier." Her eyes took on a wistful gleam.

I said, "Never lose sight of your faith, though. We live in the most amazing time in history. It's only been in the last few centuries that men and women could marry who they truly love. The only relationships I've witnessed that I would call True Love were built, and I would emphasize the word *built* here, on mutual respect and similar values. The partners express their love for each other through actions, every day, for years. To me, that's love. Not a matter of words but of demonstration."

I paused for a moment to let Lea respond, but she only waited for me to continue.

"I believe the spiritual purpose of a woman is to guide her man to his heart. But I'm sure you've noticed how so many women want to fix their men?"

"Too many times." Lea shifted to sit a little taller, squaring her shoulders. "But I'm not that kind of woman."

"I believe you. Confident women never have to fix anything except their own issues. God gave women the gift of being Holy Vehicles for Divine Creation. Women hold within them the greatest altar of all, the Golden Heart. A woman's gift of love is beyond measure. Yet how could any woman expect a man to give his greatest gift, his devotion, to her if upon their first, second, or even third encounter she gives him the most precious gift she holds for him, her intimacy?"

"That all sounds great," Lea interjected. "But if a woman's spiritual purpose is to lead a man to his heart, then what's a man's spiritual purpose?"

"To lead his Beloved to God. He might do this through a display of courage, or through support for her, which manifests as respect, honor, and fidelity to her love."

"Wow," Lea breathed. "You're really intense. Ms. HonoOpono was telling the truth. 'Talk to him,' she said. 'He'll make you happy.' There isn't much you've said that I disagree with. But let me ask you this—how do I attract a man like that into my life? One who'll cherish me for who I am and not only for how I look. How do you even find a man like that?"

Lea had undoubtedly attracted countless suitors in her life, but very likely most of them had never seen beyond the surface of her beauty.

"You can't cheat the laws of the universe," I replied. "One of those laws is that like attracts like. You have to become a heart hunter. You have to prepare yourself by creating an inner and an outer space to welcome this new mate. Prepare your living space with great feelings of anticipation, as if your beloved were returning home soon. Clean house as if the most important person in your life is on his way. Make room for him; make space in your closet, your bathroom, on the other side of the bed. Even more important, create a sacred space in your heart. If he's welcome in your heart, he's welcome in your world.

"There are many available men, most of them sincerely seeking relationships. Certainly there are some who aren't sincere, but most adult men seek authentic companionship as much as women do. Many of these men, especially of the younger generations, are happy to practice equality within their relationships."

Out of nowhere, Nelo suddenly stood in the middle of the aisle, looking up at both of us.

"Nelo," I said. "What are you doing here?"

"Coach Gaston, I need you. Could you please come with me? I need to show you something."

Lea smile was reassuring. "Go ahead, Gaston. We'll continue this later."

"You're sure it's okay?"

She nodded, still smiling warmly.

Nelo grabbed my hand and dragged me into coach class. Just as we reached his seat, Ellouise arrived from farther back in the plane. She knelt in front of Nelo and placed her hands on his shoulders.

"Where were you? I was so worried about you."

Nelo frowned in confusion, not sure what he had done wrong. Seeing the chance to quickly be back at Lea's side, I decided to let them sort it out between themselves and returned to first class. As I passed through the curtains, I saw Brielle and Lea engaged in a conversation, so I smiled at both of them and sat by Mr. Toldeck.

"You're quite the cavalier," he said with a wry grin. "The boy is truly fond of you. Lea as well. I trust you are aware of this?"

Not ready to acknowledge my feelings towards Lea, I shook my head, thinking, *let's not go there*. Mr. Toldeck, taking note of my non-verbal message, returned to our previous conversation.

"I was thinking about something you told me about the orphanage. What was it like on those 'Pick a Family' days?"

I looked down at my knees, still disturbed by the memory. "They were horrible! During my first two years there, I was paraded in front of visiting families like a puppet on every one of those days. The nuns made sure we were well-groomed, especially the three to five year-olds, because they were the most likely to be adopted. We felt like little statues on display, waiting for someone to take us home.

"At first, I rebelled. Many, many couples tried to connect with me, but I never let them get close. Convinced my dad was coming back soon to take me out of there, I maintained a wall of separation between myself and any prospective foster parents. But as the months and years went by, neither my father nor my mother showed up. Eventually I transformed myself from a rebel into a people pleaser, especially on 'Pick a Family Day.' By the time I was six, my longing to leave the orphanage had led me to become a master in the art of pleasing others.

"One Sunday afternoon, I was called over the PA system to the Mother Superior's office. Earlier in the day I had gone into the front yard and clung to the fence as if I were going to be let out, I don't know why. When I got to Mother Superior's office, I found my best friend, Bruce, already sitting in one of the chairs outside. Inside I could see a young couple in their early thirties on a couch, waiting patiently for my arrival. During the interview the man asked most of the questions. When I left, Bruce went in.

"Bruce was five at the time. His capacity to love was extraordinary. During the many nights and days when loneliness overcame me, he was always there to comfort me. Whenever I thought I couldn't take it anymore, he'd make me laugh by saying the same thing every time. "Now, now, now," he'd admonish me with a wag of his finger, "what would Amelie say if she saw you like that?"

"I'd shared with him all the things Amelie did to care for me, and he could tell how I felt whenever I spoke of her. Bruce was the person during this part of my life with whom I could share my innermost feelings, especially when loneliness came to visit.

"On the Sunday afternoons when the family visits took place, forlorn hope and desperation hung heavy in the air and darkened the faces of all the children. When suppertime finally came around, cafeteria chatter was subdued. It was obvious each and every one of us had prayed in vain for God to rescue us. The desire to be loved supersedes all others, but for us it was not to be.

"After supper on those days, many boys would wander into the yard and gather by the front fence, drawn there by the invisible hand of longing to be loved by a real family. We'd watch the children adopted that day leave with their new parents. On this particular evening, as I watched several boys being escorted out, I slumped to the ground, gripped the unforgiving bars of the fence and surrendered to my tears. I wasn't the only one.

"All of a sudden I heard a group of children shouting, 'What? Bruce? How can that be?'

"I jumped up to find out which Bruce they meant, and there he was—my brother of the heart. Bruce and I slept in beds next to each other and we spent most of our time together. I had taught him how to count, how to write his name, how to read some words, and even how to hide from the nuns in our secret hiding place. He always kept my spirits up when I was desperate and lonely.

"Bruce waved at me as he walked to the parking lot in the company of his adoptive parents. I waved back. He looked so much happier and lighter than I'd ever seen him. He climbed into the car and the family drove away, taking Bruce to his new home. That night I cried as if God had taken away the last thing that mattered to me. My closest friend, whom I had come to love with all my heart, was gone. After Bruce left, I decided never to mingle with the visiting parents again.

"No matter how hard I've tried, I've never been able to fully describe these early incidents in my life. I think people never really understand them unless they've experienced these kinds of tormenting episodes themselves. It's as if every two weeks your parents come to watch you play in the front yard, and you know they're coming, and you hope maybe this time you get to go home with them. But you never do. To us boys, every visiting couple was potentially our new parents and future family.

"That same night when I finally fell asleep, I was taken out of my body by Paulji, the Vi-Guru himself. I awoke in the soul body and found him standing by my bed in his light body, wearing his usual dark blue suit and baseball cap. He consoled me for a long time, reminding me I was loved and that I was never alone. After I had regained my inner balance, he told me that I would soon depart from this place, and that all would be well.

"Mother Superior had a tradition that anyone with complaints or questions could voice them to her between seven and eight o'clock during breakfast time. The next morning, I made sure I was the first boy she saw. By 7:01 am I was outside her door, taking a seat on the big wooden bench. She let me in and motioned for me to sit in the same chair I had occupied on my very first day.

"'Strange to see you in here, Gaston,' she said. 'I don't think I've ever heard any complaints from you before. What's the problem?'

"''I am to leave this place right away,' I stated.

"'Really? And who told you this?' she laughed derisively.

"'Paulji,' I said.

At this she laughed so loud two other nuns came rushing into her office.

"'Are you okay, Mother Superior?' one of them asked. Both sisters were clearly concerned. No one had ever heard Mother Superior laugh before; it sounded like a demonic cackle.

"'I'm fine!' she snapped. Then she bent her dark gaze on me. 'Tell your saint he better give me a phone call, because no one leaves this place without my permission.'

"She made shooing motions with her hand as if she were brushing away a cockroach. 'You run along now and have your breakfast, Gaston.'

"I was puzzled. Facing her black-cloaked figure I gathered up my courage.

"'So you're telling me you need a...a phone call?' I was highly confused, never having consciously seen a phone before. Life in the orphanage was very isolated.

"'That's right, Gaston,' she said with a grating edge to her voice. 'A phone call. And a family—a family who'd want to care for you. Good luck with that!'

"She leaned back imperiously in her big armchair and crossed her arms over her chest. The ancient leather of the seat creaked and groaned as she shifted her weight. Suddenly she seemed to become aware that she had gone too far—that she had allowed her inner darkness to show through her pious facade. The other two sisters hovered in the doorway, mouths agape, uncertain what to do. Mother Superior acknowledged them with a semi-nervous glance, then in a gentler tone instructed me again to go and have my breakfast because school was about to start. I left, troubled and confused.

"That afternoon an announcement came over the PS system while I was out in the big playground.

"'Gaston Ouellet. Please come to the main office.'

"I ran to the office as fast as my legs would carry me and sat on the bench outside. Mother Superior's door opened, and my brother, Jean, stalked out yelling something back over his shoulder. Shouting seemed to be the only way he could communicate with her. He looked angrily at me as he passed by.

"'Don't believe a word she says to you! She only knows how to lie!'

"Mother Superior escorted me into her office, this time seating me on one of the red velvet couches. Without preamble she barked, 'What do you know about this family that's interested in you and your brother?'

"Surprised, I blurted, 'I don't know anything about them! All I know is Paulji told me last night that I would leave soon and everything would be okay.' Then I added, 'Oh! Did you get a phone call from my saint?'

"'No, Gaston! Not even from your angel. Just from Father Gabriel. He's in charge of all adoptions. You and your brother have been invited to live with a family, but they'll only take you if the two of you go together. So I need to ask you: Are you willing to move to a family with your brother?'

"I leaped off the red couch and bounced up and down like a crazed kangaroo, shouting, 'I'm leaving! I'm leaving! I'm leaving! I'm being adopted! When? When? When?'

"'In two or three weeks. They need time to prepare the family and make a place in their home for both of you.'

"Two or three weeks mattered little to me. I was being adopted! That's all I cared about. I had spent so much time dreaming of this day, dreaming of the ideal family and what it would be like to be adopted. And thinking of never having to return to this wretched orphanage.

Mother Superior watched me jump up and down for a while, letting my enthusiasm run out of steam. Then she said, 'I have some unpleasant news for you.'

"'How can that be? This is the happiest day of my life! Is Jean not willing to come?'

"'Yes, Jean is willing. That's not it at all.'

"'What, then?'

"'You're not being adopted. You're going to be a ward of the state, and you'll be placed with a foster family.'

"'What's a foster family?'

"The Mother Superior's voice resumed an air of superiority. 'That's when a family is paid by the state to take you in, and if either of your parents decides to take you back, they still can.'

"'So you mean I'll never be adopted?' I said, disappointed. I hadn't even seen my parents in three years. Disillusionment overwhelmed me. You know, Mr. Toldeck, when you live at an orphanage, you spend a lot of your time fantasizing about the magical day you'll be told that a family wants you. You imagine the family, the parents, the siblings, and all the good times you'll have with them. No one had ever told me what a foster family was, never mind what it meant living with one. Once this new reality settled in, I realized why my brother had been so upset.

"As I pushed open the door to leave, I turned to the Mother Superior, 'Yes, I would like to go with my brother,' I confirmed. Whatever living with a foster family was like, it had to be better than my current life.

"Within several weeks, Jean and I moved in with the foster family."

I paused to take a deep breath. There was a deeper truth to this chapter in my life that I needed to verbalize.

"When you asked me about what 'Pick a Family Days' were like, it reminded me of something important I learned during the years of being taken out of the body and escorted to inner temples. I believe that as Soul I deliberately choose every experience in each life, even the painful ones. Especially the painful ones. These experiences create opportunities for me to balance my karmic accounts, learn to give and receive Divine Love, and master the five divine virtues.

"Each of these virtues—humility, discernment, forgiveness, detachment, and contentment—has a negative counterpart: vanity, lust, anger, attachment, and greed. Whenever I've found myself struggling, I've always tried to determine which of these negative attitudes is affecting me, and which virtues I need to develop in response. The interesting thing is, every time I stopped to consider which of the virtues was important in any given situation, the solution to my dilemma appeared effortlessly. It all comes down to the fact that we're here to learn to love."

Across the aisle, Brielle suddenly interrupted her conversation with Lea and faced me.

"Can I get you anything, Mr. Ouellet?"

Past the figure of the flight attendant, I noticed Lea smiling at me. Of course I smiled back.

"Sure," I replied to Brielle's inquiry. "I would love two more of those desserts you served us earlier. You know—the chocolate mousse?"

"I'll see what I can do. Anything to drink?"

"Mmmmm, yes. How about Perrier in a glass with no ice?"

"Okay. I'll be back."

"Thank you for doing your job so well, Brielle. I'm glad I met Ms. HonoOpono at the airport, or I wouldn't be here getting the royal treatment from you."

"Remember, Mr. Ouellet" she said. "Everything happens for a reason."

"Very true! And for the moment what's happening is chocolate mousse."

Lea waved at me as soon has Brielle left.

"You want to talk with me?" I mouthed silently, pointing to my chest and wagging my head.

Lea laughed with delight. "Get over here, Gaston!"

I turned to Mr. Toldeck and excused myself.

He whispered, "You can tell me later what happened once you left the orphanage."

"Yes, of course."

Lea was still chuckling when I slid across the aisle to her row, but before I could sit down, Ms. HonoOpono waved for me to come over. I raised my eyebrows and silently indicated Lea with my head.

"Ohhh!" Mrs. HonoOpono boomed. "I get it! We all know who your favorite passenger is now. Not me anymore, huh?"

The passengers around us began to giggle, some louder than others. Self-consciously, I slumped down into the seat next to Lea.

"She just wants your attention," Lea said soothingly. "Don't let her embarrass you. She has a big heart and she means well."

Not even Lea's reassuring words could penetrate the protective cocoon I had withdrawn to. I wanted nothing more than to disappear from this aircraft. Then something magical happened. Lea touched my hand—and I was transported!

Struck with a Light from beyond the physical world, a Divine Light that brightened in ever-expanding circles, I saw the true Lea standing at the edge of this Light. The Light surrounded both of us, and as her dark brown eyes met mine I knew that, deep within me, as yet invisible worlds awaited discovery. I knew that I sought only love, and that her form was an instrument through which Divine Love would find its way into my world.

My heart stood still. I averted my eyes and tried very hard not to reveal how deeply touched I was. With an effort I kept myself from gazing intensely into her eyes. It was clear to me her intent was to comfort, not to seduce. How many times had I foolishly misled myself over a woman's kind gesture in the past? Not this time, I promised myself.

I heard her voice as if from far away, drawing me back to the here and now.

"Are you okay, Gaston?"

Shakily, I took a deep breath; it felt like the first fresh breath I had taken in a long time.

"Yes, Lea, better than I could ever describe."

When our eyes finally connected, the invisible Light that surrounded us exploded from the center of my heart. Lea jerked her hand back as if it were on fire. She realized at once that her gesture of emotional support had transformed into an intimate connection. We could no longer ignore or deny our mutual enchantment, and deep down we both knew it.

My face redder than ever, I desperately sought to anchor my vision on something else, on anything in the cabin, just so I wouldn't have to explicitly acknowledge what had just happened. This was sailing uncharted seas for me, and I was trying unsuccessfully to make sense of the miraculous new world I found myself in. I had no instruments to guide me, and my old tools no longer worked.

Like an angel of mercy, Brielle appeared at my side and placed two rich, chocolate mousses on our trays.

"For both of you," she said. Recognizing something was going on, she continued, "Oh, did I interrupt something?"

Lea and I stammered at the same time, urgently trying to convince Brielle she hadn't interrupted anything special. Brielle's smile was warm, a twinkle flickering in her eyes.

"Well, from where I'm standing, one might assume differently. You two probably want to get your stories straight next time."

"What next time?" Lea and I blurted in unison. Then we looked at each other and started laughing like a couple of teenagers. We had been caught; even if we weren't quite sure exactly what we had been caught at. Lea's expression told me she was no longer concerned what people might think.

Brielle walked away, shaking her head, still smiling. Lea and I took up our spoons and dove with gusto into the chocolate mousse, a creamy delight which sent us into a state of near ecstasy.

We devoured the dessert in contented silence. I had always been convinced one can measure the essence of a true friendship by the length of comfortable silences spent in each other's company. By that measure, a deep new friendship was born.

LEARNING TO SHARE

VII

 Our silence grew deeper and seemed to merge into the starlight outside the window. We sailed together through the glittering darkness, 35,000 feet above the Pacific Ocean. I was moved by new sensations and by dormant feelings I thought I had left behind. The moonlight and the stars, Lea sitting next to me, the taste of chocolate mousse lingering on my tongue all combined to bring this moment to the edge of perfection. Then the moment, like all moments, came to an end.

 Brielle reached in to remove our dessert cups, noticing that we both seemed to be lost in a daze. Nevertheless, she leaned close and whispered in my ear, "I hate to disturb your chocolate bliss, Mr. Ouellet, but Ms. HonoOpono asked me earlier and I forgot to tell you. She wanted to know if you could stop by and spend some time with her. She said to tell you that she has more questions." She smiled an apology.

 Despite Brielle's whisper, Lea overheard her and was already looking at me when I turned to her. In response to the unspoken question in my eyes, she nodded in support of Ms. HonoOpono's request. I rose and stepped into the aisle.

 "Well, it looks like someone's jealous of our chocolate mousse treats," I said to Brielle. "I better leave right away and give the mousse inspector a detailed report of our appreciation. Thank you, Brielle."

After a few steps I turned to wave at Lea, but she was already engaged in a conversation with Brielle. When I reached Ms. HonoOpono's seat, she was fast asleep. This time none of her bulk extended into the aisle. I decided to take the opportunity to stretch my legs and explore the opposite aisle.

To my surprise, I found another familiar face among the passengers there.

Who would have thought? I wondered. *First Ellouise and Nelo, and now here's Melisange.* Melisange, a dark haired French-Canadian women, was deeply engrossed in a novel. As I approached, she placed her book on her lap, smiled and gestured toward the empty seat next to her.

"You weren't just going to walk by without saying Aloha, were you?"

Melisange looked like a typical surfer girl: about 5' 5", strongly built, and perfectly tanned. I always ran into her at Hookipa Beach whenever I took my children there to surf. If you liked direct, straightforward conversation, you'd find her company quite enjoyable.

"I certainly was not," I returned. "I'm not like that, as you probably know."

"I know. Just kidding."

"So, Melisange, where are you headed on this marvelous evening?"

"Japan. I've been hired to teach English in Imasato, a little town near Osaka."

"I really like Japan," I said. "It's clean everywhere you go. The Japanese practice a sense of order and of cleanliness that should inspire all industrialized nations. How did you ever come across the opportunity to teach English in Japan?"

"Believe or not, in a surfing magazine, of all places. Remember how I've been looking for opportunities to leave Hawaii? Raised on Maui most of my life, all I know is my Valley Isle and I really wanted to get another view of the world. I'm ready to expand my horizons." She paused, smiling mischievously. "So what do I do? I'm—moving to another island!"

We laughed together at this.

"Living abroad will definitely open you up to a new understanding of yourself and the world," I assured her. "It had a major impact on my life. Transformed me completely, really." After regarding her for a moment, I continued, "So, what's the great concern about your relocation?"

Melisange raised her eyebrows and sucked in her breath just a bit, as if she were wondering if I had read her mind.

"Funny you should ask. I've been trying to calm myself down all night over that very subject."

"What is it, Melisange?"

"Come with me, Gaston; let's go to the back of the plane. I'll feel freer to talk back there. Besides, my legs need a wakeup call."

As I followed her down the aisle to the rear, her concern was evident in the tension of her shoulders and back. At the small aft galley she stopped and turned to look intently into my eyes.

"During this flight I discovered something. I thought I feared death very much, but now I realize I'm far more afraid of not being understood." Her upper lip trembled just a bit. "I don't speak a word of Japanese. I mean…not a single word!"

"Well, Melisange, the Japanese generally don't speak a word of English either, so you and your new students start out on an equal footing. The wish to be understood is one of the primal desires of all humans, but one desire supersedes all others: the desire to be loved. I think they're actually one and the same, you know, the wish to be understood and the desire to be loved. Through their desire to learn English, your students will show you love, and because of that, you'll experience a sense of being understood.

"All you'll be asked to do in return is to love them back, like a mother hen—in English of course! You'll lead them out of the shadow of ignorance and into the light of understanding English one step at a time, for them and for you. You and your students already share knowledge of the most important language: the language of love. You'll just be translating it into English and Japanese. Don't worry, you'll be understood."

"Wow, Gaston! I didn't expect that kind of response from you. That was so cool. It's the kind of advice my father would probably give me."

"You know, Melisange, your destiny is leading you to Japan. You're really going because you've agreed to fulfill your mission there. So view your adventure as if everything has been taken care of ahead of time. Just like you're flying through the sky on this airplane with no effort on your part, you can choose to do the same with moving to Japan."

Melisange's face lit up with a big smile. "Wow! When I look at it that way, all my fears just go away. I can relax and let my adventure unfold. It's just like surfing! Like letting the powers of the wave carry you."

"You got it," I confirmed. "No matter what we decide to do on this plane, it will land according to the will of the Great Spirit of Aloha. So why sweat what's to come? Every element of your life is being orchestrated down to the smallest detail. Your job is only to discover the joy in each moment. That's easy if you see your life as an adventure, as your greatest adventure."

"I'm ready to parachute right out of this door if need be! My worries are gone. Now I'm ready to go back to my novel. Mahalo, Gaston! You brought the spirit of adventure back to my journey. I'm very grateful."

She leaned forward and gave me a big hug. As I accompanied her back to her seat, I couldn't help but wonder why I didn't just listen to her, and to my own advice.

Back in first class, Brielle, Lea, and Ms. HonoOpono were where I left them, so I returned to my own seat.

"Welcome home, traveler," Mr. Toldeck greeted me.

His warm voice and calm face made me realize I had missed him.

"So," he said. "What happened after you left the orphanage? Where'd you go and what kind of experiences did you have?"

"I left the orphanage in the early spring of 1966, several weeks after my sixth birthday. One day during lunch, Jean and I were called over the PA system to Mother Superior's office."

I interrupted myself to take a deep breath, searching Mr. Toldeck's eyes. His questions struck me as sincere and his countenance even more so. Nevertheless, after only two sentences emotions were already rolling over me like a scouring wind on a winter day. It seemed I was unable to stop myself from disclosing the details of my childhood to this man.

Though I knew in my heart opening up to him would inevitably bring great sorrow, I proceeded with my story in the hope this wouldn't occur. For too long I had clung to the perception that I and only I must heal everything in my life.

"Some of the other boys were spreading the rumor that I'd been adopted. But my best friend, Bruce, told me months prior to his departure that it was rare for a family to adopt two brothers. After hearing about foster families from Mother Superior, I'd rekindled the all-but-lost hope that my father would come pick us up. How I longed for this dream to come true as I made my way to Mother Superior's office! Maybe he was there right now! I desperately clutched at the thought that the life altering event the Vi-Guru had forewarned me about in my dreams would be a return to my father's care.

"In the office I found my brother, Jean, arguing vociferously with Mother Diane. When I entered, they immediately fell silent. The Mother Superior instructed me to sit down.

"'You're both leaving today with the family who came to visit you a few weeks back. Go pack your belongings.' She pointed to large cardboard boxes on the floor.

"My voice heavy with disappointment, I said, 'Yes, Mother Diane.'

"All sorts of fears pressed down on me as I approached the empty boxes. What was I afraid of? The unknown, of course. My brother, angry rather than fearful, stormed out of the office.

"Before I left the orphanage, I was able to say goodbye to all my brothers. When you live in a dorm where seventy or eighty children sleep under one roof, you can't help but become a family.

"As I pushed my two full boxes through the empty corridors, I stopped to scan one last time the pictures of the saints who had accompanied me through so many lonely nights. My new family was waiting in the hallway outside Mother Diane's office.

"They introduced themselves as Joanne and Michel. Jean sat on the wooden bench staring sullenly at the floor. In contrast, I rejoiced at the fact that I was finally leaving, even if it wasn't with my father or via adoption.

"It took around thirty minutes or so to drive to Marieville, the town where our new home was located. For Jean and I the most difficult part of this transition was adjusting from an institutional regimen to a family lifestyle and learning to share. We lived with the family for almost a year and a half.

"Being institutionalized had created many dysfunctional behaviors in me, along with a fierce instinct for survival. By survival instinct I don't mean the *all for one and one for all, circle of trust and love* support that families are built on. One of my behaviors was a falling-asleep routine that involved rocking my head and body back and forth. Since I hadn't received much affection in my early years, this mechanism provided me with the emotional comfort to let me fall asleep.

"If you ever visit orphanages in various countries, you'll observe all kinds of physical motion the orphans engage in to make up for the lack of affection in their lives. Some I've witnessed are very awkward to watch, while others are downright disturbing.

"Jean and I had to sleep in the same bed, which meant of course he was unable to fall asleep with me rocking back and forth. At first he politely asked me to stop. However, my bedtime ritual was so ingrained he eventually resorted to beating me up to make me stop. The result was that *he* could sleep but I didn't. By winter, I began to sleep on the floor. Those were the coldest months of my life. The floor was bare wood, and in the mornings the room was so cold we could see our breath. In most rural homes in 1966 the bedrooms weren't heated or well insulated.

"Learning to share was the most difficult part for me. In my new family, meals were a sacred ceremony, and with our solid religious foundation from the orphanage was this was nothing new. What was different was that we were asked to share our food with every member of the family, since money was tight and there wasn't enough to go around. Being the youngest, I was expected to share the most at every meal. At the orphanage we'd each had our own food tray and our own belongings, no matter how few. The nuns' philosophy was 'what's yours is for you to care for, because no one will come to replace it.' However, in our new family the philosophy was 'what's ours is for the welfare of the whole family and meant to be shared.' It was many years before I could make peace with the fact that to share was okay and safe.

"For my seventh birthday, Joanne baked a beautiful, three-layer chocolate cake. The love in her heart was her secret ingredient—her devotion to her family manifested in chocolate form. There were nine family members, so the cake had to yield nine slices. It was the first time in my life I had ever been honored with a birthday celebration, much less with a home-baked birthday cake.

"Our dining table was rectangular with seating for twelve. Everyone was sitting down waiting for the long-anticipated ceremony to begin. At one end of the table sat Michel, the father, while the chair on the other end was decorated and reserved for the birthday person. Joanne brought in the spectacular cake with seven candles and placed it in front of me. I blew out the candles, and she cut a piece and placed it on my plate.

"When she moved the cake aside to cut another slice for the next person, I shouted, 'Hey, that's my birthday cake!'

"The collective reaction to my outburst was as if I had set the kitchen on fire. The other children all started talking at once, while Michel exchanged a disappointed glance with his wife.

"Joanne's voice turned stern. 'So it's your birthday cake, is it?'

"Across the table, Michel gave me a meaningful look and shook his head to elicit the correct response from me. He knew his wife very well and already anticipated what would happen if I didn't follow his advice.

"'Yes!' I replied stubbornly, shoveling in another mouthful of the delicious cake.

"Joanne asked the kids to sit back down and pulled up the nearest chair.

"'You say it's your cake. Well, then you're going to eat all of it,' she ordered.

"The other children had waited all day for a piece of her famous chocolate cake and were very angry with me. Michel knew better than to argue with his wife. Each time I finished a piece, she placed another one in front of me while the others watched. To everyone's disappointment, nothing was going to stop me from eating the entire cake! Of course I was sick throughout the night and into the next morning, but there was no compassion from the family members. I even had to go to school. Through this experience I learned the consequences of taking others' joy away with my own selfishness.

"In the following months, each time we celebrated a birthday, Joanne made sure my piece was small. She committed herself to teaching me about generosity and gratitude, which she demonstrated through her own generosity toward everyone. It took time, but eventually I began to understand."

As I finished the sentence, Brielle tapped me on the shoulder.

"Forgive me once more, Gaston, but Ms. HonoOpono has asked again if you could go over and sit with her."

I smiled up at the flight attendant and unbuckled my seatbelt.

"You don't have to go right away, you know," Brielle said.

"I know."

Rising, I found Lea giving me an inquisitive look. With a smile I tipped my head towards Ms. HonoOpono. Lea returned my smile and I melted just a little. I glanced at Mr. Toldeck.

"Please, do go," he said politely. "However, I still want to know more about the experiences you had in that family."

"Thank you for being so generous in listening to all my childhood stories," I returned. "I'm usually the one who does all the listening."

Ms. HonoOpono seemed to eagerly anticipate my arrival. She began probing immediately.

"I told you, didn't I, that Lea was a special princess?"

All I did was nod in agreement. It was my turn to love and to listen.

"Tell me everything, Gaston," she continued breathlessly. "Do you realize how beautiful she is?"

Again she was asking me questions to which she already knew the answers. I just smiled in return.

"But before you tell me everything you see in Lea, I want to hear more about those exercises you mentioned."

"You mean the Spiritual Exercises, Ms. HonoOpono?"

"Yes, that's it! I remember them all—I mean, I wrote them all down."

She pulled out her worn journal. "I'm determined to try your Spiritual Exercises. My grandfather used to tell me, 'When you stumble upon wisdom, it's your responsibility to make every possible effort to learn from it.' And he'd also say, 'To ignore a great truth you've become aware of is like walking in the dark with a lit torch in your hand but choosing to keep your eyes closed.' Oh, and another thing he'd say, 'Dare yourself to learn what lies behind the wisdom and discover what kind of Mana you've stumbled upon.' I think that's what's happening to me—I've stumbled upon you and you're Spiritual Exercises."

She regarded at me eagerly and tapped her pen on a blank page of the journal.

I said, "You know, Ms. HonoOpono, our meeting and our conversations are of the Divine Order. Really, if you think about it, there are no other kinds of encounters in life but the ones determined by the Divine Order."

"Go on, Gaston." Her usually stentorian voice was soft for a change.

"Here's an exercise that's lots of fun: intuitive listening. Everyone practices intuitive listening in some form or another, some people many times a day. If you listen to your inner voice when it gives you a subtle nudge, it'll give you another, then another, providing more and more insight on how to run your life harmoniously. On the other hand, if you tell yourself the subtle signal wasn't real, or if you don't act on it, the Holy Spirit will try to reach you by more direct means or actions. When I remember to listen to my inner voice, life for me is a constant path of stepping stones in the shape of hearts, reminding me that love is the way home to God."

Ms. HonoOpono cocked her head and thought for a moment. "Sort of like what happened with you and your realtor friend."

"Exactly like that!"

"So you're telling me intuitive listening is that easy?"

"Well, I could simply answer *yes*, but that wouldn't be completely accurate," I cautioned. "Intuitive listening can be easy, but we often make it difficult by expecting logical answers or facts. The spiritual worlds aren't based on logic;

they're divine. We have to learn when the Holy Spirit sends us a nudge it reflects the truth for us and for no one else, and that it is the truth no matter how illogical it might seem. Of course, we do have to use common sense in our decisions. For example, if you hear within that you should harm another person, that's not a divine communication. Should your inner voice persist in telling you this, it's time to seek professional help. But by listening to our true inner voice, we get better and better at being a coworker with the Great Spirit."

Ms. HonoOpono's eyes turned inward in thought. Then the corners of her mouth edged up the tiniest bit and her crow's feet crinkled.

"I wonder what the heck a co-worker with the Great Spirit eats at a luau?"

She laughed at her own joke, louder than I'd heard her laugh before, and I couldn't help but join in. Lights flickered on all over first class as bleary eyed passengers turned and cast displeased glances at us. It was in the middle of the night, and most of them had been asleep. Brielle rushed down the aisle toward us.

"You've got to keep your voices down, both of you!" she admonished us in a stage whisper, although she was looking directly at Ms. HonoOpono when she said it. Ms. HonoOpono in turn tilted her chin in my direction.

"It's this man's fault, Brielle. He's the one making me laugh."

She didn't lower her volume one bit. The other passengers were even more upset now. I could hear rude comments directed at us like little poison darts. Lea popped up out of her seat and was at our side in seconds.

"That's it, you two! You're both having way too much fun. Time to split the kids up. Let me sit here, Gaston." Her voice was stern, but I could see she was working hard to keep from bursting into laughter herself.

"Of course, Lea," I acquiesced, rising to make room for her.

As I passed Brielle, she caught my arm and pulled me close. "Thank you Mr. Ouellet. I'm sorry for the inconvenience." Evidently she felt responsible for the disturbance.

"Don't worry," I said, patting her arm. "Lea will take care of Ms. HonoOpono, most likely in a much quieter way."

At my seat I found Mr. Toldeck wide awake, awaiting my return.

"It sure sounded like you had a lot of fun back there. I always enjoy listening to people laugh." He hesitated, perhaps waiting to see if I wanted to comment on the latest fiasco. When I remained silent, he changed the subject. "Tell me about other experiences you recall from living with Joanne and Michel."

And just like that, I was back reliving my past in the presence of this remarkable stranger.

"So many lessons learned with that family have stayed with me throughout my life." I shook my head in wonder. "The one that comes to mind right now is that working hard always pays.

"I got my first job when I was only seven years old, in the summer of 1967. We lived way out in the countryside, where every couple of weeks or so a man with a candy truck would come by. He had two big speakers mounted on the roof, broadcasting the treats he had on offer. We could always hear him coming from miles away as he traveled down every back road in our area. The driver either stopped at our house or at our next-door neighbor's. Once parked, he replaced the loud advertisement with enticing music, similar to the jingle the ice cream truck played.

"The driver's name was Mr. Harold, but everyone called him the 'Sweet Man.' He was the happiest, most generous man I ever met in my early youth, bringing joy to everyone wherever he went. Even grandparents and farmers up and down our dirt road knew the Sweet Man.

"The first time he pulled up in our driveway, I watched in fascination as his customers stepped into his blue truck and walked out with fists full of candy. After all the kids in our neighborhood had made their purchase, I was still sitting on the grass nearby with an expression of wonder on my face. I hadn't witnessed such a concentration of joy in a long time. Mr. Harold stepped out of the big blue truck and noticed me sitting there with a smile on my face. He said something to me I have never forgotten.

"'Soon you'll share all your candy with everyone!'

"Hearing this, I jumped up and shouted, 'How can that be when I don't have a dime or a nickel or even a penny to my name?'

"Mr. Harold got in his truck and called back to me from the rear window, 'Money? Money is everywhere, my son, for those willing to work hard for it. Working hard always pays.'

"That moment it was as if I had been hit by lightning. The truth of his words resonated like thunder in my heart. I dropped to the ground as if an actual lightning bolt had struck the core of my being. Gathering my strength, I sat up and yelled back to him with all my passion. 'How and where Mr. Harold? How and where?'

"He slid into the driver's seat and put the truck in gear. As he drove away, Mr. Harold shouted his reply out the window to me.

"'Pick up all the empty bottles you can find in the ditches. On my next trip I'll buy them from you.'

"From then on I donned my black rubber boots every day after school and trudged up and down the ditches in the neighborhood, searching for empty bottles. One Sunday afternoon after church while digging through one of the trenches, I slipped and fell on my back into the muddy water. Smelling of manure and probably worse, I pulled myself out of the muck and climbed the embankment up to the dirt road.

"Plodding along the side of the road, heading home to clean myself up, I clutched the plastic bag with my haul of the day. Towards the far end of our dirt road I saw a huge dust cloud, raised by a car speeding in my direction. As it approached me, the car slowed down and came to a complete stop near me. The dust billowed around the vehicle, making it impossible for me to see the driver or even what kind of car it was. Then, out of the dust a familiar voice reached me.

"'Working hard always pays.'

"The swirling dust thinned, revealing a sky-blue '67 mustang convertible. It was the coolest car a kid could ever imagine—the very symbol of abundance. A sudden gust swept away the remaining dust, and I recognized Mr. Harold, the Sweet Man himself, in the driver's seat. He favored me with a smile that lit up my whole day and made me forget the filthy state I was in. Without saying another word, he put the Mustang back in gear and he continued on his way, leaving me standing in the road with my mouth hanging open.

"As I walked the rest of the way home I kept telling myself, *if a candy man can give himself a gift of this magnitude, so can I.* Later, in the fall of that year, I learned that many people in our farming community had heard of me from stories spread by Mr. Harold—about the welfare kid who cleaned up ditches by picking up bottles.

"Farmers began to leave their empty bottles by the side of the road for me to pick up. Most residents in the area were aware of our poor living conditions, but they admired hard work.

"Several weeks after my dusty encounter with Mr. Harold, he pulled the candy truck into our driveway once again. The neighbor kids were upset with him because it was the second time in a row he parked in our driveway, but their complaints fell on deaf ears. The Sweet Man was the master of his own life, and no one told him how to do his job.

"As usual, he let only one kid at a time into his truck while the others milled around outside. I sat in the same spot in the grass I had several weeks earlier, waiting for all the kids to finish purchasing their treats. Then it was my turn.

"Mr. Harold stepped out of the truck to welcome me.' So, I guess you'll find out today how working hard always pays.'

"'I hope so, sir,' I said.

"'Where are your bottles?'

"I raced to our weather-beaten garage where I'd hidden them, and then I ran back to his truck with a bag of bottles. I placed it at his feet. He pulled them out and began to count.

"'You have twelve one-penny bottles, and three two-penny bottles,' he announced.' That gives you a total of eighteen cents for your hard work.'

"'What? Eighteen cents? That's not fair!' I exclaimed.

"As a seven year-old, I didn't know what eighteen cents were worth, much less what I could buy with them. It just seemed like a very small amount for the many hours I'd spent in the ditches.

"'I don't set the prices, kid,' Mr. Harold said sympathetically. 'The market does, you know?'

"He was addressing my back, because I was already running to the garage to get two additional bags filled with empty bottles. They clinked and clanked as I dragged them through the dirt towards the candy truck. Mr. Harold was grinning widely when I reached him, for he knew even more than I did what this small treasure meant to me.

"He completed counting the bottles and said: 'Son, you have a total of seventy one cents.'

"'Aw, I don't even have a dollar's worth?'

"He laughed.' No, you don't, kid. But come on in with your seventy-one cents and discover what hard work tastes like.'

"I scampered into his truck like a kid boarding a merry-go-round, happy to finally be inside. The ice cream truck jingle was playing and multi colored lights splashed the interior. Candy of all colors, flavors, and sizes filled the shelves on both sides of the aisle. Heaven had descended and parked in my driveway. I bounced on my toes, barely able to contain my excitement. An amazing combination of aromas overwhelmed me. The smells were so rich and abundant I could almost taste them. Sunlight streamed through the windows and played over the candy like fairy dust. I couldn't tell which were brighter, the colored lights or the candy. All the while I was rushing up and down the aisle swiveling my head this way and that, Mr. Harold kept repeating the same thing over and over.

"'Hard work always pays, son. Hard work always pays.'

"I had definitely discovered what hard work looked and smelled like; now I would find out what it tasted like. Back in 1967, one penny could buy ten to twenty different kinds of candy. Most kids walked into what we called the 'Magic

Truck' with a nickel or less, and that was sufficient to fulfill their candy needs until the next visit.

"The candy I purchased added up to more than five pounds.

"When I returned to our house with my bulging bag, it was like I had set fire to the kitchen floor again. The other children were enraged over the apparent injustice of my wealth of candy while they had little in comparison. In response, Joanne ordered me to share most of my candy with the other kids.

"While Joanne was dividing the candy among everyone, I remembered the comment Mr. Harold had made when we first met.

"'Soon you will share all your candy with everyone.'

"That moment had come.

"It didn't even bother me that Joanne made me share the candy I'd bought with my own hard-earned money. I had learned that hard work always pays, and I knew I was going to taste the fruits of my hard work if I kept it up. There were plenty of other ditches I hadn't explored yet, and the farmers were going to leave more bottles for me to pick up. Besides, I was learning that sharing the fruits of my labor with others only brought me joy, especially when I was sharing something everyone greatly desired.

"Some people seem to only want what others have, without being willing to work for it themselves. But I had learned my lesson well. In the summer of 1967 I picked up a lot of empty bottles and ate mountains of candy. In addition to learning to share with the people I loved, and that hard works always pays, the most valuable lesson I received came from observing how Mr. Harold led his life. A man can only teach by example who he already is, not who he might aspire to become. What I learned from Mr. Harold's example was that only through perseverance can a man ever become what he aspires to be."

Mr. Toldeck mused, "How many 'Mr. Harold's do you think we meet in our lifetimes? You know the type of person who shows up in your life to give you a helping hand, or to teach you a lesson?"

"Thousands of thousands of them. Each day of our lives Divine Spirit sends us many sweet people such has Mr. Harold to show us Divine Love in action. We can witness it in their selfless acts and let it inspire our hearts. These days television and the internet are degrading our belief in people's goodness by the constant meanness and violence they display, making it harder than ever to see the kindness in others. But I'm convinced 99 % of the people are good to the core of their being, no matter where you go in this world.

"Every night before I go to sleep, I replay the events of my day in my head to remember how many Mr. Harold's came into my life to demonstrate love. And every night I'm transformed by the realization of just how many people and even animals have demonstrated Divine Love.

"You see, Mr. Toldeck, today you're my Mr. Harold. You're allowing me to share for the first time in my life experiences that have caused me much pain and sorrow. For reasons I don't yet quite understand, I find myself very comfortable with that. I know it's okay to continue this dialogue with you…even if it seems we're constantly being interrupted."

Both of us chuckled because it was so obvious. Then his piercing eyes searched mine again, and I got lost in the Light and Sound. Time stopped as I met his gaze. Emotions began to swirl within me once again, so I closed my eyes to compose myself. But even with my physical eyes closed, I continued to witness a colorful celebration of Divine Spirit through my third eye.

Silence reigned within our shared, inner realm. We were bathing in each other presence. It felt like the air conditioning had shut down and my seat was in flames. No, not the seat; the fire was inside me! The heat increased until it was almost unbearable. Still, I wasn't going to open my eyes or disclose to Mr. Toldeck what was going on with me. I decided just to flow with it, as I had done previously.

In the middle of this profound moment, I faintly heard tiny footsteps approach. Struggling to maintain my focus on the Light and Sound, I sensed a little hand touch my knee as if it were happening in a faraway dream. It wasn't long before I was jolted out of my inner bliss: Nelo began shaking my leg as if he were trying to wake me up.

Brielle appeared almost immediately, instructing Nelo firmly to return to his seat. Lea spoke up from across the aisle, assuring Brielle Nelo and I were friends. Signaling to Mr. Toldeck that I would return soon, I took Nelo by the hand and walked with him back into the coach section. Behind me I could hear Brielle and Lea engage in a debate as to who was allowed in first class and who was not.

As I let Nelo walk ahead of me, I remembered something I had learned from my spiritual guide, the Vi-Guru. Time and time again he had told me my heart would open whenever I wished to serve the Light and Sound. Someone would always be ready to receive the spiritual fire fueled in my heart. At this moment in time it was Nelo who was drawn to this roaring fire. When we reached the entrance to coach I leaned down to gather him up in my arms.

Ellouise was fast asleep in her seat, so I took Nelo to the rear of the plane where we could speak without disturbing anyone. I set him on the floor.

Nelo said, "Coach Gaston, do you know when we'll land at the airport?"

"No, but I'll find out for you."

Turning to find one of the flight attendants, I saw Brielle hurrying down the aisle towards us. She apologized for her displeased tone earlier when she ordered Nelo back to his seat.

"It's okay," Nelo said. He blessed her with a sunny smile. "Don't be sorry. Just be happy."

Brielle smiled back. I think her eyes may have been a little misty at Nelo's good-hearted forgiveness.

"How long before we land?" I asked.

"About three hours."

She smiled again and began to make her way back to first class. Watching her uniformed figure retreat I noticed Nelo pulling on my pant leg.

"Coach Gaston, how long is that? Three hours?"

"Three hours," I answered. "Well it's like…"

Then I stopped. How long was three hours in terms a six-year-old could understand? Then it hit me.

"It's like two soccer games back to back. Like our last championship, remember?"

Nelo's whole body sagged at the memory. "Oh, yes, Coach Gaston. Whew! That's a long time. I was so tired after that."

"A good reason for you to get some rest like your mom's doing," I suggested.

"Okay," he replied without hesitation. "I will."

Together we went to his row, where I picked him up, placed him in the middle seat and tucked two blankets around him.

"Nelo," I said. "Promise me that when you wake up you'll come see me."

"I will, Coach Gaston, I promise."

The boy cuddled up to his sleeping mom's shoulder, hugging his teddy bear. I waved and returned to my seat. It was the only one with its reading light on. All the other passengers were fast asleep, even Lea. Quietly I slipped in, acknowledging Mr. Toldeck with a glance, and closed my eyes. Within moments I entered the dream state for a journey into the Far Country.

GRATITUDE LEADS US TO LOVE

VIII

When I opened my eyes from my inner journey, my attention was immediately drawn to Mr. Toldeck. He was alert, chin resting on his hand, contemplating the view outside our window. Although I was certain he knew I was awake, neither of us spoke for quite a long time. Brielle, noticing I had stirred, headed over.

"Mr. Ouellet would you like something to drink or a snack of some sort?"

"Only green tea, please. Thank you, Brielle."

She was back in no time, and I gratefully took a warm sip.

"I was amazed at how fast you fell asleep once you closed your eyes," Mr. Toldeck remarked.

"Yes, I know," I concurred. "It was amazing—the first time I ever slept on a plane. I've never been able to do that before."

"Looks like this flight has a lot of firsts for you."

His reply sent a shiver down my spine, as if he knew something about me that I didn't. That feeling usually indicated something important to me, but at the moment I had no idea what it might be. Still, in the back of my mind I was wondering if perhaps I was going to die on this airplane tonight. Was that too farfetched?

Finally I said, "For myself, I try to view everything I do in life like it's my first time."

Mr. Toldeck digested this comment for a moment, then decided to take up our previous topic.

"Before your rest, you were talking about the family you lived with in the countryside. Where did you go after that?"

Taking another sip of tea, I resumed my story. "On a Sunday afternoon in the summer of 1969 my brother and I were asked to come to the kitchen. Joanne and Michel told us we had to leave because the family was no longer able to provide for us. This didn't come as a great surprise to me, since their financial struggles had been evident for quite some time. Jean would be going to live on the neighbor's farm where he'd worked for most of his summer vacation. Joanne told me I would move in with a family in the suburbs the following day. I had no idea what suburban life entailed. I only remembered what Paulji foretold in my dream a few nights earlier:

"'A new spiritual adventure is coming. Remember that I am always with you. Remember that this adventure will be imperative for your growth.'

This turned out to be true in more ways than one.

"Whenever I cried out of loneliness, Paulji would always appear in my third eye and assure me all was well. His favorite expression was, 'I am always with you.' His reassurance resonated in my inner ear like the rush of a waterfall of light.

"The night before my departure to the suburbs, my brother allowed me to sleep in the big bed with him. By now I'd been sleeping on the bare wooden floor for over a year and half, and the bed felt like a haven of softness and warmth. The next morning after breakfast, tears flooded my eyes as I watched Jean cross the plowed field to his new home on the neighboring farm. Joanne held me in her arms, her own tears dripping onto my head. Then a stranger in a brand new station wagon pulled into our driveway; it was my turn to leave.

"Michel walked me out to the car. I looked back to see Joanne framed in the kitchen window, sorrow written across her face. As I climbed into the front seat of the wagon, familiar feelings of abandonment washed over me. *I would have eaten less if only they'd asked,* I thought. But it was too late for that now.

"After Michel loaded the boxes with my belongings into the back, he came over to my window and shook my hand. He turned his head and wiped each of his eyes against his raised shoulders, first the left, then the right. I had never seen Michel cry before. Now it was the last thing I saw as we drove away.

"I cried during most of the hour and a half trip, even though the driver tried everything he could think of to cheer me up. When we arrived at my new home, the whole family awaited us seated in the living room. My new foster parents, Raymond and Valerie, had three children of their own and one more girl from the same welfare agency I came from.

"Within a few days I found great comfort in Raymond's presence. He had a heart of gold, but his wife was the spitting image of the most evil witch imaginable. I stayed far away from her for the first few days, like a wounded animal sensing a stalking predator, even when she called to me. Raymond kept telling her, 'Give him some time. He'll come around.'"

"It must have been very painful for you to be around her," Mr. Toldeck sympathized.

I nodded. "Within a few weeks she began to beat me up night after night. It became a nightly ritual."

"Why was that?"

"As soon as I moved in with my new family I began having recurring dreams of a past life as a race car driver. Every night for months I'd fall asleep and wake up in a dream speeding down a racetrack, careening through a sharp right turn and then crashing into a wall. I'd wake up screaming in horror. Valerie would hear me and come upstairs to slap me around for the disturbance I was causing. I'd only be spared when Raymond accompanied her. He could see how terrified I was, so he'd talk to me to calm me down.

"After numerous beatings I developed all sorts of methods to stay awake and avoid the dream. Eventually, sleep would always overtake me and I could only hope that the nightmare wouldn't revisit, or that Valerie wouldn't hear me scream. But the dream always came, she always heard, and the beatings always followed. It wasn't until much later that I discovered why she was always awake at night—she was an alcoholic and stayed up late to drink."

"Did your nightmare ever stop?" Mr. Toldeck asked.

"Oh, yes! I remember that night very well."

"What happened?"

"I discovered that if I waited past one o'clock in the morning, Valerie would pass out. Then I could safely fall asleep and be spared my daily beating. One magical night, she was already drunk before I went to bed and warned me she didn't want to hear one peep out of me. Of course I was terrified; several nights ago she had broken one of my front teeth in her drunken rage and scratched my face with her wedding ring. I lay in bed crying, begging God to come to my rescue. Just as I was about to slip into my nightmare, Fubee appeared in the door of my room."

I stopped for a moment and looked inquiringly at Mr. Toldeck. "You remember who Fubee is?"

Mr. Toldeck nodded a faint smile on his lips as if he were harboring a secret. What was it? I hoped eventually I would find out.

"Anyway," I continued, "there was Master Fubee in his white robe, looking right through me as always.

"'Are you ready to resolve your karmic situation?' he said.

"I knuckled the tears out of my eyes and let out a big sigh. I'm not sure if I understood mentally that my prayer was being answered, but physically I certainly did. My whole body relaxed in Master Fubee's presence.

"I nodded in the affirmative.

"For many months now I had dreamed of this same past life. I learned where I had lived and visited the people I had loved. Every aspect of my inner experience about this life was familiar. In that life, I had suffered a severely broken heart. The love of my life had left me. So instead of executing the right turn on the racetrack properly, I had crashed the car and ended my life.

"As soon as I agreed with Fubee to resolve my karma, I dropped off to sleep and found myself hurtling down the track in my race car once again. Everything was the same. Except… this time I found the resolve to make the turn correctly. The moment I drove safely out of that curve, the curve where before I had died every night in my dream, I woke up.

"Fubee was still in my room, glowing bright in his white robe. After that experience I slept like an angel every night. Even better, from then on I had the courage to choose love, no matter what circumstances I was in. That's a gift I still carry with me today."

"How do you know it was a past life and not just some crazy nightmare?" Mr. Toldeck inquired.

I smiled. "The truth is hidden in the details. Once, when I was in my early twenties, I visited my mother at the hospital. She brought out a very old book, opened it to the page dated April 9, 1960, and showed where next to the date she had written the name *Harry*. Her finger traced over the faded paper, back and forth between the name and my birth date.

"'I've kept this old book for so many years. I'm not even sure I know why.' She stopped sliding her finger across the rough paper and tapped the name. 'When you were born, I wanted to name you Harry so bad. But your dad wouldn't hear of it, so we called you Gaston.'"

Even now, decades after first learning this fact from my mother, I still got goose bumps whenever I thought or spoke about it. Mr. Toldeck waited patiently for me to continue, smiling as if he almost knew what I was going to say next.

"The race car driver in my dream was named *Harry*," I revealed.

Mr. Toldeck shook his head slowly and let out a low whistle.

"As you can imagine," I went on, "I was quite shaken when my mother told me. I never forgot my race car crash dream, and I made the connection immediately. But the name was only the first detail that convinced me the dream was about a past life.

"The next detail was revealed to me when I returned to the San Francisco Bay area where I lived with my wife, Joan. She had a dear friend named Katie King, a British woman with a distinct accent and a lively personality. For months Katie and Joan would talk on the phone, and each time Joan hung up she'd say, 'I can't wait for you to meet her in person.'

"One afternoon Katie called to invite us over for supper at her apartment in Redwood City. Joan was so excited; I was finally going to meet her friend. They knew each other from years ago in New York and had developed a very strong bond. At the time, Joan and I had known each other for only nine months. She was thirty-one and I was only twenty-two. The deep friendship between her and Katie had me worried that I wouldn't be accepted as her husband because of my relative youth and inexperience. Besides my insecurity there was something else: in a strange way I felt drawn to Katie.

"Whenever Katie called and I picked up the phone, I would listen to her voice and see a very attractive, very familiar thirty-something blonde in my mind's eye. Since this happened every time she called, I was pretty sure I knew exactly what she looked like. That night, as we walked to Katie's front door, Joan asked me to return to the car to get something while she went ahead. When I entered the apartment, I found Ms. King sitting on an old couch waiting to greet me. To my amazement, she turned out to be in her late sixties.

"As I sat listening to her fascinating stories of her life, I soon found myself closing my eyes and listening on a deeper level. Her voice resembled the one I'd heard many times in my early dreams, except the woman in my dream had been in her thirties. At some point I couldn't hold myself back any longer and asked, 'Mrs. King, please, I would truly appreciate seeing pictures of you when you were in your thirties, if that's possible.'

"'Please, call me Katie,' she said, glancing warmly at Joan.' We're family now.'

"Smiling proudly, she left to get the pictures and returned shortly with a small box of photo albums. She pulled one out and showed me a picture of herself and her husband when they lived in New York City in 1960. I'd never told anyone that in my race car dream I lived in New York. The picture showed the beautiful blond woman I'd seen so many times in my dreams, as well as in my mind's eye each time she called. So I dared to be bold with her.

"'Kat King,' I said to her. 'Do you remember me? I'm Harry the race car driver.'

She jumped off the couch like a child and threw her arms around me.

"'Harry! It's you! Oh, it really is you! No one has called me Kat King for decades.'

"Joan was bewildered by her dramatic reaction, but as we sat for hours, reminiscing about Kat and Harry in New York, she came to accept our connection in my past life. Now I understood why I felt drawn to her whenever she called. In my past life I had always had a weak spot for her, and my feelings hadn't changed despite my death and reincarnation.

"After that evening whenever we had a chance to get together, I learned from her that past lives are as real as the seasons. She always said to me: 'We better get it right this time around, Gaston!' Several months after we met, Katie King was found in her bed, having passed away peacefully in her sleep. At her funeral I found out she had been a well-known clairvoyant and psychic in New York and London, and had made her living as such."

Mr. Toldeck gently steered me back to my story. "Even though you discovered one of your past lives through physical abuse, that still had to be traumatic. How did you manage to maintain a loving state and not fall into the trap of anger or sadness?"

"I think physical abuse isn't always as traumatic as psychological or emotional abuse. Valerie tried to break my spirit in many ways, not just with beatings. That's what servants of the dark are tasked to do. The higher we as Soul raise on the ladder of spiritual unfoldment, the greater the personal challenges we experience in our physical lives. But as I see it, we're always exactly as competent as the challenges we face at any given moment. Our consciousness is ever-expanding and evolving, which means eventually we resolve all the inner challenges we're confronted with. That's where the true battleground lies—within—the field on which the Warriors of the Light and Sound confront the servants of darkness every day and every moment.

"Honestly, though, many times the difficulties in my life were so profound that I could only keep my heart open by placing my attention on gratitude. I learned early on that if I focused on the blessings, like Raymond's golden kindness, the fact that Valerie prepared our meals every day, or my loving teacher at school, then I could survive by making gratitude my invisible shield. I spent much of my time searching for things to be grateful for and found many, but I also learned that whenever I lowered my shield of gratitude, darkness would invade and I would slide into sadness. The state of sadness is no place to live; especially when one already knows how to soar on the rising winds of gratitude.

"It may sound strange, but every time I faced personal injustice of some sort, the voice of God found a way to comfort me. One such time was during my first Christmas at the foster home. I'll always remember that Christmas Eve, because it was one of the most disturbing events I experienced as a child.

"Christmas is supposed to be a glorious time when families join together to celebrate, but whenever any of Valerie's family came to visit us, holiday or not, I was sent off to the basement. It made me feel like a dog locked outside the house so it wouldn't be a nuisance to the visitors. Banishment to the cellar was one of the many ways Valerie reminded me that I didn't belong with them, that I was an outsider.

"Raymond and the other kids sometimes attempted to mitigate this injustice by including me in family events in whatever ways they could, such as bringing me treats to the basement window while family parties were going on upstairs. They were forbidden to even open the basement door. If anyone came downstairs to the basement at all, it was Valerie coming to get things from the freezer or from her private storage area.

"On this particular Christmas day I was sent to the basement after breakfast while the rest of the family held their Christmas morning celebration. Unlike myself, the other welfare girl who lived with us was the daughter of one of Valerie's cousins, so to Valerie she was part of the family. That whole day I spent most of the time looking out the basement window, which faced the house of Raymond's parents.

"Eventually, as daylight faded and Christmas lights began to sparkle in the darkness, I watched happy families arrive at the neighborhood homes carrying bags of colorful gift packages. Upstairs in our house a festive commotion broke out. Children's' footsteps scampered around on the floor above me and then pattered out the front door. From the basement window I watched as all the kids in our household ran across the street to their grandparents' house. Valerie came downstairs to turn off the basement light. Just has she was about to shut the door, Raymond called out from upstairs.

"'Is Gaston coming?'

"'No,' she called back. 'He doesn't want to. You know what he's like!'

"'But you asked him, right?'

"'Of course, I did,' she lied, closing the door.

"I watched Raymond and Valerie walk across the street to join the children for Christmas dinner at the grandparents' house. Loneliness and despair tore at my heart. At only nine years old, I couldn't understand what I had done to deserve such callous treatment.

"I cried for a long time and eventually fell asleep, exhausted from the emotional torment. Sometime during the evening, I was awakened by a knock on the window. At first I thought maybe one of the other kids had snuck back to bring me a treat, but when I looked closer I saw the shining face of Santa Claus himself. Electrified, I jumped up and ran to the window. I still believed in Santa Claus at that age, but to my amazement and surprise I realized it was my best friend JP dressed in his uncle's Santa suit. He had come to cheer me up.

"JP was a shining example of love, even at his young age. His gentle kindness was as unwavering as the sun on a cloudless day. At school kids always drifted towards him, as if coming to drink from the fountain of love. Now here he was at the basement window to comfort me during my dark hour.

"For a while we tried unsuccessfully to pry open the frozen window. Discouraged at not being able to pass me his gifts, JP was just about to give up, when I had a flash of genius. Why not let him in through the front door upstairs? My fear of Valerie had so conditioned me to staying in the basement that I hadn't even thought about going upstairs until now. But I knew she was across the street and would be there for a long time getting drunk. So I quickly ran upstairs and let JP in. He brought with him presents and food from his family's Christmas dinner. Our celebration lasted for hours. We laughed like comics and ate like kings. Finally, he went back to his own house, taking with him the leftovers from our feast.

"God knew the one person I wanted to be with that Christmas was my best friend. So the voice of God spoke to me in the person of JP to lead me out of the darkness and loneliness. It takes a lot of patience and discipline to see what gifts life constantly has in store for us, but through hardships and the presence of friends like JP, I was being trained to be on the lookout for those gifts at all times. That evening, JP was a gift and an angel to me."

Thoughtfully, Mr. Toldeck said, "Valerie must have been in a lot of pain. No one seeks to harm another person in such a manner unless they are in the grip of great sadness themselves. You were indeed blessed to have a friend like JP. Not many people can claim to have an angel as their best friend."

I nodded, remembering JP's shining face. "I truly remember JP as an angel—in more ways than one."

Mr. Toldeck quirked an eyebrow in question.

"Early in the spring of 1971, when I was eleven, I started my second job," I responded. "It involved peeling potatoes at a nearby hamburger stand for fifty cents per five-gallon-bucket. A few days after I was hired, I asked the owner if JP could help. To him it didn't matter who pealed his potatoes, but the pay would still be fifty cents a pale. From then on, JP and I walked over to the stand every day after school and peeled potatoes together.

"One evening I had a dream with Paulji, my spiritual guide. He told me I would soon assist a close friend to cross over to the other side. He gave me specific instructions in what I needed to do. Once my dream self-accepted and understood them, I woke up even though it was still in the middle of the night.

"I lay there in the dark, trying to make sense of the dream with my rational mind but was unable to. I came to the conclusion Spirit reveals only what's needed for us to best serve as a vehicle, and nothing more. In the morning I went to school as usual, but I kept a sharp lookout for anything that might relate to my dream.

"A few days later, JP and I dropped our school bags off at home and headed to work. We came to a four-lane intersection and waited at the stoplight for our signal. During a gap in the heavy traffic I sensed JP was ready to run across and pleaded with him to wait, but he bolted into the street anyway. The next second a city bus slammed into him and knocked him close to thirty feet through the air. He thudded down in a crumpled heap on the opposite sidewalk.

"Screaming, I was about to run across the street myself, but before I had even taken three steps PJ was standing by my side, wondering what had just happened. At first I paid little attention to his presence and focused on the broken body across the street. His voice snapped me out of my daze by saying almost exactly what the Vi-Guru had told me a few nights earlier.

"'You're supposed to assist me in crossing over to the other side!'

"Time stood still and all movement stopped except for JP and myself. The accident scene hung suspended as if I had pushed the pause button on the world. I gathered my courage and turned slowly to look at JP's form standing next to me, seemingly no worse for the wear. In fact, he was smiling at me as he always did. Realizing he was with me in his Soul body, I communicated to him what I'd learned from Paulji about what awaits in the next world.

"'Okay,' JP sent back. 'Sounds good. I'm ready now. Show me how to get across!'

"Desperately, I cast about, hoping for Paulji to appear and give me additional guidance, but he was nowhere to be seen.

"JP repeated, 'I'm ready. Come on, Gaston, show me how to get there.'

"I mentally went over Paulji's instructions, hoping I remembered everything correctly.

"'I only know one way to assist you,' I finally said.

"'So tell me, already!'

"I tried to keep despair from darkening my heart. I had never done this before. There was so much at stake, and I wanted only the very best for my friend.

"'You need to open your heart and sing "HU" in gratitude for all that life has given you,' I heard myself saying. 'Then the Divine Light will appear and escort you home."

"We began singing HU together, and shortly thereafter a blue-purple light appeared before us, with a brighter white light pulsing at its center. Within the space of a brief moment that nevertheless felt like an eternity, the light enveloped our entire surroundings. JP floated forward and began to merge with the brilliant glow. A beautiful melody pulsed out from everywhere at once. Then two white shapes resembling wings appeared at JP's side just before he completely disappeared into the center of the light.

"If there is such thing as angel, well, he sure looked like one to me at that moment."

Mr. Toldeck's eyes glowed with understanding as he listened.

I went on, "During the entire time this experience unfolded before my eyes, I continued to inwardly sing HU. I was numb with grief yet somehow elated. JP, my best friend, was gone, but I had escorted his true self, Soul, to the gateway of the next world. It was my first time serving in this capacity, but not my last. At some later point I dimly felt an ambulance medical technician take me by the shoulders in a gentle attempt to comfort me. By the time the medical tech got me up and moving, most of the kids from the neighborhood had come and were surrounding me. JP's body already lay zipped in a black vinyl bag.

"For a while I still saw the blue-purple light pulsing all around me with my third eye, and faintly I continued to perceive the sacred melody, the Voice of God, welcoming home one of Its own. Then, as if awakening from a dream, I slowly began to hear the babble of everyone talking to me at once. The world wanted my attention, but I was as yet unable to respond.

"I had just experienced a miracle, one for which I had no words of description. That was all right, though; I had no desire to share it with anyone. JP had been the one person with whom I could ever discuss such matters. He seemed to always understand, no matter how strange my experiences might have been.

"A subdued crowd of children escorted me home. They were in shock too; one of their friends had just died. Incredibly, Valerie began screaming at me that this was all my fault the moment I entered the house. Barely able to look at her angry, contorted face, I felt her barrage of biting words wash over me like acid rain. Tears were beginning to roll down my cheeks, when all of a sudden I noticed purple lights flashing in the room around us. Inwardly strengthened, I deflected Valerie's vicious attack and focused on the light until it filled the entire kitchen. At that moment Raymond came rushing in, saying the whole neighborhood could hear Valerie yelling at me. He took me upstairs to my room where I could find refuge from her stream of hatefulness. I was completely battered emotionally over the loss of the most important person in my life, even though I had been taught time and time again by my Vi-Guru that we are all Souls, and that Soul lives for eternity."

Mr. Toldeck and I enjoyed a moment of silence in memory of my angel-friend, JP. All too soon, I felt a small hand shaking my arm. As if I didn't already know who it was, I turned to discover Nelo and Ellouise hovering by my side.

"Could you come with me, Coach Gaston?" Nelo pleaded, glancing up at Ellouise for reassurance. "Mom said it's okay to ask you."

"Of course, Nelo. It's always okay to ask for what you want, as long as it's not meant as an order. No one likes to be ordered around, as you know. So, where are we going?"

"I want you to come with me back to our seats, 'cause my mom says we can't stay in this section."

"What for, Nelo?"

"I want to play a video game with you, and I don't have any friends to play with here."

"Oh, really," I laughed. "Then what do you think I am? Just someone you can beat at Super Mario? I'll have you know I'm a good player at that game and I'm pretty sure I can beat you in my sleep."

Nelo and Ellouise both laughed in return.

"Oh, right," the boy said. "Come on, then, Coach Gaston, I'll show you how good I am."

I rose, nodding in respect to Mr. Toldeck, while at the same time noticing out of the corner of my eye that Lea was waving me over, and so was Ms. HonoOpono. I pointed to Nelo and shrugged apologetically at both ladies.

"I hope we didn't disturb your beauty rest," Ellouise remarked. "Nelo has been pestering me to come get you for the longest time but he didn't want to tell me why. I asked him, but I guess he knew that if he told me he wanted to play video games with you I would have said no. He's been playing for hours with his Game Boy."

In the back of my mind I wondered why she said she hoped she hadn't disturbed my beauty rest, when I'd just been engaged in a lively conversation with Mr. Toldeck.

Before I sat down with Nelo, I addressed Ellouise. "I love being here and I enjoy both your company. Anyway, I need a rest from my conversation with Mr. Toldeck."

Ellouise shook her head slightly. "With who?"

I didn't feel like starting a long explanation of what I had been talking about with a stranger in the seat next to mine, and I certainly didn't want to bring up my intimate childhood experiences to yet another person. I really did need a mental and emotional rest after the intense discussions we'd been having, so I came up with an idea to avoid answering her question.

"Hey! Ellouise, Nelo, let's play a game, all three of us together!"

"How can we do that? There's only one Game Boy and we can only play one game at a time," Nelo countered.

"Easy," I said. "Nelo, you start the game and we'll count to ten. Once you hear us say *ten*, you pass me the Game Boy. Then you and your mom count to ten while I play. Next we do the same for your mom while she's playing. Whoever has the game when it ends is the winner. Sound good?"

"Oh, yeah! I'll be the winner!" Nelo responded enthusiastically.

"We'll all be winners; because we'll play so many games that everyone will have a chance."

"I don't even know how to play this game," Ellouise said doubtfully.

"The game is called *Count to Ten*," I explained. "While we're counting, you just push some buttons and discover how the game works, just as I will."

Nelo protested, "No, it's called Super Mario Go Cart, not Count to Ten!"

Ellouise laughed good-naturedly. Aware this might be the only time Nelo was going have fun with her on this long flight, she quickly gave in.

"Okay, but you better get ready, 'cause I'm going to win first."

"No way, Mom," Nelo assured her.

"Everyone ready?" I said.

"Yes!"

Nelo began to manipulate the controls of the Game Boy with both hands, while Ellouise and I counted in unison. In the course of the next several minutes, we exchanged the device many times until finally both Nelo and I were eliminated.

Ellouise smirked. "I told you, didn't I?"

"You sure did, Mom. But don't forget I'm a winner too. Coach Gaston said so."

We played several more rounds until the flight attendant came by with a tray of snacks. "Does anyone want something to eat? We have chicken wraps, salads, carrot sticks, apple slices, and several different types of chips."

"All right, guys," Ellouise said. "I'm buying. We deserve it."

Nelo and I chose an assortment of goodies. While we ate for a while in silence, I noted that Lea was heading down the aisle in our direction. I smiled at her, but she looked deliberately the other way as she passed.

"Are you and that woman together?" Ellouise inquired.

"Not yet," I answered without thinking. Then my hand flew to my mouth, trying to catch the words and push them back in. "I mean, no," I corrected myself, attempting to regain my balance. "What I was trying to say is that we just met on this flight." I took a deep breath. "And...why would you ask that?"

"Well, when we came to your seat earlier...the way she looked at me...I could just tell she had feelings for you. You know us women have an antenna for these kinds of things."

"Funny you should mention that," I said. "When Lea saw us together earlier she said the same thing about you."

"Really," Ellouise looked into the distance for a moment. "What exactly, did she say?"

"She said, 'You have a beautiful family,' meaning she thought we were together."

"And what did you tell her?"

"I told her we're good friends and that I'm Nelo's soccer coach."

"Oh, I see."

When Ellouise continued to stare towards the horizon of her inner thoughts, I sensed our conversation had made her feel uncomfortable, as if she harbored secret feelings for me. I had never realized this might be the case. Quickly I turned the conversation back to the present, hoping it would give her time to compose herself.

"Did you enjoy the *Count to Ten* games?"

"I did," she affirmed, clearly relieved at the change of topic. "I guess I've developed a negative attitude towards video games over the years." She could look at me now and smiled. "But playing together today allowed me to see how much fun you can have with them. And I saw how much fun Nelo had."

"Fun? Yes, but these games are not only fun. They are a medium for developing new social skills among our youth like nothing ever created before. I think the only reason we adults can't recognize that is that we're stuck in the past. The only place we can have fun is the present. Pleasure can only be experienced in this very moment."

"I'm in the present moment, aren't I, Coach Gaston?" Nelo put in. His eyes sparkled with the pure spiritual presence that comes so naturally to children.

I laughed in delight at Nelo's question. "Indeed you are, Nelo. More than you'll ever know."

"All righty then, can we play another game? One more time?" Nelo begged. "Pleeeeease?"

How could we refuse? We played many more games until Brielle walked by and Ellouise signaled for her attention.

"Excuse me Ms. How much longer before we land?"

"We'll be landing in Taipei in about an hour or so. Then another four and a half before we reach Bangkok."

"Thank you."

Brielle looked at me curiously. "So this is where you've been hiding, Mr. Ouellet? I noticed your seat's been empty for quite some time." When I simply smiled, she continued on her way towards the rear of the plane.

Ellouise took this as her cue. "Well, Nelo, I guess it's time for Coach Gaston to go back to his own seat."

Nelo gave off one of his whole-body sighs. "Yes, Mom, you're right." He turned his bright gaze on me. "Thank you, Coach Gaston. I enjoyed playing with my mom, thanks to you."

I stood up and began making my way back to my seat. Just before I passed through the curtains to first class, I turned to wave at Ellouise. She smiled, waved back, then lowered her eyes.

It was nearly pitched dark in the first class section; the only light still on was mine. In passing I noticed Ms. HonoOpono and Lea were both fast asleep, as were all the other passengers except for Mr. Toldeck. I sat down and leaned over to him.

"I'd like you to know I've been finding our conversations tremendously therapeutic, even if they are sometimes difficult. Expressing the most painful moments of my life alongside the most uplifting ones is transformative to say the least. I've never before dared to confide to anyone such intimate details of my personal life."

I paused, realizing it was no accident that an encounter such as this was occurring at the beginning of my pilgrimage to Thailand.

"In the weeks to come," I continued, "when I'm fasting, and afterwards as well, I'll try to comprehend the meaning behind all this."

Mr. Toldeck said, "Feel free to stop in your story whenever you want. I can understand how difficult it can be at times, so I leave it to you to stop whenever you need to."

The harmonious vibrations of his voice resonated through me like the deep hum of a jet turbine on a journey to freedom. It seemed the more he confirmed my freedom to stop with my story, the more I wanted to continue. There were so many more experiences I wanted to tell him about. He gave me the opening with his next question.

"Did you live with that family much longer after JP was hit by the bus?"

"Not really. Valerie was very upset by JP's death, but more so by the shame she presumed was reflecting on her for my part in the accident. For weeks afterward she kept telling me, 'What will people say when they hear what you did?' An accusation like this was a great burden to carry as a young child, even though I knew the truth was I had actually tried to prevent him from crossing the street.

"Several weeks later, Paulji visited me again. As usual, his droll southern accent delighted me and made me laugh. While our meetings usually took place in the dream state, this night proved to be an exception. Just before the moment I fell asleep, he appeared in his radiant blue suit to accompany me into the inner worlds. He took me to a huge playground on the astral plane where JP was waiting for me. My best friend had arranged this meeting to thank me and to reassure me that he was very happy where he now resided. For a while Paulji let us play together as we always had before PJ's translation. The difference was that now my friend was in a Light Body that sparkled like a million tiny stars.

"Once the dream travel ended, I became aware of being at another scene. Paulji and I stood on the bank of a rushing river, where he informed me that I was needed elsewhere and would soon leave the family I was with.

"When I arrived home from school a few days later, I noted a brand new car parked in our driveway. The corridor leading to the kitchen held a small pile of boxes containing my belongings. At the kitchen table a man I had never seen before sat opposite a smiling Valerie. As I entered, my heart fluttered in my chest and I had a hard time catching my breath. Valerie darted her eyes to the empty chair already pulled out for me, and I settled into it with trepidation. Neither of the adults said anything, stretching out the silence in the room uncomfortably. As the other children returned home from school, each was directed to go play downstairs in the cellar. This fact alone indicated to me that something horrible was about to happen; rarely was anyone but me consigned to the basement. Into the painful silence I dared to ask the obvious question.

"'Tell me why this man and I are sitting here, Valerie? And why can't I go play downstairs like I'm usually told to?'

"She stared at me with a rigid, malicious smile.

"'Because you're leaving. Right away. Right now. With this gentleman from Welfare.'

"Her grin remained a frozen rictus in her face, but I could tell she had to work to keep it from spreading into one of malicious triumph.

"The other children had been listening at the top of the basement stairs, despite their orders to go and play. Now they rushed into the kitchen asking, 'Why, Mom? Why does Gaston have to leave?'

"Neither Valerie nor the stranger seemed to be willing to provide any answers. Another painful silence ensued, in which a heavy cloud of sadness filled the room.

"Suddenly, as if a dam had burst in my chest, I shouted into the stillness, 'Why? Why do I have to leave? I'm a good boy! I haven't done anything wrong! I promise I'll always be a good boy!'

"In response the other children yelled in a chorus, 'You are, Gaston! You are!'

"Even though Paulji had foretold my departure several nights before, my emotional ties to my foster family were strong and I didn't want to leave. I couldn't bear the thought of being ripped from my familiar surroundings and friends once again. Valerie remained silent, while the other children hovered anxiously, hoping this was all a mistake.

"The social worker broke the silence with a question directed at Valerie. 'What? You haven't told the boy of his new arrangement?'

"Before giving her answer, Valerie ordered the children to return to the basement. Then she turned to the stranger.

"'No, I just couldn't bring myself to tell him.'

"I slipped to the floor and began to sob. For over a year-and-a-half I'd tried everything I could to please her, but it had all been for nothing. The welfare official rose from his chair and began to pick up the boxes in the corridor to bring them to the car. On each return trip he paused a moment to glance at me as if to say, 'Let's get you out of here.'

"The whole time I couldn't stop crying. In the basement, I could hear the other children wailing and begging their mom to let them at least come say goodbye to me. But she insisted they remain downstairs.

"Once the formalities were completed and all the paperwork was signed, the man escorted me to the car. This was something I'd been through before, but it was no less heartbreaking this time around. Like the last time I'd been torn from my familiar environment, I cried most of the way while the social worker tried to redirect my attention away from my sorrow. He even asked what life had been like with my former family, perhaps hoping this would allow me to vent my anger and pull me out of my grief. Of course, that ploy had been used on me before.

"'Don't even try that on me,' I said to him, tears continuing to roll down my cheeks.

"Not long afterward, he pulled into a Dairy Queen and parked in front of the entrance. Several people were in line at the window, waiting to order. Some of them turned to watch the sad little boy sobbing in the car. Wordlessly, the man got out and left me to my tears.

"I felt completely devastated, as if I had been thrown into the street like an unwanted cat or dog. Over and over I kept asking myself what horrible thing I'd done to be cast aside so readily. There had been nothing but abuse from the first week I arrived in Valerie's family. I couldn't understand why, and not knowing the reason made me that much sadder.

"As I sat in the front seat looking at the line of people moving up to the DQ window, I heard in my inner hearing the voice of the Vi-Guru speaking softly and firmly in his distinct accent.

"'Look around. Any of these kids might be your next stepbrothers and—sisters.'

"Paulji's words ignited like a flame in my chest. Drying my eyes, I began to look at each person in line. Children of all ages waited patiently among the adults to move up and be served. Love blossomed in my heart at the mere thought of having a new family.

"*Yes*, I thought, looking from person to person. '*This could be my next stepsister and this one my next stepfather.*' As if by magic, I was lifted out of the depths of my agony. The feeling of love and inner support grew until my heart was wide open, ready to accept the new gifts life had prepared for me.

"By chance I caught the eye of a young girl carrying two sumptuous vanilla ice cream cones, one in each hand. As she passed my window she glanced over and said, 'The other ice cream is for my brother.' At this confirmation of my thoughts I began to laugh out loud. All the sorrows that had been pressing me down were lifted from me and I couldn't stop laughing.

"At that moment the social worker opened the driver's door. In his hand he held an enormous ice cream cone. When he saw me laughing he assumed it was due to the size of the ice cream. But I was laughing in happiness because once again the Vi-Guru had reached out to me in my most desolate moment. He had found a way to open my heart when it seemed closed like an obsolete factory.

"You know, Mr. Toldeck, through all my hardships I've come to believe that when hope is no longer present in one's heart, death is near. A person without hope is like a dead man walking. However, sometimes a single gesture of kindness or affection can ignite a wildfire of hope in a despairing heart. If we only knew how profoundly we're all interconnected and how positively our open hearts affect others around us, we'd always try to be with people when we're happy and seek solitude when we're at the opposite end of the emotional scale."

Mr. Toldeck said, "Could you tell me more about the role hope and faith have played in your life and how they work for you?"

I cast about the darkened cabin for inspiration. My attention settled on the China Airline Magazine in the seat pocket in front of me. The cover featured a picture of a huge, golden sunflower.

"You can compare them to little seeds," I explained, pointing to the image. "Each seed needs to be nurtured. When we nurture the seeds of hope they grow into faith. People who have faith are like little sprouts just beginning to see the Light of God. With determination and perseverance, people with faith can reach a state in which the living truth of the Divine Presence manifests in their lives. This Divine Presence expresses Itself through personal experiences that reflect the strength of their faith. Seeds of faith need not only to be nurtured but cherished, so that faith can find permanent residence in the garden of our heart. Once hope matures into faith, hope is no longer needed. At the crucial moment when faith truly supplants hope, a state of knowingness awakens deep within us. We understand that faith is the key to our inner revelation, which gives birth to an unshakeable trust between us and the Holy Spirit.

"When we nurture this state of knowingness, our inner garden blooms into what might be called beingness. Flowers in full bloom touch our heart because Soul recognizes Its own potential for spiritual unfoldment in them. Of course, not all plants reach full bloom in one season; it takes time and effort."

I thought for a moment, searching for a better example to illustrate my point.

"You remember the story of Mr. Harold, the Sweet Man?"

Mr. Toldeck chuckled, "How could I ever forget the Sweet Man?"

"Well, the Sweet Man first gave me hope and then something to have faith in, such as the job of picking up bottles. It was necessary for me to do all the work myself for my faith to turn into the reality of knowingness. Through this experience I learned that I had the ability to create my own circumstances. One day I hope to reach the state of beingness that comes from diligently practicing knowingness in daily life. I've always thought if I'm as persistent with my spiritual practice as I was with picking up bottles, then one day I'll find a bottle containing the message, 'You have now reached full bloom. Let yourself be loved by all the bees in the garden!'"

Mr. Toldeck leaned forward and laughed quietly. I joined in, keeping my volume down as well to avoid disturbing the sleeping passengers. As our laughter faded, Mr. Toldeck turned to fix me with his penetrating gaze. When I began to teeter on the edge of losing my inner balance under its power, Mr. Toldeck recognized the limits of my acceptance and asked another question to pull me back from the brink.

"What happened after the Dairy Queen?"

I took a deep breath and licked my lips. "We continued through the countryside and arrived at a village called Hemingford. There we turned down a dusty driveway to a big old farmhouse which looked like it had been built in the early 1900s. As we entered the house, the welfare official introduced me to Mr. Ken, a tall German of about six foot three inches. He welcomed us, speaking in broken French. Next to him stood his wife, Marylyn, a petit Métis woman of about five foot four. They invited us in to sit at an immense dining room table, where we made small talk. Clearly they were trying to make me feel at ease in my new environment.

"Looking around, I kept asking myself where everyone else was. No way did the two of them live in this gigantic house all by themselves. Once the social worker left. Mr. Ken took me out to the barn behind the house where he presented me with a brand new pair of rubber boots.

"My heart leapt at the thought of farm animals. Interacting with them and caring for them would be a great way for me to ease into this new world. Inside, Mr. Ken pointed to some tools racked along the wall. I was told my new daily chores were to shovel the manure from the stalls of fourteen horses and to give them hay and water twice a day, once before school and once after, seven days a week. He waved at the wheelbarrow and told me to begin right away since the stalls hadn't been cleaned in days. Then he turned his back and left me to my new work. When he was out of sight, I sat down on the nearest bale of hay and had myself another cry. Shoveling piles of manure was my latest welcome home. I was twelve.

"How long did you stay there?" Mr. Toldeck asked.

"I lived there from the ages of twelve to fifteen, when I was finally old enough to run away for good, which I'd tried several times before without success."

"How many were there in that family?"

"Believe or not, nine children lived in that home, five from the welfare office and four of their own. The oldest were all foster children, while the four little ones were theirs.

"When I finished cleaning out the barn that first day, I dragged myself into the house and met the other children. Mostly, everyone was happy to welcome me into the household. I was immediately drawn to the littlest one, Richard; he was barely a year old. He saved my life, you know. Whenever I could, I would change his diaper, feed him, and play with him for hours at a time. Caring for Richard was my salvation."

"What do you mean by that?" Mr. Toldeck said.

I paused a moment, thinking back to my arrival at the farm and the subsequent years.

"At that age my heart was so scarred by feelings of abandonment, rejection, betrayal, humiliation and injustice that I almost believed this was the inevitable state of affairs for me. Day after day these feelings fell upon me like a thick, heavy rain, and I simply couldn't shake them off. Caring for someone who needed help more than I did somehow allowed me to release my imprisoned pain. It's a strange thing, really; whenever we're stricken with sorrow, a simple act of selflessness can release us from the personal agonies of our heart. Richard became like my little brother. Sitting with him, giving him his bottle, became my favorite hours of the day. No matter how great the challenges may seem, life always provides us with the means to serve Its cause. Salvation, true salvation, can only be attained through selfless service to others."

Mr. Toldeck's attention shifted past me towards Brielle who had stopped in the aisle by my seat.

"I just wanted to inform both of you," she announced, sweeping her gaze to include Lea, "that we'll be landing in Taipei in ten minutes. We won't be there long because only a few passengers are getting off. Soon afterwards we'll be on our way to Bangkok."

I was beginning to feel a little irked by Brielle's failure to acknowledge Mr. Toldeck. I turned to apologize to him for her, but he was looking out the window, marveling at the beauty of the Taiwanese landscape below. Changing my mind, I decided to rest for a while. I raised my tray, loosened my seat belt just a bit, and made another attempt at sleep.

SURRENDER IS THE KEY

IX

I awoke from a sudden pressure, scarcely able to open my eyes as my body was pushed back into my seat. We were taking off on the final leg of our flight. Rubbing sleep from my eyes, I glanced at Mr. Toldeck. His attention was focused intently on the lights of Taipei receding into the distance, so I decided not to disturb his contemplation.

Soon we leveled out from our ascent and the seat belt sign blinked off. My excitement mounted with each mile we got closer to my adventure in the land of the Smiling People. Turning towards the aisle, I found Lea smiling at me. My heart took a little leap as she gave me a wave of her fingers.

"Come over and let's talk some more," she suggested.

My eyes never left hers from the moment I rose and moved across the aisle. In the background I could hear Ms. HonoOpono trying to attract my attention.

"Hey, Gaston," she called. "Come over here. I've got some more questions for you." Then she saw where I was headed and spoke in an even louder voice. "Oh, I see! You're going to sit with your favorite passenger."

Heads turned and most of the passengers in our section guffawed at her frankness and my discomfort. It suddenly struck me that Mr. Toldeck was actually my favorite passenger, although I certainly wouldn't share this with anyone. Settling into the seat next to Lea, I couldn't take my eyes off her beautiful, slim legs outlined under her colorful princess dress.

"It's okay if you want to go and sit with Ms. HonoOpono," she said. "She's probably more entertaining than I'll ever be."

My face had turned beet red again, and shyness spun threads around me like a protective cocoon. It seemed each time Ms. HonoOpono spoke up I received another dose of humiliation.

"I don't want to be entertained by anyone," I mumbled, staring at my hands in my lap. "I just want to be here with you, that's all."

Lea's gentle laugh soothed me immediately. "Forgive her, Gaston. She means well. She's one of those people who wears her heart on her sleeve. Plus, she's not very good with boundaries. That's very much a Hawaiian trait. In the Hawaiian Kahuna teachings we're all as one. Being ourselves is perceived as our greatest gift to ourselves, our family and our village as well."

Her sweet voice burst my cocoon of shyness as fast as it been spun, allowing my self-confidence to return. I resolved to learn as much as I could about this beautiful woman, who appeared perfect from every angle. Her voice mesmerized me. Never before had I experienced such a dramatic attraction towards anyone. There was only one thing for me to do, and that was to discover what lay behind these powerful feelings.

Lea's words snapped me out of my reverie.

"Would you mind if I asked you another question?"

"Please, go ahead. Ask anything."

"Have you ever been married?"

Ouch! Maybe I wasn't ready for anything, after all. The subject was a sensitive one for me, but I decided to answer her honestly, hoping I wouldn't be judged too harshly.

"Twice," I nodded.

"Oh, really?"

I think I might have cringed at her response, but Lea quickly waved her hand in dismissal.

"Twice," she repeated, chuckling. "Don't be embarrassed about having the courage to commit, Gaston. Marriage can be the most rewarding time of your life, as well as the one with the most growing pains." Her gaze turned inward. "I'm speaking from experience here."

There was no judgment her voice, only understanding and compassion.

After a moment, she continued, "Tell me how you met your first wife. What was her name?"

"Her name was Joan," I replied. "She was from Brooklyn, New York. I hope you like unusual stories, because that's what my whole life consists of."

Lea smiled. "I do—that's why I asked. Also, I believe everything happens for a reason, even if I don't understand the reason at the time. So come on, tell me about her."

"All right. Back in 1980 at the age of twenty, I traveled to Las Vegas to attend a spiritual conference. Between talks there were a number of different creative arts performers on the program. One was a group of singers, of which Joan was a member. After their performance, Joan came off the stage and sat three seats away from me in the same row. I was looking sideways at her when, I kid you not, my inner voice spoke to me loud and clear.

"'*She's not ready to sit at your side yet,*' it said.

"I was so surprised I nearly jumped out of my shoes. As I leaned forward to get a better look at her, she noticed me and smiled back. But shy as I was, I couldn't muster the courage to go over and introduce myself. After that I didn't see her again, and when the conference was over I returned to British Columbia where I was attending college.

Lea waved this part of my story off. "That only tells me how you saw her the first time, not how you actually met her. Come on, Gaston." She smiled mischievously and grasped my arm with slim fingers. "Let it out."

I sighed. "Okay. After I returned to BC, every time I closed my eyes to contemplate I'd see Joan's face in my third eye. When this kept happening day after day, I decided to resolve the situation in the dream state. On one of the following nights during a dream, I was instructed to drop out of college, leave British Columbia, and travel to California where the two of us would meet."

Lea shifted forward to literally perch on the edge of her seat. "And did you?"

"When I awoke from the dream I completely rejected this message. I certainly wasn't going to leave college and venture to California to meet some woman based on a vision! The next night I had another dream. It showed me that my college professor was about give me a failing grade in one of my classes. When I awoke, the dream only made me more determined to study harder and pass all my classes, including the professor's. In my arrogance, I decided to challenge the dream and take full charge of my destiny.

"Several weeks later, despite many hours of strenuous study, my professor called me into her office to notify me of her decision to flunk me out of the class. She told me I could take another course next year to be eligible for my general education certificate. While I was in her office I watched myself reacting in anger and denial, just as I had in the dream. Yet that same day I called one of my friends in California and told her I was on my way. She invited me to stay at her house. I contacted a used furniture store and sold everything I owned. Within days I was on a plane to San Francisco.

"My friend, Carol, picked me up at the airport. She lived in Menlo Park, a small town near Palo Alto and Stanford University. Once I had settled in, Carol invited me to join her meditation group which met at a center in Palo Alto. We rode over on her motorcycle and as I took my helmet off, who did I see walking into the center? Yes, of course, the vision woman!

"The strangest emotions washed over me. Here she was, the woman who had haunted my contemplations and dreams for almost a year, standing in the room on the other side of the entrance doors! I asked myself how someone would approach such a person. Probably it was best not to go with the line, 'Pardon me, beautiful lady, but I've been seeing you in my dreams and whenever I close my eyes.'

A burst of laughter escaped from Lea's throat, and she clapped her hand to her mouth to stifle it. I smiled and continued.

"That would undoubtedly send any woman running away as fast as she could, even if it were true. Maybe *because* it was true! Unable to think of a good opening line, I decided to go with the flow and trust life to work things out. As I stood on the sidewalk, waiting a moment before going inside, Carol thought my hesitation might be due to fear of attending the event. I assured her this was not the case and that I simply needed a moment to compose myself. She entered the center ahead of me, and I sat down on the sidewalk, astonished at how quickly life can manifest itself when you trust your inner voice. Still grappling with the situation, I waited until the very last second before entering.

"Inside, approximately sixty people sat in a large circle preparing to meditate together. All the seats seemed to be taken except, of course, the chair next to Joan. My heart was beating hard as I walked across the circle and sat down. After a few awkward moments of silence, I could contain myself no longer and blurted out, 'When we're through with the meditation, we need to talk.'

"Joan reacted surprisingly calmly.' I know a great ice cream place nearby on University Avenue,' she said.

"Six months later Joan and I were married at the city hall in Redwood City."

"Wow, Gaston!" Lea exclaimed. "That's one of the most beautiful love stories I've ever heard."

I sighed at the memory of that special day. Yes, it had been beautiful, but of course it was only part of the story. "Not all great love stories necessarily end beautifully, you know."

Lea nodded emphatically. "You can say that again! How did you meet your second wife?"

"After my divorce from Joan, I decided to move to Paris. I was twenty-five at the time. The strange thing was, during my entire two years there I was unable to date any French women. As a French Canadian I was used to interacting with independent women—and Joan certainly fit that bill—but what I found in Europe was that French women were a bit too submissive for my tastes at the time. So one night, desperate for companionship, I decided to ask my Dream Master to assist me in finding where my new life partner was. That same night I was told she resided in the province of Quebec. By now I trusted my dream guidance completely, so I gave two my weeks' notice at work, flew to Montreal and rented an apartment.

"Once settled in, I must have asked inwardly a thousand times, w*here is she?* I received no answer, except for one dream in which I was assured she really did live in Quebec. After that night, I traveled to different cities of the province every weekend in hopes of finding her. One evening I arrived in a town called Sherbrooke, where an inner nudge told me the woman lived.

"It happened to be Halloween, so I decided to celebrate my revelation by going to the biggest party in town and dancing the night away. Upon my return to Montreal, I was determined to move to Sherbrooke. I gave notice at work, emptied my apartment, and temporarily moved to my friend Darcy's farm in the countryside. After several days there my desire to get to Sherbrooke became so overwhelming that I packed up my things and said goodbye to Darcy and his wife, Patricia. I only got five or ten miles away when my car broke down. After towing it back to Darcy's place, we repaired it and I set out once more. Again my car broke down! This happened five times in a row! By now, Christmas was just around the corner and Darcy and Patricia begged me to put off my move and stay for the holidays. But with each breakdown of my car my determination to reach Sherbrooke only grew.

"In the early afternoon of December 31, in the middle of a big snowstorm, I decided to take my chances and make the journey. That I made it to Sherbooke at all was a miracle. At the time I was driving a 1972 Lada, a Russian-made car most reviewers agreed was one of the most unreliable cars on earth. I checked in at the Wellington Hotel and soon hit the streets to ask everyone for the best place to celebrate New Year's. Repeatedly I was told to go to the same venue where

I'd partied at Halloween. When I entered the place at 6:00 pm, there were barely any lights on and the manager was sitting idly at the bar. After I purchased a ticket for the New Year's party and was leaving, he called after me.

"'Hey! You ever tend bar before?'

"'Why?' I asked.

"He shrugged casually. 'Just looking for a fresh face for my place.'

"I'd never been a bartender, but nevertheless I heard myself say, 'Sure.'

"He hired me on the spot and two days later I started working there. One evening around eight two women walked in. The bar was still mostly empty and the three of us regaled each other with tales of the different countries we'd visited.

"Around nine the women decided to leave. I tried to convince them it would get more interesting soon when the DJ showed up; there'd be music and dancing. They were in the middle of debating when, out of the blue, one of them said to me, 'The most beautiful part of you, Gaston, cannot be seen with our outer eyes.' And with that they both walked out! It was the most beautiful compliment I'd ever received. A week later that same woman strolled back in and introduced herself as Diane. We hit it off instantly and she moved in with me the next day. Several months later she was pregnant with Melisange, my first daughter. Diane is the mother of my children, and she also lives on Maui."

"You're just a big romantic, aren't you?" Lea said.

"If following my heart makes me a romantic, then yes. However, being a romantic means far more to me than that. It means being present and being attentive to whom I've chosen to love and be loved by. It is through our actions that we demonstrate best what lies in our heart. So tell me, Lea, what about you? Have you ever been married? And how did you meet him?"

Lea shifted to a more comfortable position in her seat. "Yes, I have been married but we're divorced now. His name is Makaha, and he was the football quarterback during my days at Baldwin High. My love for him was pure, but his drive for other woman destroyed whatever chance we had at building a lasting future."

"I'm very sorry you had to experience such disrespect," I said sincerely. "How could he not have seen how beautiful, genuine and precious you are?"

"Well, thank you for your kind words, Gaston. But no matter how beautiful a woman is or not, she seeks a man with a pure heart. That's becoming as rare these days as a woman with a pure heart."

"Maybe it's just that we've forgotten what to look for in a pure heart. Maybe we've become so conditioned to worship outer appearances that we no longer pay attention to inner virtues. We think that old-fashioned stuff doesn't matter anymore, when really, those virtues make or break us."

Lea looked a little wistful. "That's true, but how can I tell a man who's pure of heart from one who's not? Can you tell me that, Gaston? Will you be the man to clarify this mystery for me?"

A little embarrassed, I laughed, looked down at my hands and shook my head. A tall order, but I'd give it a go.

"When a woman is touched in her heart by a man, it's always through his unselfish acts towards her and toward others as well. A man who serves his wife—and is served by her in return—creates a happy couple, but a man who serves himself first eventually loses her. A pure man must be capable of the self-discipline to love unselfishly, abide by his virtues and understand others with his heart. He must give unconditionally to others without trying to own them. He must learn to stand on his own and not be dependent on anyone. Within his household he must be a kind leader and teacher, but never a tyrant. That is in my view what the Aloha Spirit requires of all people. Look for these qualities next time you meet a man. Who knows, maybe soon you'll discover a man with a pure heart."

Lea's eyes glowed with passion.

"Maybe I already have!"

Reading her body language, blood instantly shot to my face and my throat constricted. My eyes darted everywhere in near panic while I searched for something to say. Had I tried to sell myself to her as such a man? Was I being that obvious? My heart raced in my chest and my hands fidgeted in my lap. Maybe I was, but how could I conceal the strong attraction I felt for her? Wouldn't that be dishonest toward myself and her? And yet another part of me all but screamed, *I'm attracted to you but so afraid of being rejected!*

Lea regarded me, waiting for a response to her last statement, but I was totally at a loss. Anxiety blew through me like a winter storm. With each passing moment the painful silence grew. Then, thankfully, Brielle arrived.

"Sorry to bother you, Lea," she said, "but Ms. HonoOpono asked me to tell you she wants very much to talk with you."

Lea rose gracefully from her seat. "Of course, I'll be happy to." Then she leaned down to me. "The more we talk, the more I believe what Ms. HonoOpono says about you is true."

A short laugh escaped my lips and warmth spread in my chest. "You know, Lea, I could say the same thing about you."

Lea laughed warmly and made her way back to Ms. HonoOpono's row. I remained where I was for several minutes, hoping Lea would return sooner rather than later. After Brielle had passed by a couple of times, I began to feel uncomfortable, so I crossed the aisle to my own seat. Just as my finger reached for the button to lower my seatback for a nap, Mr. Toldeck faced me.

"By the way, Gaston, were there any wonderful moments with that family at the farm house?"

I blinked and shook off the mental fatigue that had been beckoning me to sleep.

"Oh yeah, definitely. With nine children in the family, life is bound to be filled with all kinds of diversions and unique opportunities to learn from one another. Three specific events come to mind. But first I have to say it took me several months to be comfortable with everyone, emotionally damaged as I was. Over time, between nurturing the horses morning and night and caring for the baby, I found renewed joy in life.

"To my relief, segregation and physical abuse weren't part of Ken and Marylyn's child-rearing philosophy. In that family, everyone was on equal footing. The only differences were our levels of responsibility, which led in direct proportion to the amount of freedom we enjoyed.

"In a family of nine children there are always chores to be done, even more so on a farm. Since I'd been searching for freedom as far back as I could remember, I took on as many chores as I could fit into the day. The payoff was that the more I demonstrated my capability to handle chores, the more freedom I earned.

"The first memorable event occurred at the beginning of our summer vacation. I had just hauled all the hay up into the loft and was completely exhausted and sweaty. In the distance I heard Ken coming up the driveway with the horse trailer attached to his pickup. When I peeked out the barn door to see what was going on, I could tell he had brought home another animal.

"Discouraged and overwhelmed, I slumped down on the nearest bale of hay, not even interested in what kind it was. Besides taking care of all the horses already there, I was the oldest boy in the family and my responsibility as such was drilled into me day in and day out: 'Be responsible and kind because all the other children look up to you.'

"As I sat on the hay bale, exhausted and half in a daze, I heard Ken calling my name. Everyone else was running out of the house as if something exciting were taking place, but I slowly made my way down to the corral without even noticing what was in it.

"The other children were chattering excitedly about the new arrival, but I didn't even pay attention. My expectation was that Ken would say: 'Gaston, here's an additional chore for you.' Instead, Ken pointed towards the new animal and spoke loud enough for everyone to hear:

"That's yours, Gaston. Yours to care for and yours to ride as much as you want. It's all yours!'

"While the other children reacted with disappointed cries of, 'Why him?' and 'What about me?' I lifted my eyes from the ground and saw it was a small brown pony. Ken had bought it just for me! I was so happy! Ken led me to the back of his truck and handed me the small saddle he had purchased with the pony.

"Ken's act of generosity showed me I was appreciated for my all efforts and contributions to the well-being of the family. It taught me that taking responsibility leads to greater freedom. In this case, the freedom to own a pony and ride it to my heart's content.

"The second event that changed my life happened in church. Every Sunday, without exception, all the children were sent to church. Ken and Marylyn, on the other hand, remained at home. Who knows what they did during that time, but just having the house to themselves for a few hours must have been blissful.

"A few months after my arrival I became an altar boy, a role I enjoyed very much. As time went by, my responsibilities in our church services increased until I was promoted to altar boy in charge, the job all altar boys dream of.

"One Sunday morning while I was in the basement cleaning the floor, a girl named Helene came downstairs." I paused to sigh at the memory of Helene, and Mr. Toldeck smiled knowingly. To forestall blushing I hastily went on, "Helene was the most beautiful thirteen year-old girl in our school, probably in our entire village. She had shimmering golden hair and eyes as blue as the ocean. The priest had sent her down to ask me to bring up the sacramental wine for the church ceremony, the wine we were told symbolized the sacred blood of Jesus Christ.

"It was a sign I had earned the full trust of Father Louis, for it was a great honor to even touch the wine container. As I placed the container on the counter to get a better grip on it, Helene looked at me with those bottomless blue eyes and said, 'Why don't we drink some?' She cast her gaze down at the floor for a moment, and then looked back up. 'Just a little bit.'

"Like most thirteen year-old boys, I was unable to say no to a pretty girl. I looked around the basement to make sure we were completely alone and said: 'I will if you will.'

"'You go first,' she demanded.

"Together we searched for something to drink the wine in. The only cup we could find was the golden chalice I had polished earlier. Helene held the chalice while I poured. Taking it from her, I held it aloft in both hands, like I had seen Father Louis do during the communion, and took a big gulp. Within seconds my blood burned as if hellfire were spreading through my veins. The wine certainly didn't taste or feel like the Holy Blood of Christ, as I had been lead to believe all these years. Shaken, I passed the chalice to Helene, who did exactly as I had. We were drinking the presumed blood of Christ the same way we drank our favorite soft drinks.

"After Helene had downed a big swallow, she gave me a meaningful look. 'We'd better drink it all, or Father Louis will know.'

"To this day, I wonder why I listened to her. But then, who was I to argue with the most beautiful girl in town? So I took another gulp and passed it back to Helene. After several more swigs our states were very much altered—I had gone from altar boy to altered boy.

"When we were done we quickly rinsed and dried the chalice. Helene stepped in front of me, fixing me with those ocean blue eyes. Her body was warm and close, and she was breathing heavily. She caught her bottom lip between her teeth and drew her brows together in a combination of uncertainty and determination. Then she parted those soft lips and spoke in the most breathy, seductive voice I had ever heard:

"Gaston, will you kiss me now?"

"Every rational part of me was screaming to get the hell out of the basement! Helene touched my hand, and whatever rationality I had was lost. All strength and will to fight my runaway urge deserted me. I was enchanted under her spell, immobilized, disarmed, captivated by a force I had never encountered before. A lightning bolt shot through me, jolting all systems alert. My hands were shaking, my knees were shaking, my whole body was shaking, but not from fear. Slowly, I took the short step to close the distance and felt the softness of Helene's body press against mine. I was drowning in her clear blue eyes. I bent forward and kissed her.

"That moment I came alive like never before, reborn in the flesh! I had no idea what to do or what to say; I was only aware of how ecstatic I felt. Disengaging from the girl, I turned away and ran upstairs as fast as I could. On the main floor I almost knocked over Father Louis in my blindness and confusion. I pulled myself together as best I could and told him I would be unable to perform my altar boy duties that day. As it happened, I never returned to church after that Sunday morning. I had found God, and He was behind Helene's ocean blue eyes."

"That must have been some kiss," Mr. Toldeck commented.

I smiled, still feeling Helene's soft lips on mine during that first, forbidden kiss.

"Indeed it was the most remarkable kiss of all. My first."

Mr. Toldeck and I observed a moment of silence in honor of first kisses. At length he drew me back to the conversation.

"You said there were three events. What was the third one?"

"In our village we were definitely one of the poorest families, materially speaking," I took up my narrative. "But by being entrepreneurial at an early age, I developed survival skills to assist me in fulfilling my needs. For instance, I wanted very much to own a bicycle and must have asked, begged, and beseeched my foster mother, Marylyn, a thousand times a month, to no avail. Her reply was always the same: if she gave me a bike, everyone else would ask for one as well. Then, late one evening, after annoying Marilyn yet again for hours, she said out of desperation, 'Just get a job, Gaston. Save up for one and you can buy whatever you want.'

"Certainly I had worked for money before, but I had never thought to save any. My motto was, what use is having money in your pocket when the stores are full of candy? The following morning, after my chores were done, I went over to the golf course, planning to wade into the small ponds to search for golf balls. A friend at school had told me golfers were willing to pay up to twenty-five cents per ball if they were in good condition. As I approached my first pond, a player not far away called out:

"'Hey, kid! You want to make some money caddying for me today?'

"Caddying? I had no idea what that was. 'What do you want me to do?' I called back.

"'I'll give you twenty-five cents per hole if you pull my golf bag on the course and give me the clubs I ask for.'

"That was all? I agreed almost before he could finish the job description. That summer I caddied every single day. Once I even caddied for Jean Beliveau, a famous hockey player who'd played for the Montreal Canadians. By the second month, I had saved enough money to buy my bike. Along with it I also purchased all the decorations a young boy would want to mount on it. The experience of having a paid job was fulfilling in so many ways. I discovered that if a man wants something, he can acquire whatever he desires as long as he works hard. At that time, the only thing I wanted to acquire was a bike.

"Now I had greater mobility and freedom, riding around on the coolest bike in town. I was free to roam wherever I wanted in our village, without ever having to ask for a ride. It was a freedom I had earned."

"It sure sounds like this family was good to you," Mr. Toldeck said. "But you mentioned earlier that you ran away.

Why would you run away when you were being given so much freedom at your age?"

"It's true that I had a certain freedom of movement," I conceded. "But each step toward greater freedom came with corresponding responsibilities. By the early spring of 1976, when I was sixteen, the burden of responsibility I had taken on to achieve my limited freedom had become so overwhelming that I decided to run away."

"Where did you go? How far away did you run?"

"I ran 2300 miles away, to be precise."

Mr. Toldeck's eyebrows rose in surprise. "Wow! That's not running away. That's moving to another world. Where did you go? And how did you get there?"

"Having demonstrated that I had the money for whatever I really wanted, I was told in the summer of 1975 that from now on I'd have to buy my own clothes. So I looked for another job and found one as a gas station attendant. For months I saved the money I made there. At the time I didn't really know the true worth of how much I had in savings, but it would soon become clear when I used them to travel.

"The week before Easter of 1976, I told my friends I was running away. I asked my girlfriend at the time to come with me, and also my best friend, but neither wanted to. Undeterred, I bought a bus ticket for Montreal that weekend. When I arrived at the Montreal bus terminal, I had no idea where to go next. On the way to the exit I passed a ticket counter and decided to take a chance.

"'Where is it sunny this time of year?' I asked the ticket agent.

"'South Carolina is very warm this time of year,' she replied from behind her glass partition.

"'One ticket, please,' I said promptly. 'One way.'

"When the bus arrived at the US border, the passengers were asked to go through customs. As I stepped up to the counter, the customs officer took one look at me and his mouth drew down in a disdainful expression that indicated I wasn't going anywhere.

"'Do you even have a dime on you?' he inquired gruffly.

"'Sure I do,' I said. 'I have a lot more money than you think.'

"'All right, then give me your home phone number so I can call your parents.'

"This caught me off guard. If he spoke to my foster parents, my grand plan of running away was finished. Soon after he made the call he returned to tell me he'd informed them he wouldn't let me into the US. For the next two hours I sat there on a cold steel bench waiting for someone to pick me up. We only lived fifteen miles from the border crossing and I felt someone should have been here by now. Then a flash of genius hit me. I walked up to the customs officer who had placed the call.

"'Excuse me, sir,' I said politely. 'Who did you talk to at my house?'

"'I spoke with a young lady,' he answered in his gruff, no-nonsense voice.

"I tried to contain my sudden excitement. 'Are you sure it was a young lady, sir?'

"'If I tell you it was a young lady,' he said with the full weight of his authority, 'it's because it was a young lady.'

"'Thank you.' I smiled, overjoyed. He had talked to one of the welfare children, Huguette, who spoke barely any English except *yes* and *no*. After two hours it was clear no one was coming to pick me up because she hadn't understood a word the customs agent said. My great plan wasn't finished after all! I hitchhiked back to Montreal and cashed in my bus ticket at the terminal. Next I headed to the train station and bought a ticket out west, to Vancouver. That weekend I celebrated my sixteenth birthday on the train. For most of the three days it took to cross Canada I hung out in the bar section, where a constant party atmosphere reigned eighteen hours a day. I was celebrating my newfound freedom.

"However, once we arrived in Vancouver, which was as far west as the train would go, I had to face the fact that my freedom was a delusion. I found a bench outside the train station and unfolded my map, on which I had carefully highlighted my entire journey. Hemingford and Montreal were only a half inch apart on the map, while Montreal and Vancouver were fully three feet apart. The stunning reality of how far I was from home began to sink in. My greatest fear—being abandoned and alone—was coming to life. Again and again I tracked the vast distance between Montreal and Vancouver with my finger, lost in a sea of anxiety. I sat on the bench and fought back tears of desperation, not knowing what to do or where to go next.

"Not much later a sweet-looking college girl came by, carrying a backpack.

"'Are you waiting for the bus to the youth hostel?' she asked me solicitously.

"'What's a youth hostel?'

"As she described the youth hostel in Kitsilano, a great weight seemed to be lifted from my shoulders. The majestic process of life had once again come to my rescue."

Mr. Toldeck thoughtfully stroked his chin. "Have you always been able to see what you call the majestic process of life and what impact it had on your destiny?"

"Well, to the first part of your question, I would have to say *no*. Before I could begin to see the majestic process, I had to discover that the will of God supersedes all. At that time I had not yet discovered that. But the impact of it on my destiny was profound to say the least."

"How did you take care of your financial needs, since you were only sixteen and living at a youth hostel?"

"Most of my savings were gone after a few months. From a graduate student I met at the hostel I heard that the Canadian National Railroad was hiring in Edmonton, Alberta. It took me two days to hitchhike there, but within a week of my arrival I was hired. The CNR provided room and board: we ate, slept, and lived in railroad cars. Not having to pay rent, I was able to save most of my earnings, but the work was a summer job only."

"What did you do once the working season was over?"

"Most seasonal railroad workers came from different colleges and universities," I explained. "At the end of the season, some returned to school while others headed south with their savings to winter in Mexico. Since I didn't have anywhere else to go, I was planning on joining them. However, one evening one of the older men in our group came to talk to me.

"'Gaston, don't you want to go home instead of coming with us to Mexico?'

"Filled with youthful pride, I declined to answer. I didn't want to admit to the men how much I missed home. But in my heart I knew I was only fooling myself. The next afternoon I mustered my courage and called my foster family to ask if I could come home. My stepmom's response caught me by surprise.

"'If you're ready to come home, we're ready to welcome you.'

"I had expected to be severely scolded for running away, but nothing of the sort happened. I was welcomed back with no ifs, ands, or buts. The following day I boarded a train back home."

"Did you return to school?"

"I did, if not for long," I said. "I also took up my old job of pumping gas for a while. Sometime in the fall of that year, I received a phone call at the gas station from one of the other foster children telling me Ken had thrown all my clothes on the front lawn and I was being kicked out of the house. Shocked and hurt, I went outside to sit on two big tires behind the garage, trying to suppress the tears welling up in my eyes. I didn't want anyone to see me and I hoped no customers would come around for gas.

"After a while I heard a familiar voice. It was Denis from Montreal, one of my regular customers.

"'Come on out, Gaston!' he called. 'I know you're back there. I saw you earlier.'

Setting my face in a semblance of normalcy, I walked out. Denis and Lucille were a young couple who came to town every weekend to visit their family and always stopped by the station. The man unscrewed his gas cap and told me how much gas he wanted. As I slowly reached for the pump, Lucille noticed my despairing mood and asked: 'Are you okay, Gaston?'

"Her simple act of concern nearly broke the dam holding back my tears.

"'Ken just kicked me out on the street and everything I own is scattered on our front yard,' I managed to choke out, my breath heaving. 'I don't have anywhere else to go.'

"Lucille got out of the car, her concern deepening. 'Well, that doesn't surprise me, coming from Ken. But don't worry, Gaston. Denis and I will go pick up your stuff, and you can come with us to Montreal tonight if you want. We have a spare bedroom in our apartment.'

"Denis paid for the gas and they left, returning in half an hour with all my worldly possessions in the back seat. After I finished my shift we drove to Montreal together, and a new chapter of my life began. The Holy Spirit had once again come to my rescue. Sometimes I wonder why I worry so much. Whenever I truly surrender a situation to Spirit, I experience the abundance life has in store for me."

Glancing up, I noticed Brielle heading in our direction carrying a tray piled high with snacks.

"Speaking of abundance," I said with a chuckle, gesturing toward the flight attendant. A quiet answering chuckle came from Mr. Toldeck.

"Do you need a snack, Gaston?" Brielle inquired. "We'll be landing in Bangkok in less than an hour."

I clapped my hands together and rubbed them vigorously. "One hour! How exciting! I could use a snack for sure!"

Checking with Mr. Toldeck, I noted he had shifted his attention to the window as he usually did when Brielle stopped by. He was watching the twinkling lights of the nameless cities, towns, and villages that rolled by thousands of feet below. I had learned not to disturb him when he was in a contemplative state, so I turned back to Brielle.

"I'd like pretzels, please."

"And would you like something to drink with that?"

"I'll have a Perrier."

"No ice, as usual?" Brielle retrieved the bottle and twisted off the cap. "Here I'll get your pretzels from the galley."

While Brielle walked away I realized Mr. Toldeck hadn't eaten anything during the entire flight. Maybe he didn't like airline food. Come to think of it, why didn't I invite him to have dinner with me in Bangkok? The thought of spending some more time with him brought me great joy.

Brielle brought me my pretzels, and I savored them one at a time, knowing that soon I'd be starting my three-week fast. Each time I put another pretzel in my mouth, my palate rejoiced at the explosion of pleasurable sensations—sensations specifically designed to convince me not to follow through with the fast. The strangest feelings arise when we decide to stop eating. Everything suddenly tastes richer, as if new taste buds were developing in every corner of our mouth; all to remind us how attached we are to our old eating habits.

Once I finished my pretzels, I leaned over to Mr. Toldeck, but his attention was still fixed on the view outside. I decided instead to stretch my legs one last time before landing.

A few rows down, Ms. HonoOpono and Lea were still in the midst of their conversation. Ms. HonoOpono waved to me as I passed by but Lea merely glanced up. Yet, even though her expression didn't seem to change, I thought I detected a secret smile in her eyes. Ellouise and Nelo were intertwined, Madonna and Child, fast asleep. At the back of the plane I was peeking through the small round window to get a glimpse of the landscape below, when a man in his late sixties exited the restroom. On the way to his seat he noticed me and stopped.

"Hi! My name's Earl. What's your name?"

"Gaston."

"Are you concerned at all about our landing in Bangkok?"

"Of course not," I retorted. "What do you mean?"

"Well, I don't want to frighten you, Gaston," Earl said earnestly, "but did you know that most major airline accidents occur during landing?"

"No, actually I didn't know that." Thinking that perhaps our earlier incidents of turbulence had upset him, I attempted to address his concern: "Are you afraid we'll experience more turbulence when we land in Bangkok?"

Earl waved the notion away. "I'm not worried about it, but my wife is still very much shaken. I've never seen her pray to God before this flight, and we've been married forty-two years."

I arched my eyebrows. "Forty-two years! Wow! Now that's a successful love story! What have you learned over the last forty-two years about how to maintain a successful relationship? I'm eager to learn."

"Well young man, it's pretty simple really," he said, folding his arms and leaning a shoulder against the bulkhead. "I call it the love secret. It's all about being present. A harmonious relationship with a woman requires re-learning each day how to listen with your eyes."

"What do you mean by listening with your eyes?"

"It's like this: a woman needs to communicate extensively with her mate each day. It's her nature. I've discovered over and over that when we wake up in the morning, she needs to talk. Not just wants to, mind, she needs to. If I don't look into her eyes when she's talking, she'll keep going on and on because she feels she isn't being heard. And if she doesn't feel heard, she doesn't feel loved." Earl held up his index finger. "However, when I make the effort to look into her eyes and listen to her, her need is fulfilled. Now she knows she's loved. More importantly, she knows that I love her. I've tried to tell each of my children about the love secret, but they always come back with the same answer: 'It can't be that easy, Dad!' But it is, Gaston. It is! How about you? Do you have someone dear to your heart?"

I weighed my words for a moment, then smiled. "Indeed I do, but I'm scared stiff of her."

Earl laughed good-naturedly. "Well, I certainly feel for you. What's her name? And why are you so afraid of her?"

"Her name is Sandrine, and I've been in love with her for the longest time," I confessed. "But each time I see her, I literally run away and hide. I haven't even spoken to her yet. This mysterious fear has plagued my very Soul since the first time I laid eyes on her. She's the most beautiful woman I've ever seen."

Earl pushed himself off the wall and scratched behind his ear. "So you're telling me you've met the most beautiful woman in the world and your heart beats like crazy whenever you look at her, but you're afraid to talk with her or spend time with her. Am I right?"

"That's about the size of it."

"Well, pardon my French," he said, "but let me just say with a hundred percent certainty that you are a fool, Gaston! Remember this: when your heart beats for a woman in this way, within that rhythm lays the potential for great love. So what is it then: are you afraid to love or to be loved?"

"Probably both, but especially to be loved by a woman with a high degree of purity. Partly my fear is that I won't be able to live up to her expectations and that she will then reject me. I'm also apprehensive about where the transformative experience of such love would lead me in the future."

Earl smiled as if I had discovered a great secret but not yet realized it. "You are right in one thing: love is indeed a transformative experience, my friend. Indeed it is." He paused for a moment to make sure he had my full attention. "But only if you let it happen. Only if you let it happen!"

His words blew through me like a cool wind waking me from a bad dream.

He continued, his eyes twinkling with wisdom, "Next time you meet her, just let your heart do the talking and your eyes do the listening. Then you'll see clearly where her heart stands. It'll reveal itself right in front of you—or it won't. But you'll never know if you don't try, so you have to find the courage to approach her."

I took a deep breath, at the same time relaxing and finding fresh hope.

"Thank you, Earl I really needed to hear that. Next time I see her, I'll ask her to have coffee with me. And I'll listen with my eyes and see where it takes us."

Earl nodded in satisfaction at my response. "And remember this, Gaston: if you listen with your eyes when she speaks, you will connect with her through her eyes, which are the window of Soul. Who knows where your destinies will take you? Just look at us: forty-two years and she's still the love of my life."

Hearing footsteps, we both turned at the same moment to witness a distinguished elderly lady in an elegant dress of Asian design approaching us. She stopped in front of Earl.

"Mr. Earl Goodman," she smiled. "Your fiancée requests your presence by her side."

With that she turned around and walked right back to where she had come from. Earl looked at me in mock helplessness and held up his palms. It was evident to me they had developed an easy manner with each other over the years.

"By the way, don't forget to use humor," he said. "It'll save you in many disagreements." He stuck out his hand. "And now, as you know, my presence is requested elsewhere. Good bye, Gaston. Good luck to you on your quest."

I shook his hand and watched him stroll down the aisle to join his wife. To me they seemed to have the wonder of newlyweds coupled with the wisdom of a journey spanning forty-two years. Love radiated from them like a magical corona. As they took their seats, I looked out at the sky and pondered the reason for my fear of expressing myself to Sandrine. Right then and there I made the commitment to overcome my fear the next time I saw her.

Unless, of course, I overcame that same fear with someone else first.

Suddenly a rush of feelings flowed through me, making my heart pound. I had finally surrendered to the solution for something that had haunted me for a long time. Permitting myself to be loved by someone who truly moved me would lead to the life my heart yearned for, I was certain of that.

Aware of a presence behind me, I turned from the porthole to find myself confronted by one of the flight attendants from coach.

"Excuse me, sir, you can't stay back here. You'll have to return to your seat now."

When I arrived at my seat, Mr. Toldeck glanced up, noticing immediately that something in my demeanor had changed. "Well, you certainly seem to have had a good time stretching your legs—your face is filled with joy. Do you want to continue with our previous conversation?"

"Sure," I agreed. "Before I do that, though, I want you to know that the joy my face reflects is the result of a commitment I just made with myself back there. Now, are you sure you want to continue with my childhood stories? I don't quite see why a complete stranger would be so interested in my youthful history."

"You and I, Gaston," he said warmly, "are no longer strangers."

The truth of his statement put me at ease. Yes, we were no longer strangers.

Mr. Toldeck added, "I think the best is yet to come. Tell me what happened next, after you moved in with that young couple in Montreal."

An unexpected discomfort arose in me as I realized where our conversation would lead. Whether he knew it or not, he was asking me to share the deepest secret of my life, the most transforming experience I'd ever had. How could I explain to anyone, even to him, my initiation into an ancient order of masters? It seemed impossible, but the look in his piercing eyes convinced me he must know more than he let on. His gaze seemed to see through me so completely I had to close my eyes to focus on what to reveal and what to keep to myself. Hundreds of images flashed on my inner screen. Suddenly I knew exactly where to begin, and my discomfort disappeared as fast as it had risen. I was about to revisit a realm to which I had longed very much to return, and I was about to share that experience with the world, starting with one person. I was glad Mr. Toldeck was that person.

SOUL TRAVELS

X

Before I could begin this part of my story, Mr. Toldeck held up his hand to stop me.

"First, tell me what you're feeling right now."

I had to laugh at how well this man was reading me. Surely he could see my heart was opening wider with each breath and my excitement was surging upward like a vortex. How to describe my current state of elation? I yielded to the first image that captured my attention.

"Right now, I'm experiencing a deep yearning to share with you some of the most transforming experiences of my life. It feels like a dam inside me is about to burst, or a river is about to overflow its banks." Drawing a deep breath, I reigned in my feelings. "But, first things first. You asked me what happened when I moved in with the young couple."

"Yes."

"Well, let's see: I lived with them through the winter of 1976-77. When spring came, I returned to work for the Canadian Rail Road out west. The following winter I again stayed with Denis and Lucille in Montreal, trekking west in spring for work. By the early summer of 1978, I had worked for the Canadian Railroad for three years and was promoted to a crew which operated a huge crane that laid quarter-mile-long rails. At eighteen, I had traveled alone across Canada several times and was financially responsible for myself. I considered myself confident and capable.

"In my new job, the Ukrainian foreman heard I had been working for the railroad since the age of sixteen like him, so he kind of took me under his wing. There were about a hundred and twenty workers on the crew, altogether. I worked very hard, always striving to earn the foreman's trust. After a while it became apparent to the crew that our foreman had developed some favoritism towards me, but they didn't begrudge me his favor. I was the youngest kid in our work gang, and the rest of the crew was fond of me as well.

"In my free time I read Lobsang Rampa and other authors who wrote about esoteric topics. Speculation about what existed beyond our physical perception fascinated me. One night I lay on the roof of a railroad car gazing at the firmament, transfixed by the brightness of the stars, when a familiar voice began speaking to me. It was the distinct voice of Fubee, the master who had forewarned me so often of imminent major changes in my life.

"Your world is about to change completely," Fubee said.

For some reason, I failed at first to recognize the owner of the voice. I scrambled to my feet on the railroad car and cast about, trying to figure out who had spoken. Sometimes railroad crew members played pranks on one another for entertainment while working in the bush; this could be such a trick. After several times of asking aloud who was out there and hearing no response, I sat back down. Immediately, Fubee's voice spoke again.

"Your world is about to change completely," he repeated. Truth resonated in the words, leading me to accept that the speaker was, in fact, Master Fubee, who had come once again to share his blessings by forewarning me of an imminent change. How often had I foolishly taken his warnings lightly? Every time I had done so, I paid dearly for my lack of discipline. Now, hopefully, I had grown a little bit and would heed his words with the diligence they deserved.

"When the master said nothing further, I lay on top of the railroad car until almost daybreak, wondering what was going to happen this time.

"Once I finally made it to bed, I was taken out of my body for a journey with Fubee. He escorted me to a man he introduced as 'Z.' I paid little attention to the man other than to notice he was tall, wore glasses and was dressed in a bright blue suit. Much later in life I was to discover the importance of this person and the role he would play in my spiritual education, but for now I hadn't the slightest idea.

"The next morning, I found a brand new pair of construction boots at the door of my rail car. The other workers teased me about my new boots, but I was unashamedly proud of them. It had been six weeks since I started my new job, and I had been made to wait for them all this time. Everywhere I went in the rail yard the new boots drew comments, until I began to suspect Divine Spirit was trying to convey a message to me. It made no sense otherwise that a mere new pair of boots would generate so much interest. Over the years I had learned to listen to the subtle symbols through which Divine Spirit communicated, so I decided to be open to any message that might come to me. By the time I reached the place where all the employees gathered before work, I believed I'd deciphered Its message: 'A brand new way of walking.' Did it ever turn out to be true!

"We all boarded our designated construction machines and took off toward the job site. The equipment traveled along the railroad tracks and took about twenty to thirty minutes to reach the site. About halfway along, a loud horn could be heard blasting from up ahead. The sound vibrated through my whole body, giving me goose bumps. My spiritual teachers taught me that all sounds are of a divine nature—the instruments of the Holy Spirit expressing Its presence. Most of the time we're not aware of this fact, but this particular sound struck me so intensely I couldn't help but be aware of its greater significance.

"The construction machines we rode on came to an abrupt halt in a curve in the middle of the Rocky Mountains. I stood on the forward part of the mobile crane peering at the rail curving around the cliff ahead, wondering if what Master Fubee foretold was about to happen. His words 'your world is about to change completely' echoed in my head, tying my stomach into a tight knot. With each passing heartbeat, I became more certain that a great life change was upon me. Yet a different part of me was still convinced it couldn't be possible. Everything seemed to be normal. Loud horn blasts weren't *that* unusual, this part said.

"What transpired next took place in less than a second. Racing at me around the curve of the hill was a 12,000 pound spike machine. This in itself was not out of the ordinary: the spike machine often moved towards me at a good clip before coming to a halt in front of the construction equipment. However, this time it didn't stop. The massive machine slammed into the crane with a boom that seemed to shake the very mountains on both sides of the valley. Caught between the two giant, metal beasts, my body of flesh and blood provided about as much resistance as a bug crushed under a shoe.

"As the sound of the crash reverberated around the valley, the shaken crew members came running to the front of the crane to see what had happened. Our Ukrainian foreman was close to tears as he ordered the machines to be slowly drawn apart. In his years of service to the railroad he had witnessed many accidents; one glance told him this one was very, very bad.

"Slowly, the crane and the spike machine inched away from each other. Looking down, I could see my lower left leg dangling, barely hanging on as if attached with rubber bands. In a state of complete physical shock, I felt no pain whatsoever. From the look of it, I immediately knew my left leg below the knee was gone, even if it was still semi-attached.

"Screams sounded from all directions among the crew gathered around me. Two of the most courageous workers carried me away and placed me gently on the ground until a decision could be made on how to evacuate me. And then, lying on the ground in the middle of the Rockies, with my crushed and dying leg hanging on to my living body by a thread, I had the most majestic experience of all."

Shaken and moved by the vivid memory, I took a deep breath to continue. Before I could say anything, however, I noticed Mr. Toldeck's gaze shifting away from my eyes to something above and behind me, his eyebrows quirking up. Following his gaze, I turned to see Lea arriving at her seat from visiting with Ms. HonoOpono.

Instantly my mood changed and my desire to go on with my story flagged. I was riveted by Lea's radiant smile and the inviting look in her eyes.

"Come over, Gaston," she suggested quietly. "Let's talk some more, okay?"

"Of course, Lea," I heard myself saying, a little too eagerly. "I want to talk more, too."

Rising, I offered Mr. Toldeck a lopsided half smile to acknowledge my obvious weakness: Lea had me under her spell and I had no control over her effect on me. Mr. Toldeck smiled indulgently and wagged his eyebrows in understanding. I crossed the aisle and settled into the seat next to Lea.

"I've just come from Ms. HonoOpono," she said. "You know, Gaston, she claims you are a Master Kahuna. She says when she was a young girl, her grandfather taught her how to recognize one."

"Oh, really? How's that?"

"Her grandpa taught her that a Master Kahuna can only speak wisdom, and that our duty is to listen to his messages as well as to discover the gifts he brings."

"Well, Lea," I said. "Don't believe everything you hear; learn to trust your instincts."

Lea let loose a delightful little laugh. "You see," she said. "You can't help but express wisdom. That's your true nature, you know."

I smiled. "God knows Lea I'd love to be trained in the ancient art of becoming a Kahuna, but that hasn't been the case. However, I do know a little bit about this ancient art. Would you like me to tell you?"

"Yes, please, I'd like that very much."

"I was once invited to a very special location where, long ago, all the Kahunas of the Hawaiian Islands came for their training. It's on Maui near Makena Bay. The site is built with lava rock and has a special doorway. At its center stands an altar where the Kahuna-in-training would take his place. The experienced Kahunas would sit in a great circle around it so they could give him instructions. The native Hawaiian elder who invited me told me to bring offerings to the Aloha Spirit and to the guardians of this sacred site when I came to visit."

"I've never heard of this place, and I've lived all my life in Hawaii," Lea said in surprise. "Why is that?"

"I don't know," I shrugged.

"What happened when you went? I'm assuming you went there, right?"

"Indeed, I did. I was instructed to go during a full moon with offerings in hand and to have a specific purpose in mind. The night I arrived it was past midnight with a full moon high in the sky. As soon as I drove up, I became aware of a strong presence surrounding the sacred site like nothing I had ever experienced."

Lea drew in a quick breath in anticipation. "And what did you see?"

"Before I even got out of my van I sensed this whole assembly of beings approaching. Once I opened the door, a mob of what seemed like hundreds of Spirits surrounded me, pressing up against me, telling me I wasn't welcome and to get out. With each step I took towards the site, the fear and dread emanating from these beings grew in strength. My whole body was trembling, urging me to turn around and flee, but I kept moving forward, one step at a time. Eventually, I spoke out loud to them.

"'I was invited here. So let me through.'

"It was the most invasive psychic attack I'd ever gone through. According to the elder, I needed to walk around the site three times and ask for permission to enter. Unfortunately, he didn't inform me what an ordeal that would be, but fortunately for me, the more the malevolent pressure to leave intensified, the more my inner strength rose to resist it.

"When finally I entered the sacred site, the storm of spirit guardians vanished instantly. A deep, calming peace pervaded the interior of the shrine. I placed my offering on the altar and sat down nearby. Through most of the night I played my wooden flute and waited for whatever was going to happen."

"Did anything happen?" Lea asked, delicate fingers touching her lips.

I searched her eyes. "What I'm going to tell you now may sound untrue, even borderline crazy, but I assure you it's exactly what happened."

Lea nodded mutely.

"After playing my flute for a long while, I decided to move over to a spot I had been subtly drawn to the moment I walked inside. Believe it or not, when I sat down many Kahunas began to appear out of thin air. They were of all ages and sizes and appeared to be from many different time periods. It was the strangest thing, seeing them sitting in a circle around the periphery of the shrine, dressed in colorful ceremonial attire.

"After my astonishment at this mystical tableau had subsided a bit, the tallest one rose to his feet. His height must have been sixteen feet or more. He told me the ancient Kahuna training had come to an abrupt halt ever since the Hawaiians had stopped believing in the Aloha Spirit and their sacred link with the Menehune and the Tall Brothers. He said that since the passing of Tall Brother John, the sacred teachings had been placed on hold. In addition he revealed to me that in the near future a young Kahuna-in-training, whose belief in the Hawaiian traditions was strong, would take it upon himself to revive some of the ancient Hawaiian spiritual teachings, which are some of the oldest on earth."

"What else did you learn?"

"I was taught many things that night. One of them was that several centuries in the past, thousands of Hawaiians lived in the special area we now call Makena and Wailea on Maui. It was a region that was very lush and verdant before it became the desert it is today."

"What happened when you left the shrine?" Lea asked, leaning closer.

I grinned. "As soon I stepped out of the doorway, the guardian spirits set upon me again. They hounded me all the way to my van, then disappeared the moment I closed the door. As I drove away I promised myself never to return unless accompanied by another person, which the elder had warned me to do anyway. Of course I had followed an inner nudge to go by myself, which turned out to be a good thing, but I'd do it only this once."

"Why did you say the Hawaiian teachings are some of the oldest on earth?"

"Well, today's historians believe civilization only goes back maybe six or eight thousand years. The Hawaiian culture is far older than that, but if this truth were revealed it could upset many established religions. Very little is known about the continent of Atlantis and even less about Lemuria, or Mu. The continent of Lemuria is where the original Hawaiians came from. Much of this knowledge will be revealed in the future so the present Hawaiians can rediscover their ancient roots. The Kahunas told me there are many hidden sacred sites in valleys all across the Hawaiian Islands, some even older than the pyramids of Egypt. There will come a time when the young Kahuna will reveal to the world where those ancient sites are located, and many of them will be rediscovered and put to use."

Lea's eyes were wide with wonder. "But…how can that be, Gaston?"

"Don't ask me," I said with a laugh. "I'm only the recipient of the message, not the originator. But I've also learned over the years you only need one thing to discover your roots,."

"As a Hawaiian I really want to know, what is it?"

"It's a connection with Spirit, Lea. Spirit is the essence that governs our reality. Long ago Hawaiians didn't just have faith in the Aloha Spirit, they knew intimately of Its existence. They led their daily lives in harmony with IT by paying homage to It each moment of the day. Those were the days some religious scriptures refer to as the Golden Age or the Garden of Eden."

"Did you ever go back to the shrine?"

"Since that night I've never gone back, and I've never told anyone these stories."

"Would you consider taking me there, if I asked?"

"Yes, I'd be honored to take you. Before we land I'll give you my email and phone number so we can plan it, if you're still interested in going when you get back to Maui."

"If I'm still interested?" she exclaimed. "Of course I'll be interested! Are you kidding me?"

At that moment Brielle approached us from the galley.

"Would either of you like something to drink before we land?"

Lea requested tomato juice and I was about to order another Perrier when Brielle was called towards the back of the section by Ms. HonoOpono. Their conversation started out as a low murmur, then rapidly became as loud as a bullhorn.

"Ask Gaston to come back here," Mrs. HonoOpono shouted.

She sounded frustrated, as if the flight attendant wasn't listening to her. Brielle looked around in slight embarrassment.

It was clear she had tried to keep Mrs. HonoOpono's voice down to not disturb the other passengers, but she had failed.

Lea let out a laugh like silver bells chiming. "Go ahead, Gaston. Go be with her. It's okay."

I got up and went down the aisle towards Ms. HonoOpono's seat, exchanging a secret smile with Brielle as we passed each other.

"Well, Gaston," Ms. HonoOpono said when I sat down. "We'll soon land in Bangkok, and I wanted to tell you how much I appreciate all you've done for me during this trip. My worries are still very high regarding my little Lulu, because I don't know how my granddaughter will find the strength to deal with death. When you're old like me it's different, but she's barely lived yet."

She paused to wipe at the tears that began rolling down her cheeks. I held her hand, moved by her profound pain.

"Cancer has taken so many in our family," she sobbed. "Before modern medicine people lived, got sick, and died. Now they get treatments hoping to live longer, but so many don't. My sister, Hana, went through chemotherapy, and the treatment made her sicker than she was before she was diagnosed!"

Trying to calm herself, Mrs. HonoOpono continued, "Sometimes I worry what I'd do if I were hit with cancer. Since I weigh over four hundred pounds the chances of me going through the same thing my sister went through is very likely. But for now all my focus is on Kimo's hardship and Lulu's happiness. All I really want is to make Lulu happy. That's why I'm on this flight."

After a brief interval of quietly looking out the window, Ms. HonoOpono turned back to me and told me more about various members of her family. Eventually, though, she fell silent again, and I sensed a certain desperation in her as she inwardly grappled with the cause of her concerns.

At last she said, "Gaston, now that you know more about my family, and since I trust your vision, tell me how you understand this cancer epidemic?"

Caught off guard, I didn't know what to tell her. Any wrong or thoughtless response on my part might only further contribute to her pain. What could I say that would ease her mind and not raise her fears even more?

Out of nowhere, I heard myself saying, "To me, cancer is a great blessing from the Aloha Spirit."

Her response was immediate and forceful.

"How can you say that, Gaston? That can't be true!"

I searched for a rational answer but couldn't come up with one. So I spoke from the heart.

"Look at it this way: for thousands of years, humans have died without ever being told they had only a few months to live and to make the most of the remaining time they had. Now with modern medicine people all around the world have this chance. Mankind's consciousness has evolved to the point that some Souls choose to know ahead of time approximately when they'll translate into the higher worlds. Deep inside, these Souls know they have a mission here, and most of them try to fulfill their spiritual commitments in the time they have left."

"Are you telling me my sister agreed to suffer the way she did?" said Ms. HonoOpono.

"Well, did you ever ask yourself what would have happened if she hadn't known she was going to die? How she would have lived her life? What she might have done differently? Her entire experience during that time would have been completely different, not just for her, but for you and your family as well."

Ms. HonoOpono's mouth opened to snap another rebuttal, but she caught herself as the meaning of my words sank in. She looked off into the distance, no doubt remembering precious moments with her sister. After a moment, she said:

"Everything she did after she found out was different. I'd never seen her go to the beach so much, or watch the sunset with her children. The rest of our family all did the same just so we could be with her. We did so many things together we hadn't done since we were kids. I think we lived more intensely during those two years than we did in the rest of our lives." She paused, then launched our conversation in a different direction. "Do you think we can heal cancer?"

"Of course," I replied promptly. "Not just place it in remission but completely reverse it. People believe cancer can be healed with chemical pills and radiation treatments, just like they think years of unhealthy eating can be undone with diet pills or liposuction.

"Cancer can be directly linked to the devastating effects of the over-consumption of processed food. The body needs natural food to stay in balance. Therefore, the solution to me is simple: eat healthy food, drink lots of water—perhaps two or three liters a day—and clean out your digestive system as often as you need during the year. This can be done through salt water cleanses, also known as 'salt water flushes.' A salt water cleanse is one of the easiest and quickest ways to clean out the colon at home. Not only does it clean the colon, but it cleanses the stomach and small intestine as well. In other words, it disinfects the entire alimentary canal (the digestive system) by removing the accumulated toxins, parasites and undesirable bacteria from the digestive tract.

"The physical body is a vehicle for Soul created by God specifically for our own individual purposes, so each person must learn to listen within to receive their own personalized instructions from the Holy Spirit Itself. Many of us know this already, but we're hoping instead for a magic pill or a medical treatment so we don't have to do the work of changing our habits. Only when cancer knocks at our door do we start taking responsibility for our own health."

Ms. HonoOpono had been listening intently. "I've never heard such a unique viewpoint on cancer before. It's sure worth thinking about, but you also said something about Hana fulfilling her spiritual commitment. What do you mean by that?"

"Our spiritual commitments come from the contracts we make in the higher worlds with the Holy Spirit and with the Souls we love. We as Soul travel down here to the physical world for spiritual education. To further that purpose, we create agreements with other Souls so we can fulfill our mission of learning what we need to make the next step in our spiritual unfoldment. Before Souls are born on earth, they enter into agreements with other Souls who will be their family, friends, co-workers, neighbors, and even their enemies and antagonists. They set up a contract between the Holy Spirit and each other to engage in actions that will help each of them learn the necessary spiritual lessons.

"That's why people with grave illnesses sometimes hang on for quite some time. They're working right up until the last second to fulfill their spiritual contracts. We all make these agreements, whether we're aware of them or not. Some of us are here to learn great spiritual lessons, no matter how great the cost to our physical well-being."

"It's funny you should mention traveling as Soul," Ms. HonoOpono said. "My grandfather often spoke of the powers Kahunas had, one of which he referred to as Soul Travel. I wish I had learned more from him about these powers, but he passed away when I was in my early teens and not really interested in such things yet. What do you know about Soul Travel?"

"It's pretty simple, but it takes true devotion and persistence to learn. We travel as our true self, Soul, by contacting a desired location or state of being through the initial use of our creative imagination. Once contact has been achieved, we let the Soul Travel experience take over and lead us to places and states we haven't been to before. This ability can only be developed through daily practice of spiritual exercises, such as the ones I mentioned to you earlier. A strong love for the Aloha Spirit is the medium that enables us to travel to any place in the universe. This connection isn't gained through observation; it can only be established through practice and experience."

I expected Ms. HonoOpono to ply me with a host of further questions, but Brielle pre-empted her by letting us know we would be landing in Bangkok soon.

"Oh," Ms. HonoOpono said, her brow furrowing. From her tone I sensed the prospect of our imminent landing was raising her worries for Kimo and Lulu to be uppermost in her mind again. Sounding worn, she said, "You know, Gaston, I think I'd better catch another snooze before we land."

"That's fine," I said, rising to return to my seat. "I hope you'll be well rested when we land."

Mr. Toldeck was waiting for me, patient as an old comrade.

"I've been anticipating you're arrival with great joy," he told me as I sat down.

"Why's that?"

Mr. Toldeck spread his hands in an expansive gesture. "Before you left to sit with Lea, you were going to tell me about the miraculous experience you had after you were hit by the spike machine. Did you really experience a miracle?"

"Yes, indeed," I replied, instantly back to reliving my story. "To me, a miracle is a change of consciousness. That's exactly what happened to me, on many different levels."

Mr. Toldeck smiled eagerly. "Tell me every detail. I can't see how anyone could describe being maimed in a train accident as miraculous, but I look forward to hearing your reasons."

"All right! I should warn you, though, that this story may sound even stranger than any of the others I've shared so far."

As Mr. Toldeck leaned toward me in anticipation, the sudden realization struck me that I had divulged every major incident of my early life save this one to a man who was a complete stranger to me. It occurred to me how little, if anything, I knew about him, yet I felt the strongest urge to tell him everything, without reservation. My entire life I had held myself back from sharing this particular experience, maybe out of fear of reliving the traumatic incident that preceded it. Or more likely, because I longed so much to return to the place I had visited that I didn't quite dare speak of it, lest speaking of it would make me miss it that much more.

"The strange thing is," I began, "when they laid my injured body on the ground, I felt exhilarated, caught up in a kind of euphoria that was exciting and comforting at once. Before I knew it I was floating free, gazing down at my prone body. I watched the assembled crew members look at my body in anguish, feeling the concern and pain each held in his heart for me, but I knew they were in the physical world while I was in another dimension now.

"As I became more comfortable with this new state, I began to take in my surroundings. Not far off to the side were two familiar Masters—one my old friend Rebatarz in his maroon robe, the other Fubee, dressed in white as usual. Peace and love radiated from their light bodies.

"'Would you like to come with us?' Fubee said.

"I glanced over my shoulder to be sure the invitation was directed at me, not at some other disembodied being behind me. In my state of ecstasy I had no concerns about where we might be going, no doubts at all. I had traveled with both of them many times before, if not with the clarity and awareness of the 360 degree vision I was enjoying at the moment.

"'Yes, please,' I answered without hesitation.

"In a flash, we were standing at the steps of a monastery which I knew to be in the foothills of the Himalayas in northern Tibet. The structure resembled a medieval castle perched high on the edge of a cliff. How anyone could reach it, let alone live there, baffled me, yet somehow they managed. The beauty of the place inspired me; I felt more alive than I'd ever felt before.

"As we approached the steps leading to the temple entrance, I noticed an artfully carved, wooden bench at the foot of the stairs.

"'Do you wish to rest a moment before entering?' Fubee asked.

"The bench seemed like an old friend I had known for many lifetimes, so I nodded, went over and sat down. Within me, the Sound Current roared like surf crashing on the beach. Looking around at the hills and the towering, snow-capped mountain peaks beyond, I wondered if I was in a dream or if this was real. If it was a dream, I certainly didn't want to ever wake up.

"After a timespan in which I was allowed to acclimatize to the higher vibration of the monastery's vicinity, Rebatarz led us up the stairs to the arched entrance. Each step radiated with a different color, raising my vibratory level ever higher as I climbed. On the ninth stair at the top I paused to look around once more. The sun shone in vibrant, golden hues above the glorious mountain landscape. I felt as if I, Soul, was on fire; my only desire was for the sacred flames to consume me entirely and eternally.

"The Masters had brought me to a Golden Wisdom Temple, a place of learning where Souls can go to acquire the knowledge they need to reach their highest spiritual potential. The temple doors opened as we approached the archway, closing behind us after we passed through. I followed the Masters to what they called the Sound Room, where Rebatarz directed me to lie down on a white, oval table. Immersion in the Sound Current, he told me, would help heal my subtle bodies, which were in shock due to my physical injury. How long I lay there I don't know, but at some point the treatment was over and Fubee led me to a classroom in another part of the monastery where I joined other Souls who had also traveled here.

"Classes went on during my entire stay at the monastery, the subjects varying with each class. The adepts teaching the courses each specialized in a specific field of spiritual wisdom. When a class ended, the attendees usually dispersed to various corners of the monastery to assimilate in private the wisdom they had received. Fubee's classes held the most attraction for me and I often returned to them when I had a choice. I loved the way he taught, always with a gentle smile and a glint of good humor in his eyes."

Mr. Toldeck smiled appreciatively. "Do you remember any pearls of wisdom from his lectures?"

"Oh, my, there were so many. One thing he told me was that this ancient Golden Wisdom Temple was the origin of all earthly faiths. He said every great religious leader in earth's history had Soul Traveled there and some even journeyed in their physical body there prior to beginning their spiritual mission. The temple's only purpose has always been to teach Souls about the Holy Spirit.

"My stay there seemed to last for a long time—months, maybe even years; it was hard to tell since time is perceived differently on other dimensions. During my visit I encountered many others like myself whose desire for the knowledge of God drove them to explore higher realms. We were taught Soul is our true self, and as such we are eternal and cannot be injured or harmed in any way. Of course this isn't true in our physical bodies, as I could readily attest to. In this regard the adepts helped me understand that I had nothing to worry about as well. Though I had lost a leg, I would be walking again very soon.

"One day I was sitting on my favorite wooden bench outside the monastery, enjoying the overwhelming love that permeates the atmosphere around this temple, when I saw Rebatarz striding towards me. He is a tall, dark-skinned man, with short, black hair and a thick beard. Each time, he was clad in a maroon robe and sandals, and as always he got right to the point.

"'The time has come for you to return.'

"I was aghast. 'Return? Oh no, Master! I desire no such thing. I want to stay here with you and Fubee.'

"The love in his liquid eyes warmed me and broke my heart at the same time.

"'I understand,' he said. 'However, you require many more lessons in your physical existence, and the moment has come for you to return to them. Rest assured you'll be back here soon.'

"My physical life wasn't something I desired to return to. I longed only to remain here at the temple and continue my education. No one in his right mind would want to give up this marvelous new body, I thought, or the love and freedom experienced at the Golden Wisdom Temple. Unless, of course, he was being asked to by his spiritual master. Bowing to the inevitable, I wordlessly assented to his request. This phase of my experience had come to end. Instantly, I found myself on the return journey to my body the physical world.

"I awoke in a soft bed, unable to pry open my eyes. A moment later a loud alarm sounded overhead, and I heard thunderous footsteps pounding down the hall like a herd of buffalo. A door slammed against its doorstop, the shock causing my eyes to snap open. I was in a hospital room, lying in a white, metal-framed bed, a drip IV attached to my arm. Looking down, I immediately noticed the missing hump of the bed sheets where my left foot should have been. It was gone. Still, this was the most glorious day of my life because I'd just returned from the most inspiring out-of-body experience I'd ever had. My heart was overflowing with joy.

"Nurses rushed into the room, solicitous, their eyes brimming with tears. They surrounded my bed, their concern clearly evident at how I would take the news of my amputation. Would I be horrified or despondent? Expecting to soothe and comfort me, they were unprepared for the wide smile I gave them and for the grateful hug I offered each of them. Many cried in my arms, more anguished at the trauma I had experienced than I was. It was one of the most touching moments of my life.

"Eventually, everyone stood back from the bed so I could pull away the blanket to see the result of the surgery and touch my cast. Experimentally, I moved my leg and was told by the doctor the knee joint still functioned normally, although it was swollen and sore. The realization I was now an amputee struck me as surreal in light of the fact that I had just spent long periods of time in a perfectly fine body, walking around and studying at the Golden Wisdom Temple.

"Curious, I asked the nurses: 'How long have I been gone? Was it weeks or months?'

"They laughed.' You were unconscious for two days, not weeks or months."

"Two days! The time dilation experienced in the higher dimensions was truly astonishing. To me the two days I had lain "unconscious" in the hospital had seemed like months or years of the most intense and exhilarating of conscious activities.

"I spent most of the first day after regaining physical consciousness pondering Rebatarz's final words: 'Rest assured you'll be back here soon.' The day wasn't yet half over, and already the longing to return to the temple wrenched at me like a child torn from his parents. I ached to return to my spiritual family."

"Did you ever get to go back?" Mr. Toldeck inquired.

"During the first day, many of the doctors, nurses, administrators and even the janitorial staff came to offer their support to the eighteen-year-old kid who had just lost his leg. They brought me a lot of goodies, so my attention was pretty much focused on the hospital room. By nightfall I had stuffed myself to the gills, my visitors had left, and I was finally alone. I turned off the light and went to sleep. Within seconds I slipped out of the body and hovered in the air next to it. Hands on the bars of my hospital bed, I stared down at my sleeping form lying under the blanket like a mannequin made of clay. Rebatarz was standing at my side. The moment I became aware of his presence, we were transported back to the temple. I traveled there every single night during my stay at the hospital, which was around six weeks or so. Then I was transferred to a rehab center to learn how to walk with a prosthetic limb."

Mr. Toldeck said, "Those were rather extensive out-of-the-body experiences you had. Did you ever encounter the two Masters again thereafter?"

"Oh, yes. On the night before my release from the hospital, as I lay in bed worried whether I would ever walk again, Fubee and Rebatarz came to visit me and escort me to the temple once more. It was rare for both to visit at the same time. At the end of the Soul Travel experience they told me I wouldn't need to come to the temple any longer, since from this moment on they would frequently visit me in their Light Bodies.

"When I awoke, I rejoiced in the fact that I had been visited by two of the most venerated spiritual Masters. Years later, I learned that Rebatarz had been in charge of training every Vi-Guru for the past 500 years, and that Fubee was the abbot of this Temple in northern Tibet.

"Later that morning, as I lay in bed waiting to be wheeled out of the hospital and driven to the airport for the flight to Vancouver, I kept seeing blue and white lights in the air around me. Some flickered in a corner of the room, others by the window, still others right next to the people coming and going. Each time one of the hospital staff came to my room to wish me good luck, I asked them if they could see these lights, but none ever did. The fact that only I could see the lights assured me they represented the Masters' presence. From that moment on I truly knew the meaning of my teacher words: 'I am always with you.'

"Soon I realized if I focused directly on the lights they quickly vanished. I could only observe them by glancing at them obliquely, or out of the corner of my eye. This technique allowed me to remain in their presence continually. I'm convinced had I insisted on talking about the lights in the room to the hospital staff, they would have transferred me to the mental ward. 'Poor kid,' they'd probably say. 'Not only did he lose his leg, he lost his marbles too.'

"To this day these lights appear around me to warn me of potential danger, or to assure me of the presence of the Master and his Divine Love. Since my stay at the hospital I've never shared this with anyone, but telling you has awakened within me wings of Spirit that have been dormant for decades."

I paused to catch my breath and steal a glance at Mr. Toldeck. "It's taken all my courage to share these experiences with you, but it feels good to liberate myself from long-held secrets. Opening up to you has created an expansion of consciousness within me, just like a Soul Travel experience. My heart is filled with profound gratitude for you and your genuine companionship. Your sincere desire to listen and discover what I've gone through has changed me profoundly. Mahalo, Mr. Toldeck. This has been a very special flight for me, one I'll never forget."

"The same is true for me, Gaston," he said gravely.

Suddenly, heat welled up in my body and my head swam as if all the lights in the cabin were aimed directly at me, even though I knew mine was the only one on. A tsunami of emotions rolled over me, thrusting me into a state of near ecstasy that was fast becoming unbearable. Was this Mr. Toldeck's doing? I couldn't understand what was going on.

Fortunately, Brielle chose that moment to walk down the aisle, retrieving trash from passengers. The sensation of heat and overwhelming emotions ended abruptly as soon as she reached our row.

"We'll be landing in thirty minutes," she announced. Glancing down at the floor by my feet, she bent and picked up my leather folder. "What's this?"

"Oh," I said, retrieving the portfolio. "That's my notebook."

After Brielle had gone, I handed the folder to Mr. Toldeck and placed it on my seat.

"You can write any questions you think of in my folder if you need," I offered.

Feeling restless, I rose from my seat for a walk towards the back of the plane.

EXPERIENCE, THE MOTHER OF CONSCIOUSNESS

XI

Though I didn't understand exactly how or why, a great burden had been lifted from me. I stared for a while through the little window in the exit door at the rear of the plane, adjusting to the electrifying energy spinning inside me, gradually gaining control of my emotions. Then I noticed Lea standing beside me.

"We'll be in Bangkok soon," she said. "I just wanted to tell you how much I enjoyed our conversations."

"Me too, Lea. I truly enjoyed your company as well."

"Before we part, I wanted to ask you one more question."

"Sure. Go ahead."

"Earlier we talked more about the philosophical aspects of relationships. What I want to know is: how do you think good relationships should actually look in day-to-day life?"

I thought for a moment. "There are several steps to my plan for a future relationship. The first step is called *Learning to Tame the Heart*. During this phase I intend to court my future beloved for ninety days, so we can discover each other's' weaknesses and strengths. I want to spend the first three months imprinting every detail of her face and body onto my heart. I want to become familiar with her mannerisms and let her inner beauty inspire me. These three months also give us the opportunity to visit each other's' families. It's amazing how much you can learn about a person just by having supper with her family. You get a sense of the environment in which her personality was formed. After the courting period, if we still like each other, I'll invite her to build a 'love nest of intimacy.'

"Building a love nest is the beginning of the second step, which is called *The One Year Commitment Vow*. By pledging a full year of commitment, we prove to each other that both partners are looking for true commitment. Every year after that, we renew our vow. Renewing our commitment vow each year will allow us to take incremental steps toward a lifetime commitment to our beloved. Our renewal day will both mark our yearly anniversary and begin a celebration where we spend two or three weeks together in a romantic setting. Every month, we will spend the day we made our vow honoring the contributions each partner brought to the relationship during the past month. It becomes our very own monthly Valentine's Day."

Realizing I might be rambling on I checked myself.

"I hope I'm not boring you will all of this?"

"No, not at all," she said quickly. "This is all very interesting. Are there any other steps on this road map to a perfect relationship?"

"There are three more." I gave her a lopsided smile, half apologizing for what almost seemed like a sermon. "The next step is called *Creating the Dream*. In this step, we disclose to each other what makes us happy once we've moved in together. To reach our goal of being happy together, we need to see our goals clearly. The best way I know how to do this is to create a dream board. We create our dream board together, then write a simple plan of how to achieve the dreams outlined on the board.

"The next step is *Pursuing Our Life's Missions*. Once we've revealed what we consider our life's missions to one another, we devote ourselves to helping each other accomplish them. For example, for you a mission might be opening your own Hula school. For me it might be creating educational games for children.

"The last step is called *Sharing a Common Passion*. For this part, we agree to donate some of our time together to a nonprofit organization, such as our church or some other cause greater than ourselves. Selfless acts, especially when performed by a couple together, inspire a deep passion for life and cement relationships in many ways. The power of love works its magic through service. In my view, a loving couple needs to find ways for their love to flow outward, not just within the closed loop of their relationship or family. It's true that love keeps people in each other arms; however, manifesting love in acts of giving to the wider world is a great foundation for a solid relationship."

Lea swept her hair back over her shoulder and tugged thoughtfully at her earlobe. "Do you really believe a modern, financially independent, emotionally stable woman would exchange vows with a man after only one year of commitment? That seems hardly enough."

Her resistance seemed to indicate she might have commitment issues. Perhaps she had been hurt or disappointed in a previous marriage.

Confidently, I replied, "Yes, I do, because I believe the process I've outlined will ensure my beloved and I never ever take each other for granted. How often do we see couples no longer express gratitude or affection towards each other simply because they assume their partners will always be there? *The One Year Commitment Vow* allows each person to demonstrate each year, each month, and each day how important their partner is to them. Expressions of gratitude and respect for our beloved become part of our daily experiences. When we're nurtured with love at home, we can't wait to reunite with our beloved at the end of the workday. Love is all that people desire, no matter how rich or poor they may be. That's what I think the Aloha Spirit is all about: sharing what's inside—love."

Lea appeared less than convinced. "That all sounds great, Gaston, but I need to believe in something more than sharing the love that's inside. There's got to be more to it."

"You're right, there is something more to believe in," I said.

"What's that?"

"God, the Creator, the source of the Holy Spirit. Unlike people, the Creator will never disappoint us or let us down. The human consciousness we take on as Souls when we incarnate on earth is imperfect; in fact, it's designed to be fallible so we make mistakes we can learn from. Hence, a relationship between humans will always be imperfect and limited to some degree. Within the Spiritual worlds, relationships were created so all parties involved would learn about the sacred art of unified cooperation. If we place all our beliefs, hopes and aspirations in life on our relationship with another person, we're bound to get hurt. It's just human nature. There's no possible way a man or woman can completely fulfill our need for love, no matter how great that person might be. We need to draw upon something greater than a finite relationship: it has to be an infinite one, an eternal relationship. A human being will never be able to love us to the same extent as the Eternal Spirit does; he or she can only inspire us to achieve the state of Divine Love."

"I think I see the point you're trying to make," Lea acknowledged, running her fingers through her lustrous hair. "I'll have to think more about that."

At that moment the same flight attendant who had previously shooed me away from my favorite spot at the rear of the plane approached and instructed us curtly to return to our seats at once—we would be landing soon. Together Lea and I headed back toward First Class.

"Where are you staying in Bangkok?" she inquired.

I shrugged. "I haven't decided yet."

"We're booked at the Bangkok Hyatt downtown. I'm sure Ms. HonoOpono would really enjoy your company." Lea paused and gave me a sidelong glance. "I know I would."

I swallowed, suppressing a deep sigh.

"Thank you for your kind invitation, Lea, no not this time, I need to focus on my fast. It is the primary reason for my trip. I'll pick a hotel once I get into Bangkok, because I prefer to adapt to the unexpected when I travel. But I want you to know I'm very grateful for your offer."

Lea's posture sagged minutely in disappointment. "I can see this fast is very important for you," she sighed.

Despite myself, my shoulders slumped in response. Inside my head a small voice whispered, *Why not just say yes? You know you have feelings for her.* It belonged to the part of me that wanted very much to yield to her sweet temptation, but there was another part of me that felt an equally strong desire to spend more time with Mr. Toldeck, perhaps over dinner. There was no possible way I could explain this to Lea, because I was highly confused about it myself.

Not knowing what else to say, I suggested lamely, "Should we continue to our seats now?"

Lea nodded mutely and took the lead down the aisle. I followed, riveted by the flow of her raven hair and the sinuous movement of her dress shifting over her delicate curves as she walked. Other passengers looked up from what they were doing to watch her pass. No wonder—she was radiant, like a graceful bird gliding on the currents of the wind, barely disturbing her environment.

Suddenly I felt a small hand snag mine in passing; it was Nelo. I squatted down next to his seat, bringing my eyes level with his.

"Hey, Coach Gaston," he said. "I really hope I see you in Thailand during our vacation."

"You never know what kind of surprises life has in store for you when you travel," I replied.

"Are we going to land soon? I'm tired of sitting here."

"Just a few more minutes, Nelo."

"Yes!" Nelo punched the air with his fist. "Should I wake up my mom?"

"Um, why don't you let her sleep until the seat belt sign comes on? And try to take a little nap yourself until then. I have to return to my seat now."

The boy held up his hand, thumb and index finger extended in the Hawaiian sign for 'hang loose.' "Okay, coach."

When I entered first class, the only lights on were Ms. HonoOpono's and mine. Lea's space was dark, clearly indicating she wanted to be left alone. I tried to sneak past Ms. HonoOpono, but she was alert and flagged me down.

"I wanted to ask you if you would consider coming with us to the Hyatt hotel," she said. "You'd have the opportunity to spend time with us and get to know Kimo and Lulu. It would mean a lot to me, Gaston. You've been my angel during the entire flight. Please? Would you consider it?"

Again, I muffled a sigh. "Lea just asked me the same thing and I had to tell her I can't. It would be very impolite for me to say *yes* to you and *no* to her."

Ms. HonoOpono looked astonished. "What? You said *no* to Lea? Have you lost your mind? There isn't a man on this plane who would have denied her wish. Am I to assume you're meeting someone special in Bangkok?"

"No, of course not." I waved the suggestion off. "I'm simply trying to focus on my fast, that's all. A big part of me wants nothing more than to go to the Hyatt, but I've convinced myself for months now that I'll be a different man after this fast, so it's very important for me not to be distracted from it. I'm sure you understand."

"If you put it that way, Gaston, I do understand. Alright. I'll let this one pass."

I smiled gratefully at her. "You know, I think by letting it be you're helping both of us adhere to the will of the Aloha Spirit. My experience has been that to become the cause instead of the effect of others in our lives we have to allow some things to follow their course. We have to accept the responsibility of being ourselves and choosing our own path, rather than simply reacting to other people's emotional viewpoints and efforts to control us."

"That's not always easy. How do you manage it?"

"Experience is the mother of consciousness," I replied. "By that I mean I've learned through trial and error to keep myself free from other people's emotional appeals. When Lea asked me to join you at the Hyatt I was very tempted to say *yes,* not just because of my attraction to her, but also because I didn't want to hurt her feelings. However, my inner voice told me to reply 'No not this time', and if there's one thing I know by now it's to listen to its subtle nudges. In the past there were so many times when I didn't listen for one emotional reason or another, but then circumstances invariably developed to prove my reasoning was wrong and I should have followed the course Spirit intended for me in the first place. I believe sometimes our role is simply to do what you did earlier: let it be." I smiled at her. "So, thank you for your kind invitation. We're landing soon and I need to make my way back to my seat."

Ms. HonoOpono sighed in acquiescence. "All right, Gaston. I guess I'll see you on Maui, or who knows where else we might run into each other."

I patted her hand, then stood and headed down the aisle. Lea was still resting, so I slipped into my seat. Suddenly something crackled under me and I realized I was sitting on my leather folder. Mr. Toldeck must have left it there. I pulled it out and began to open it, but Mr. Toldeck touched me on the arm to gain my attention.

"So, you were all alone at the hospital with no family," he prompted, returning to the point in my story where I had left off. "That must have been difficult at the age of only eighteen."

"In some ways it was, and in other ways it wasn't. The hospital was in an isolated town, tucked away in the Rocky Mountains of Northern British Columbia, surrounded by native Indian reservations. Not much ever happened there, so my accident was big news. I was the talk of the town. Within days of being hospitalized, my co-workers had pitched in to buy me a cassette player and a stack of popular cassettes so I could listen to music. Then our work crew threw a full-blown party in my hospital room, which became so raucous the town's Royal Canadian Mounted Police were called in.

"That same week, the local newspaper published a front-page article about my accident and encouraged its readers to visit the young French Canadian boy who had just lost his leg and had no family or any kind of support. In response, dozens and dozens of people came with their families to visit me. They brought fresh-baked cookies, muffins and gifts of all kinds, even a beaver pelt! More importantly, these kind strangers gave me the gift of companionship during the dark days immediately following my injury.

"What they couldn't provide was the answer to my fear of whether any woman would ever want to have a relationship with a man with a handicap such as mine. Sure, beautiful young nurses visited me every hour, very concerned and friendly, but their concern came from pity. The last thing a handicapped person wants is pity, especially while he's trying to forge a new identity for himself under trying circumstances. It was in this context that I received a special gift from Spirit for which I'm still extremely grateful today. Many people have personal stories illustrating how the Holy Spirit took a hand in their lives, but sometimes we're so focused on our loss or pain that we don't see the miracles that occur for our benefit. In this instance, though, I was acutely aware of the origin of the gift.

"After a week in bed, I was able to transfer to a wheelchair and propel myself to the veranda outside my room. Often I'd sit there and admire the valley with the breathtaking Rockies in the background. Other times I'd get up with the help of crutches and go for walks on the hospital grounds. I've always been adventurous, so early one morning I decided to hitchhike a mile or so down the hill to the nearby native sacred site called Kispiox Village. Hobbling along the side of the road on my crutches, I was picked up by the first passing driver, a local farmer. He told me something I've never forgotten: 'When you use desperate measures to get somewhere, it's because something important is waiting for you.'

"Kispiox Village is situated on a spit of land between two major rivers, just before the junction where they merge into one. Since I couldn't walk the grounds without discomfort, the farmer gave me a tour of the village in his pickup. When the time came for him to return to cutting his hay, he asked me where I wanted to be dropped off. My first impulse was to name the hospital, but then I hesitated. It was only about a mile to the hospital and I was sure I could find my own way back. What I really wanted at the moment was just to sit by myself and look at the totem poles and the long houses I had heard so much about. An empty picnic table beckoned at the end of the site's parking lot, so I asked him to drop me there.

"As I sat alone on the bench, enjoying the spectacle of the two blue-green mountain rivers rushing from their respective valleys towards their junction, I noticed a beautiful young woman riding a bicycle in my direction. Immediately, I felt self-conscious. I was handicapped. The stump of my left leg had a big cast around it covered in scribbled signatures. My crutches had slid off the picnic table and lay askew on the ground. At first I pretended to ignore her, but it became impossible when she braked to a stop at my table.

"Calling a cheerful greeting, she laid her bike on the grass and came over to pick up my crutches. My nervousness subsided considerably as we fell into an easy conversation. I learned her name was Reagan, that she was twenty-four, from New York City, and that she worked for the Katimavik Organization. This civic organization had come here to build housing for impoverished native families. Her youthful beauty and the sense of adventure emanating from her were like a breath of fresh air to me. When I told her I was staying at the hospital up the hill, she laughed; I guess it was pretty obvious. We could hear ambulances, police cars, and fire trucks driving up and down the roads somewhere above us.

"After a while, we observed a small pickup truck from the fire department racing towards us. When it screeched to a halt, the fireman jumped out and yelled at Reagan that what she had done was unacceptable. The whole town, it seemed, was in a state of emergency. Every available person had been mobilized to locate the amputee who had just absconded from the hospital. Two police cruisers pulled up behind the fire department pickup, sirens blaring, and the Mounties, too, got out and weighed in against Reagan. It was completely irresponsible, they repeatedly told her, for a girlfriend to take her boyfriend out of the hospital, especially when he's on medication after having undergone recent major surgery. The poor girl could hardly get a word in edgewise to defend herself.

"At first I found it kind of amusing, but when Reagan began to look desperate in her efforts to convince them this was all a misunderstanding, I stood up on one unsteady leg and lifted my palm.

"'Stop! That's enough. She had nothing to do with my leaving the hospital—I came down here by myself. We've only just met and we were simply having a conversation. All we wanted was to be left alone for a while. You guys can understand that, can't you?'

"The two police officers instantly backed down and stopped their scolding. The fireman shook his head, grumbling, and got into his truck. One of the officers asked Reagan if she wanted him to put her bike in the trunk of his car.

"'Why, yes, of course!' she answered uncertainly, not knowing what to make of the offer. The Mountie's intent became clear when we settled into the back of the police car: he was giving us a chance to sit together for a while longer on the way back to the hospital. I was moved by his kindness.

"Back at the hospital the staff was amazed to hear that I had hitchhiked down to Kispiox Village on my own, and even more amazed to see that I had returned with a girlfriend. None of the locals had ever seen her before, which made it seem as if she had appeared out of nowhere. My doctor, the head nurse and many of the other nurses on duty stopped by to see if I was okay, and, of course, to meet this mysterious new girlfriend.

"It didn't take long for me to completely fall in love with Reagan. She was about five foot five, with long brown hair and brown eyes that sparkled like gold-flecked amber in the sun. She came to visit me every single day. When we made love it was as if God were saying to me: 'Look, I love you no matter what. You'll be fine just the way you are.' This gift of love from the Holy Spirit had a profound impact on my self-perception as a man and on my attitude towards my handicap. I felt whole again. I was in love with life again.

"During my stay at the hospital I experienced a wide spectrum of thoughts and emotions, but the most important discovery I made was that I am loved. Life demonstrated this to me time and again. In my heart the truth I had learned from the Vi-Guru, that 'Soul exists because God loves It,' was augmented by the greatest gift of all, the certainty of God's love through personal experience. I became determined to share that gift with the world."

Mr. Toldeck fixed me with an intense gaze. "Have you, Gaston? Have you found a way to share your gift of love with the world?"

His pointed question completely derailed my train of thought. Momentarily at a loss for words, I looked past him out the window, searching for comfort in the night sky. This very question had haunted me for many years now. Every day I woke up with the strong desire to find a way to share this gift of love with the world, but over the years I had spent so much time and energy denigrating myself and my abilities that I always put it off. How could I, small and inadequate as I was, inspire the world to accept Divine Love? Still, the overwhelming yearning to pass on what I had received grew in intensity as the years passed and it seemed there was nothing I could do about it. After a moment, I managed to find my voice.

"What I know, Mr. Toldeck, is that the Holy Spirit sends small miracles our way every day to assure us that each of us matters. Yet I'm daunted by the idea of undertaking the enormous task of bringing this to the world. Who am I to take on such a grand mission? I have no skills in that regard, no formal training. It's as if God is asking me to do something It knows I can't."

My throat constricted with long held emotions. During our flight Mr. Toldeck had asked me many questions, but it appeared they all had been leading up to this one. It was as if our whole conversation had been designed to walk me across the one bridge I had avoided all my life. I trembled at the mere thought.

"Please, Mr. Toldeck," I pleaded. "How can I resolve this dilemma that has haunted me for so long?"

With the echo of my plea still ringing in my ears, I was suddenly overcome by the strangest sensation. It felt like all the old, depleted energy drained from my body and was replaced by potent new energy. I felt lighter and freer, as if on the verge of stepping out of my self-imposed prison.

Mr. Toldeck said, "Your dilemma can only be resolved through the expression of your gifts. You can do this while engaging in the activities you already do in your daily life. Your doubts will vanish once you begin to share your gifts of love with the world in your own way, without measuring yourself by the yardstick of others. But think about this: only when you're willing to fully accept the gift of love yourself will you be able to share it with others."

Again his words touched a nerve within me. More than anything in life, I wanted to pass on the gifts I had been given to anyone who would listen, but were my feelings of unworthiness linked to an inability on my part to fully accept love for myself, as Mr. Toldeck seemed to indicate? Had the traumas of my childhood and youth led me to wrap myself in an impenetrable cocoon of untouchability, to avoid being hurt again? Under the stranger's penetrating gaze I had to admit I had not been willing to see this truth before. Perhaps it meant I was now ready to break out of my cocoon.

Eyes shining with compassion and reassurance, Mr. Toldeck remained silent, appearing to wait for some inner nudge to give him direction for what to say next. Finally, he continued: "Receiving and fully accepting a gift is one thing, but having the courage to share it is another matter entirely. Courage is a trait with which you are quite familiar, however. Therefore, all you have to do is listen closely and persistently, and you will resolve all your life's dilemmas."

Looking down at the folder in my hands, I pondered. How would listening persistently resolve my dilemmas? I had no idea, but in my heart I knew he spoke the truth. It felt absolutely right. Perhaps it was because I had known this truth all along.

We lapsed into a welcome, contemplative silence.

The captain announced we were beginning our descent into Bangkok; all passengers were to return to their seats. I brought my seatback upright while Brielle moved up the aisle, performing her final check. After she passed us Mr. Toldeck broke our silence.

"I must get back to where I was prior to sitting with you. Before I leave, however, I want you to know that many people could benefit from your experiences. Sharing them is the greatest gift you could give to others, as well as to yourself."

An aura of grace and mystery seemed to surround him as he stood. Though he hadn't left the seat for many hours and hadn't had anything to eat or drink the entire time, he looked fresh as a daisy. Even his blue suit had remained unwrinkled. Everything about him proclaimed the fact that he was no ordinary man.

As soon as he stepped into the aisle to leave, I felt a deep sense of loss. I told myself I had no reason to feel this way: we were about to land, and my adventure was about to begin. Yet the feeling persisted.

A few minutes later, while the plane taxied down the runway, I again considered inviting him to dinner. Then I could give him the opportunity to talk for a change, and I would discover more about this stranger who had become my friend. After all our time together I was acutely aware that I barely knew anything about him.

Just before we pulled into our gate, I reached across the aisle and touched Lea's slender arm. She opened her eyes.

"Are we in Bangkok?"

I nodded. "I thought you might want to be awake before they opened the door."

"That's very nice of you," she said, stifling a yawn. She stretched and then gathered her long hair together with both hands.

"You're beautiful when you're sleeping," I blurted on impulse.

She smiled, fastening her hair clasp. "That's the loveliest compliment I've received on this flight."

Emboldened, I said, "There are more where that one came from."

Lea laughed. She held out her hand to shake mine just as the plane jerked to a final stop. We both stumbled a little and ended up hugging instead. As we said our goodbyes, Ms. HonoOpono called from her seat behind us; she needed Lea's help. I lifted my carry-on from the overhead bin and joined the line of passengers at the exit. Since this was first class, only three passengers were ahead of me.

When the door opened, a wave of warm humidity rolled in like a thick tide. I stepped off the plane and positioned myself just outside the door in the corner where the gangway curved to the right, determined to wait for Mr. Toldeck's emergence. There were so many questions I wanted to ask him. If I could set up a few meetings, I would perhaps even delay my fast for a day or two.

A steady stream of passengers flowed by, some of whom I had become familiar with during my occasional strolls. Melee passed by and I waved a 'hang loose' to her, but she didn't see me. A while later, Nelo burst out of the line and jumped into my arms.

"Coach Gaston! I told you we'd meet in Bangkok. I told you, didn't I?"

"You sure did, Nelo," I said, setting him down. Over his head, I continued to scan the moving line, nervous I might miss Mr. Toldeck.

Ellouise noticed my anxiousness.

"Don't worry, Gaston, if you're destined to be with her, you will."

I blinked at her. "What do you mean?"

"You seem nervous," she replied. "You're waiting for the woman you were speaking to in first class, aren't you? She hasn't come out yet, right?"

"Oh, I see. No, she hasn't come out yet. But I'm not waiting for her."

Ellouise gave me with a dubious look. "Yeah, right. Of course you aren't."

"No, really. I'm waiting for a friend."

"Oh, now she's just a friend," Ellouise retorted sarcastically.

"Really, I'm waiting for someone else, not Lea."

At the mention of Lea's name Ellouise's expression lit up in recognition.

"Is that who was sitting by you? Lea Kapua? Miss Hawaii herself?"

"Yes, it was."

"Wow! Why didn't you introduce me to her when I came by? She's my idol, you know."

"I had no idea," I said, keeping one eye on the throng of moving passengers.

"I've always been envious of her beauty, grace and humility," Ellouise gushed. "In my mind she's the most beautiful Miss Hawaii of all time! But since you're not meeting her, who is the special lady you're waiting for?"

I laughed. "Not a lady at all! I'm waiting for Mr. Toldeck, the man who was sitting next to me by the window."

Ellouise looked askance at me. "That's funny; I don't remember anyone sitting next to you at all. But who's to say? Maybe all my attention was on Miss Hawaii. You know how jealous women can be. See you around, Gaston."

Ellouise followed Nelo down the corridor, still looking doubtful.

Weary of standing on my prosthetic leg, I sat on the carpeted floor and continued watching passenger after passenger shamble past. I wanted so much to see Mr. Toldeck again. After fifteen minutes, hundreds of people had walked by right in front of me, but there was no sign of him. The flow was down to a trickle now. Could I have missed him? What was I to do? Run to the baggage claim or to the customs area to search for him, or should I remain here and wait?

TOGETHER OUR MISSION IS TO LOVE

XII

Still trying to decide what to do, I heard a familiar voice through the door of the plane and got up from the carpet. It belonged to Earl, debarking with his wife.

"What are you doing here, Gaston?" Earl asked.

"Earl," I said, shaking his hand. "Good to see you. Do you know if there are any more passengers left on the plane?"

"How do you two know each another?" Earl's wife put in.

"We met in the back of the plane," I explained, continuing to keep an eye out for Mr. Toldeck.

Earl said, "This is the young man I told you about, dear. The one I was talking to when you came to get me in the back of the plane? I told him about our life's mission."

His wife cocked her head to the side. "And what, may I ask, might that mission be, my dear Earl?"

"Why, Faith, my darling, together our mission is to love each other, of course."

"Oh, I get it now," Faith said. "This is the young man who was eager to know how we managed to stay together for forty-two years."

Earl nodded. "Yep! Gaston, this is my beloved Faith, wife of the luckiest man on earth."

Faith linked her arm with Earl's and pulled him closer, smiling up at him.

"So, tell us why you look so stressed, Gaston," Earl inquired.

"I've been waiting for a very special friend to exit, and I'm starting to get worried. Well, not so much worried as anxious to reconnect."

Faith chuckled. "If it's that beautiful women I saw accompanying the elderly Hawaiian lady, then your patience will be well rewarded."

"Actually, it's not," I said, wondering if every single person on the plane was hooking me up with Lea in their mind. "It's a man whose conversation had a very healing effect on me. I want another opportunity to express my gratitude to him."

"If that's it, then you have nothing to worry about," Earl declared. "There are a lot more people still to come out."

"Thank goodness," I sighed.

Earl nodded, picking up their carry-ons. "Relax. Be patient. We'll see you later at the baggage claim."

After they had walked away, my patience began to quickly unravel again. Passengers continued to trickle out, but Mr. Toldeck wasn't among them. Unable to stand still, I decided to re-enter the plane and find him myself. As I stepped through the hatch I almost bumped into the male flight attendant standing by the door. He raised his hand to stop me.

"Hold on, you can't go back in there. Not allowed."

It didn't make sense to me, but I wasn't about to argue with him. His face was stern, and his Chinese accent made him hard to understand anyway. Mutely, I returned to my waiting place.

He nodded without changing his expression. "That's fine. You wait there."

Several more passengers came out, none of them Mr. Toldeck. Then Lea appeared in the doorway. When she saw me, her eyes lit up and her smile could have melted a glacier. She made her way over to my corner of the gangway, Ms. HonoOpono following close behind.

"Hey, Gaston," Ms. HonoOpono said in her battlefield voice. "I was just telling Lea we'd see you again. Our meeting on this flight was just the beginning, not the end. She didn't believe me. We even argued. She said, if you were interested you'd have waited. And here you are!" She gave Lea an I-told-you-so look.

As usual, she had managed to completely embarrass both of us. For a moment, we stood there in an uncomfortable silence, then Lea changed the subject.

"Come on, Ms. HonoOpono, let's go find your family." She began heading down the corridor.

"Wait!" I blurted. "Lea, please wait. Could you help me?"

Lea spun back around, giving the hem of her bright dress a quick twirl that revealed her lovely legs. Both she and Ms. HonoOpono raised their eyebrows at my unexpected request.

"How can we help you, Gaston?" said Ms. HonoOpono.

"I've been waiting for someone to come out, and there's no sign of him yet." I looked pleadingly at Lea. "Could you go back and see if a tall, distinguished man in a dark blue suit is still inside? His name is Justin Toldeck. I've been waiting for him for more than twenty minutes now. The flight attendant won't let me back onto the plane, but maybe you can charm your way past him. Could you, please? I really need to see him and I want to be sure I haven't missed him."

Ms. HonoOpono gestured to Lea. "Go ahead. I'll wait out here with Gaston."

"Are you sure?" Lea said.

"No problem. It's not like an extra two or three minutes will make my family mad at me. Gaston has been kind to both of us. It's the least we can do."

Lea nodded and disappeared into the plane, smiling her way successfully past the Chinese door guard. To take the weight off my leg, I sagged down to the carpet again.

"What's really going on here, Gaston?" Ms. HonoOpono sounded concerned.

"I'm really not sure, Ms. HonoOpono. I have this strange feeling I'll never see my friend again, and it's making me kind of sad and confused."

Ms. HonoOpono bent down and patted me on the shoulder. "Don't worry about a thing, Gaston. Lea is very capable. If your friend's in there, she'll find him."

A couple of minutes later, Lea stepped through the hatch and I roused myself from the floor.

"No passengers left in first class, and only nine in coach," she reported. "None of them is a tall man in a blue suit. Your friend must already be off the plane. He's probably at the baggage claim by now."

"No, that can't be. I watched everyone exit right from the start, and I never saw him."

"Maybe he slipped by while you were talking to another passenger?" Lea suggested.

"Did you talk with anyone while you were waiting?" Ms. HonoOpono prodded.

"Of course," I said. "But…"

Now I began to doubt myself. Could it be that Mr. Toldeck passed by without me noticing? It was definitely possible.

On the other hand, he surely would have said "hi" or at least waved to me. Then again, maybe not if I was talking to Nelo and Ellouise or Earl and Faith at the time. Hope that I would yet meet him again rose in me.

"Come with us, Gaston," Ms. HonoOpono urged. "Let's see if he's at the baggage claim."

"That sounds like a good idea," Lea agreed.

I nodded. "It makes sense to me too. Let's go."

As we walked down the corridor, the image of Mr. Toldeck's piercing blue eyes appeared in my inner vision.

"Lea," I said hesitantly. "You know the man who was sitting next to me for most of the flight? He's the one I'm looking for."

Lea gave me a puzzled—even a little irritated—glance. "What man, Gaston?"

"Come on, Lea, didn't you see me talking with him? He was sitting right next to me."

"As a matter of fact, Gaston, I didn't," she replied. "But now that you mention it, I was wondering why you always seemed to be looking in the opposite direction from me."

She was disappointed I hadn't paid more attention to her.

"He was sitting in the window seat," I defended myself. "I had to look in that direction to talk to him."

Lea frowned in frustration, as if she could hardly believe I was telling her this story in all seriousness. Ms. HonoOpono observed we were about to have an argument and would have none of it.

"Let it go, you two," she admonished. "Let's go to the baggage claim and get our luggage. Who knows, Gaston, your friend might even be waiting for you there."

Lea gave me a little facial shrug and I lifted my palms in response. We both knew our small disagreement was insignificant compared to what Ms. HonoOpono was facing with the illness in her family. Lea waved her hand in the hang loose sign, and I smiled and hefted my carry-on. Probably Mr. Toldeck *had* walked right by me unnoticed; surely we would catch up with him at the baggage claim.

As we made our way slowly along the vast concourse of Suvarnabhumi International Airport, Ms. HonoOpono chattered nervously and Lea kept quiet, gazing at the ground with a quizzical look on her face.

Finally, she said to me, "I'm certain if there had been a man beside you on the plane I would have seen him from across the aisle. Besides, wouldn't I have heard you talking?"

She swept her hair back over her shoulder with her free hand and looked at me tentatively. I stopped abruptly in the middle of the concourse. Her observation made a lot of sense, yet how could I doubt the presence of a man I had talked to for hours? A man who looked as solid and real to me as any of the other passengers? The mystery was beginning to eat at me inside.

"I'm sorry, Lea, Ms. HonoOpono," I said, turning in the opposite direction. "I have to go back to the plane."

"Why?"

"I need to see for myself whether he's on that plane or not, or it'll haunt me the rest of my life."

I made a gesture of apology, settled my carry-on over my shoulder, and started back the way we came.

Ms. HonoOpono waved in the direction of the baggage claim. "Come on, Lea. We'll see Gaston later. Right, Gaston?"

"Yes," I called over my shoulder. "I'll be there soon. Go ahead. Don't wait for me."

The last few passengers were exiting the plane when I arrived at the door. Mr. Toldeck was nowhere in sight. I crossed the threshold and was immediately confronted by the flight attendant who during the flight had shooed me away from the back of the plane.

"I don't know what you think you're doing," she said, "but you're not allowed in here any longer. You need to leave immediately or I'll be forced to call security."

I held up my hand placatingly. "You don't have to call security. I'm leaving."

Out of the corner of my eye, I saw Brielle in the cockpit talking with the pilots. I stepped back over the threshold and took up my now-familiar position just outside the door. A few minutes later, my nemesis flight attendant came out, rolling her carry-on bag behind her.

"What are *you* still doing here?"

I said, "I'd like to talk to Brielle. I need her help with something."

"Are you okay?"

I nodded. "Yes, but it's important that I speak with her."

"All right, I'll go get her for you. But you stay right here, understand?"

"Sure."

The stewardess hesitated a moment, glanced over her shoulder into the plane, then back at me.

"Look," she said, holding my gaze with hers. "I want you to know that Brielle just ended a serious relationship. She's very vulnerable right now, so be nice to her, okay?"

My heart lifted a little. The woman had seemed like a stern and rigid taskmaster up to this point, but now I was seeing another side of her—a protective side that worried about her friend getting hurt. *Love is everywhere*, I thought, *sometimes in the least expected places.*

"Don't worry, I will," I assured her. "I'm not after her affection, only her help."

She nodded once, set her carry-on aside and disappeared into the interior of the plane. Shortly afterward, she came back out to tell me Brielle was on her way. Then she left, trailing her wheeled bag behind her.

Through the small window in the service door of the gangway I watched the sparkling lights of Bangkok at night, made surreal by the muffled howling of the jets taking off and landing outside. Amid this strange juxtaposition, words of wisdom the Vi-Guru had once told me came to mind:

"You must have a burning faith in the Light and Sound if you want to achieve liberation, the true destiny of Soul."

What had reminded me of his words at this particular moment? The lights of the city and the sound of the planes? Or was it simply his way of making me aware of his presence? As the Vi-Guru, the avatar of his time, he is concerned with the spiritual development of the Souls under his guidance as well as the resolution of their karma during this lifetime. Perhaps there was there a karmic debt I was to resolve here? If so, I certainly didn't know what it was.

When Brielle emerged from the door, my heart leapt as I clearly heard my inner voice say: *she'll hold an important message.*

"Aloha, Brielle," I greeted her enthusiastically. "I've been eagerly awaiting you out here."

"So I hear," she smiled. "How can I help you, Mr. Ouellet?"

"Please, Brielle, call me Gaston."

"All right then, Gaston. What can I do for you?"

"I'm looking for someone who hasn't come out yet. Can you take me back inside and help me find him? It happens sometimes, doesn't it, that there are passengers still inside when you thought the plane was already empty?"

"Yes, Gaston," she agreed. "But I can assure you everyone is at the baggage claim by now, along with most of the crew."

Not ready to back down and abandon my quest, I stood my ground. Brielle could see I wasn't going to take no for an answer.

"All right," she sighed. "Come on, let's go have a look."

"I'll take the coach section. You check first class," I suggested, certain if he were on the plane he'd be in coach. I wondered down the empty cabin all the way to the back, making sure no one was in the lavatories there. When I turned around, I saw Brielle at the entrance of the coach section. In her hand she held the leather folder I had left under my seat. Again, the Inner Master's voice came through loud and clear: *she'll hold an important message.*

The folder contained the secret!

My breath caught with the excitement of anticipation, like a theater goer before the curtains rise on a highly touted play. Only now the rising curtains wouldn't reveal a stage set and actors, but the future course of my life!

In moments I glided down the aisle to Brielle and took the leather portfolio with trembling hands. In my mind I reviewed the events of the flight: my deep, healing conversations with Mr. Toldeck; the way Brielle had always seemed to ignore him; Ellouise worrying about disturbing my beauty sleep; Lea's insistence she hadn't seen anyone next to me; Mr. Toldeck's uncanny ability to see directly into the heart of my every concern; his knowing smile whenever I spoke of the Masters. These moments all collapsed in on each other to shape a single, shining truth, a truth my heart had known all along but which I finally accepted with my mind: Mr. Toldeck was another of the remarkable beings who were the guardians and guides of my spiritual journey. Like Gopal, Rebatarz, Fubee, Asanga, and Paulji, Justin Toldeck was a Master himself, a member of the ancient order of spiritual adepts who had blessed me with their wisdom for so many years.

How was it possible I hadn't recognized who he was, especially for as long as we were together?

Knowing what I did now, I struggled to process the effect he'd had upon me over the long hours of the flight. Most of the time, it seemed, I had done the talking. I raked my brain to remember what pearls of wisdom he had bestowed upon me during the precious moments he had spoken, but I couldn't recall anything specific. Determined to discover the next stepping stone on my journey in a private setting, I tucked the leather folder under my arm. The message it contained would be the most precious gift of all!

Brielle's voice intruded into my thoughts. "So he's not here, right? He's probably at baggage claim for sure by now, don't you think?"

It took a second or two for my eyes to focus on her. Inhaling deeply to calm myself, I replayed her questions in my mind to extract meaning from the sounds. Ah, yes—in her view, I was looking for a physical person, a passenger who would be in baggage claim by now. Until a minute ago, I had thought the same thing.

"You're right," I confirmed. Then I couldn't help but ad, "He's a remarkable being who's presence I was blessed with. Often we meet extraordinary people in life and don't realize how remarkable they are until we've parted."

"That's true," Brielle said.

Together we walked off the plane and into the gangway. Like our friends who had preceded us, we each dragged pieces of our lives behind us in a wheeled suitcase. After exiting the corridor, Brielle turned toward a magazine store nearby while I continued down the concourse toward the main terminal. Something inside me made me stop and turn back to her.

"Hey, Brielle!"

She paused on the threshold of the magazine shop.

"Yes, Gaston?"

"Was there anyone sitting next to me during our flight?"

"Yes, of course there was," she said.

My heart skipped a beat. Had she seen Mr. Toldeck all along?

Brielle continued, "There was a truly magnificent person—Lea Kapua. That's who you were seated next to. Like you said, Gaston, sometimes we are fortunate to be in the presence of remarkable beings. Lea is one of the most remarkable beings I've ever met. Now, be on your way." She gestured toward the main terminal. "Go, find your friend. And if you're lucky, you might still catch Lea as well."

"Thanks, I will. Bye."

As I walked down the huge concourse lined with shops and thronged with hundreds of travelers, exultation began to rise within me. With my new awareness I tried to recall my entire conversation with Mr. Toldeck again, but once more the details of what he said seemed to hover just outside the borders of my awareness. Even so, I knew my experience with him was finding its way into my heart, its proper resting place, and it would coalesce there to add to the fundamental substance of my life.

Unable to restrain my curiosity, I stopped and pulled the leather folder from under my arm. I just had to know what its message was! Before I could open it, however, I heard Lea call my name from where she stood just inside a set of automatic doors. The timing of her appearance was too uncanny to be coincidence—it had to be a sign. I replaced the folder under my arm and began walking toward her.

Watching Lea standing there, waiting for me, I felt a definitive shift take place within me, caused by the realization that I was finally ready to surrender to what my feelings had been telling me the last few hours: the love pouring through my heart from the worlds of God was meant for her. There was nothing I could do but get out of the way and let it through.

In the blink of an eye, it seemed, I was at her side. The love shining in her light brown eyes mirrored my own. We stood facing each other in a timeless moment, heedless of the passengers parting and flowing around us like a river of humanity. Bits of what Mr. Toldeck told me filtered through my consciousness, specifically the statement: "Soon you will be spending time with Lea."

His prediction was becoming reality sooner than I had expected.

Lea was the first to find her voice.

"Ms. HonoOpono asked me to come back and get you. She's determined to introduce you to her family."

Her words seemed to reach my ears from far away, as if originating in some wondrous place.

"I would be delighted to meet them," I managed shakily, trying to tamp down the welter of emotions constricting my throat. Quickly getting ahold of myself, I continued, "And regarding your earlier invitation, I would be very pleased if you'd allow me to change my mind and come with all of you to the Hyatt. It would be great if I could spend some time with you before I leave for Koh Samui."

"Really?" Her smile was more beautiful than the sunrise. "I would like that very much, Gaston. Oh, by the way, what do you think Ms. HonoOpono said to me just before I left to get you?"

I laughed. "I truly can't imagine what. She's so…unique… in many ways."

"You can say that again." Lea's laugh was a silvery answer to mine.

"So, what did she say? You never know, there might be some truth to it."

Lea smile widened. "First she told me you'd be coming to the Hyatt with us and that you and I would spend some time together. But then she said something even stranger."

"Well, the first part isn't all that strange," I remarked. "You probably knew I wanted to spend time with you."

"That's true, I did."

Lea shyly dropped her gaze to the ground, as if her admission somehow made her vulnerable. Wishing to reassure her, I reached across to lightly touch her hand. Amazingly, even this slight physical contact with her caused my breath catch in my throat and heat to spread throughout my body as if my veins were on fire. At my half-suppressed gasp, Lea raised her eyes and looked into mine. A spark jumped between us like an electric charge. Startled, we both jerked our hands away as if from a hot stove. It seemed the love that existed between us was so strong and pure that for the moment we could only endure the smallest exchange.

When I was able to draw enough breath to speak again, I said, "What was the other thing Ms. HonoOpono mentioned? The even stranger thing."

"Get ready, because it's pretty strange."

"Once she said we would spend time together, that's all I needed to hear. So, go ahead. No matter how strange it is, it won't faze me."

Lea took a deep breath. "She said the reason she knew you would be coming to the Hyatt and that we would be spending time together was because, and I quote, 'the distinguished man in the dark blue suit told me.'"

"Which man?" My heart was suddenly thumping in my chest.

Lea replied, "I asked her the same question, and she said, 'You know, the one sitting with Gaston during our flight.'"

"She really said that?" I exclaimed. "The man in the blue suit told her? That's what she said?"

"Yes, Gaston. I wouldn't lie to you."

"Of course I believe you," I said quickly. What I could hardly believe was that after all the emphatic denials from everyone, including Lea, Ms. HonoOpono had actually seen and spoken to Mr. Toldeck! Her testimony wasn't exactly a vindication—I had been absolutely certain of his presence—but it felt good to have my experience corroborated by someone else. Lea looked as if she still had her doubts, so I decided not to pursue the issue, changing the subject instead.

"Let's go to the baggage claim and say hello to Ms. HonoOpono's family. Who knows who else we might meet there?"

As we walked side by side through the sliding doors towards the baggage claim, I felt as if an aura of unconditional love surrounded us. I felt as if we were two Souls just beginning to unite in the common purpose of serving one another and accompanying each other through life's trials. Then a familiar voice spoke to me on the inner and I stopped and closed my eyes to listen. On my mental screen I saw Mr. Toldeck gazing at me with piercing blue eyes, a brilliant purple halo surrounding his light body. The Sound Current, the sacred love song of the Great Spirit, roared in my spiritual hearing, yet I could understand his words without difficulty.

"Fulfilling your life's mission is your gift to the world," Mr. Toldeck said. "Read what you wrote in your notebook."

He vanished as quickly has he had appeared. I opened my eyes to find Lea had gone on a few steps ahead of me.

I called after her, "Lea, please wait—just for a moment."

Lea stopped and looked back.

"What is it? Are you okay?"

"Yes, I'm okay, but I need to read something in this folder, right now."

I set down my carry-on and pulled the folder from under my arm with a shaky hand. On the top page was the to-do list I had planned to compile on the plane before Mr. Toldeck came to sit with me. As the heading I had written "During your Fast," and on the left side of the page I had listed the numbers one through nine with several lines between each. All the line items were blank except for the first one. There, scribbled in blue ink as my first and highest priority, was the answer to my life's dilemma:

"Write your childhood stories."

Through the years I'd been asked time and again to write down my stories, but deep down I'd never felt worthy enough. Now it was as if I had stepped out of a dark mine shaft into bright morning sunshine. The limitations I had clung to all these years no longer applied. Freedom was within reach by simply choosing to express what lay within me. Sighing with the release of lifelong tension I closed the folder and slipped it back under my arm.

"Everything all right?" Lea's look of concern changed to a smile when she saw me relax.

"Yes, never better."

I didn't elaborate, and Lea didn't pursue the matter, content for the moment to let whatever I had learned stay with me.

We continued down the hallway to the baggage claim. Shortly before arriving at our flight's designated conveyor I saw Ms. HonoOpono and what had to be Kimo, her son, and Lulu, her granddaughter waiting for us. All three of them waved excitedly.

"Look how beautiful they are together," Lea said.

"Yes, they are." I stopped and turned to Lea. Taking both her hands in mine, I looked into her eyes. "But, so are we, Lea. So are we."

As we made our way through the crowd of passengers toward the Hawaiians, I suddenly heard a deep humming sound, like that of a heavy engine revving up. Before my eyes the airport seemed to dissolve, and I found myself in my light body back at the temple of Jart Chiong in the eighth dimension. I was in the corridor near the great hall where I had met the Silent Ones just before incarnating into my current physical body. Something small pulsed in my palm, and when I looked down, I saw the tiny pearl of light Master Asanga had placed in my hand at the time. The pearl glowed brighter and brighter until it engulfed my whole world with pure white light. Through the light I heard Master Asanga's voice like thunderous orchestral music, repeating the truth he had given me so long ago:

"If you forget your spiritual heritage, you will struggle in the lower worlds longer than you need to. Therefore, dear Soul, imprint these truths onto your heart: First, you are eternal—without beginning and without end. Second, when you align yourself with the Light and Sound, you remain in the spiritual worlds no matter where you are. Third, you have neither past nor future, only the eternity of the present moment. Remember these pearls of wisdom, dear Gaston. If you lose yourself along the way, remember the Law of Love: You are Soul, and Soul exists because of God's love. Finally and most importantly, remember to sing the love song to God. Remember to sing HU."

Master Asanga's last word, HU, resounded louder and louder, until it became one great roar of all sounds combined into one. The luminous pearl in my palm continued to flood my vision with pure white light. I bathed in this ocean of Sound and Light for a timeless, eternal moment. Eventually the light resolved into an array of multiple colors, and the roar separated into individual sounds. One of the sounds was a voice was calling my name.

"Gaston! Gaston, are you okay?"

The swirling blur of colors came into focus. Images of the temple of Jart Chiong receded into memory. I was in an airport—the Suvarnabhumi International Airport in Bangkok.

Only a half a day before, I had begun my adventure in another airport, Honolulu International. I hadn't known Mr. Toldeck then, or Ms. HonoOpono, or Lea. Now each of them was an important part of my adventure; each had become a guide and a fellow traveler on my journey.

Lea's beautiful face swam into focus before me.

"Are you okay, Gaston?" she repeated.

"Sure," I said, hearing my voice from far away. "I'm perfect, absolutely perfect."

Master Asanga Kaya's seed of wisdom had reached full bloom in my heart. I was ready to give and receive love in ways I had always held back from. Now I was ready to be loved by all the bees in the garden.

"That certainly is good to hear," Lea laughed. She pointed toward a beaming Ms. HonoOpono and her family. "Look at them! Are you ready to be loved? Because the hugs we're about to get from those three are full of the Aloha Spirit, I can guarantee you that!"

"I am," I said. "I'm ready to be courageous and let myself be loved. Once and for all, I choose to be loved."

Lea nodded approvingly at the choice I had made. She squeezed my hand and giggled.

"So am I, Gaston. So am I."

We stood together, holding hands, observing the flow of Divine Love between people from all around the world as they followed the course of their spiritual destiny. Just as I had done in Honolulu, I wondered at all the places they came from, but now I no longer wondered where they were going. Regardless of the destinations written on their tickets, I knew they were all on a journey home to God.

From this moment on, I vowed I would always remember that I am Soul, the master of my own life, the captain of my destiny. And I hoped that in Lea I now perhaps had a partner with whom to share my journey.

The Beginning

Would you like to see your manuscript become a book?

If you are interested in becoming a PublishAmerica author, please submit your manuscript for possible publication to us at:

mybook@publishamerica.com

You may also mail in your manuscript to:

**PublishAmerica
PO Box 151
Frederick, MD 21705**

www.publishamerica.com

PublishAmerica